[redacted]

Oral Presentations for Technical Communication

[redacted]

THE ALLYN AND BACON SERIES IN TECHNICAL COMMUNICATION

Series Editor: Sam Dragga, Texas Tech University

Thomas T. Barker
Writing Software Documentation: A Task-Oriented Approach

Paul M. Dombrowski
Ethics in Technical Communication

Laura J. Gurak
Oral Presentations for Technical Communication

Dan Jones
Technical Writing Style

Charles Kostelnick and David D. Roberts
Designing Visual Language: Strategies for Professional Communications

Carolyn D. Rude
Technical Editing, Second Edition

Oral Presentations for Technical Communication

Laura J. Gurak
University of Minnesota—Twin Cities

Allyn and Bacon
Boston ▪ London ▪ Toronto ▪ Sydney ▪ Tokyo ▪ Singapore

Vice President: Eben W. Ludlow
Editorial Assistant: Grace Trudo
Editorial-Production Service: Omegatype Typography, Inc.
Manufacturing Buyer: Suzanne Lareau
Cover Administrator: Jenny Hart

A Pearson Education Company
160 Gould Street
Needham Heights, MA 02494

Internet: www.abacon.com

Between the time Website information is gathered and published, some sites may have closed. Also, the transcription of URLs can result in typographical errors. The publisher would appreciate notification where these occur so that they may be corrected in subsequent editions.

Library of Congress Cataloging-in-Publication Data

Gurak, Laura J.
Oral presentations for technical communication / Laura J. Gurak.
p. cm.—(The Allyn and Bacon series in technical communication)
Includes bibliographical references and index.
ISBN 0-205-29415-4 (alk. paper)
1. Communication of technical information. 2. Public speaking. I. Title. II. Series.

T10.5 .G84 2000
601'.4—dc21

99-046796

Printed in the United States of America

10 9 8 7 6 5 4 3 2 1 04 03 02 01 00 99

Dedicated to my students, past and present

CONTENTS

ILLUSTRATIONS

FOREWORD BY THE SERIES EDITOR

The Allyn & Bacon Series in Technical Communication is designed for the growing number of students enrolled in undergraduate and graduate programs in technical communication. Such programs offer a wide variety of courses beyond the introductory technical writing course—advanced courses for which fully satisfactory and appropriately focused textbooks have often been impossible to locate. This series will also serve the continuing education needs of professional technical communicators, both those who desire to upgrade or update their own communication abilities as well as those who train or supervise writers, editors, and artists within their organization.

The chief characteristic of the books in this series is their consistent effort to integrate theory and practice. The books offer both research-based and experienced-based instruction, not only describing what to do and how to do it but also explaining why. The instructors who teach advanced courses and the students who enroll in these courses are looking for more than rigid rules and ad hoc guidelines. They want books that demonstrate theoretical sophistication and a solid foundation in the research of the field as well as pragmatic advice and perceptive applications. Instructors and students will also find these books filled with activities and assignments adaptable to the classroom and to the self-guided learning processes of professional technical communication.

To operate effectively in the field of technical communication, today's students require extensive training in the creation, analysis, and design of information for both domestic and international audiences, for both paper and electronic environments. The books in the Allyn & Bacon Series address those subjects that are most frequently taught at the undergraduate and graduate levels as a direct response to both the educational needs of students and the practical demands of business and industry. Additional books will be developed for the series in order to satisfy or anticipate changes in writing technologies, academic curricula, and the profession of technical communication.

Sam Dragga
Texas Tech University

PREFACE

Most students (and professionals, too) suffer from a public speaking deficit. Although writing can be difficult, especially in areas of science and technology, most people have been practicing writing ever since they learned to spell their names in kindergarten. But when it comes to speaking and giving presentations, the same cannot be said. Think about all the papers students have written in high school and college, and compare this number with the number of speeches or oral presentations students have given. When it comes to standing up and giving a talk, most people simply lack experience and, therefore, confidence. No wonder people continually rank public speaking as the task that makes them the most nervous! Add to this the complexities of speaking about scientific or technical topics, and the job becomes even more challenging. Then, add to the mix once again, this time the skills and experience required to use computer presentation software (such as PowerPoint), and it's obvious that oral presentations in technical communication require a complex set of skills.

Yet despite our lack of attention to oral presentations in science and technology, most professional technical communicators would agree that presentations are essential in the high technology workplace. The skills required to present complex technical information in a personal, professional, and accessible manner are invaluable in today's information-saturated society.

Although the discipline of technical communication has grown dramatically in the past ten years, the breadth of the discipline has in some regards not kept pace. Most undergraduate programs and courses in technical communication have remained true to their historic roots in English departments, focusing on technical writing. Although B.S. programs in technical communication have expanded to areas involving computer graphics, international communication, cognitive science, and usability testing, few have looked to the work in speech communication as a way of enhancing the oral presentation components of their programs. This book is thus designed to combine knowledge from rhetoric, technical communication, speech communication, and the use of computer software by drawing on the best principles of each. It combines the most important and appropriate information from the normally distinct courses in public speaking, technical writing, and the use of computer technologies. By doing so, this book offers a theory and rubric for oral presentations that go beyond Public Speaking 101 and beyond the narrow chapters on oral presentations contained in most technical writing books. More specific than a course in Advanced Public Speaking, this book focuses primarily on the technical communication student, emphasizing audience and purpose, forms of technical presentations, issues of science/technology/the public, and the complicated task of using presentation software.

Audience and Purpose

This book is designed to teach presentation skills to students of technical communication, whose careers will involve making complex scientific and technical information accessible to a variety of audiences (including lay audiences). Most technical communicators are very good *technical writers* but often lack the skills needed for good oral presentations. Although this book is designed primarily for the working technical communicator and for technical communication students, science and technology professionals will also find these concepts extremely useful in terms of how to present expert knowledge to general audiences.

Traditionally, instructors and students in technical communication had few choices when looking for a textbook on oral presentations. There are a wealth of textbooks on public speaking, yet although these books are appropriate for a large introductory public speaking course, they tend to be too general and are written at too basic a level for the upper-division technical student. In addition, public speaking texts are designed to teach students how to give *speeches,* not oral presentations in technical communication. Recently, a few books that focus on presentations have emerged, yet these texts are also not entirely suited to technical communication, as they tend to include managerial and business presentations as well. In addition, these presentation books are often overly prescriptive and tend to ignore important concepts from rhetorical theory and technical communication studies. Finally, there are many books on how to use various types of presentation software, but these books are designed solely to assist with the technical aspects of a presentation.

This text focuses exclusively on technical communication and provides a rich, interdisciplinary approach to the subject. Unlike general speech texts, where examples are taken from any number of subject areas, examples in this book are drawn especially from the areas of science and technology. In addition, this text offers a rhetorical perspective, addressing certain basic presentation types in specific chapters. Yet the presentation is broad enough so that these concepts and techniques can be applied in a variety of settings. For no matter how much a textbook tries, no one book can capture the unique situations and types of presentations that take place from job to job or from organization to organization. Thus, a rhetorical approach, balanced with some specific examples and outlines, provides the most useful tool for learning about oral presentations in technical communication.

In addition, most technical communication instructors come to the classroom with a good deal of professional experience. Many have spent time in industry as technical writers, editors, consultants, or research specialists. Even those instructors who have never worked in the field per se become quite familiar with the practice of technical communication through their students' internships and jobs. Because of this, technical communication instructors often prefer textbooks that provide the essentials of instruction but that leave room for them to include their own examples, handouts, and experiences. Thus, this book, while providing the needed tools for giving technical presentations in a variety of circumstances, is purposely not overly heavy-handed or bogged down with irrelevant examples.

Feature boxes sprinkled throughout the chapters offer additional study aids: FYI boxes provide more information and resources on a topic; Scenarios present short cases that illustrate the techniques being described; Checklists summarize key points and serve as memory joggers of important items students need to know. Yet the use of these features is purposely light, because this book is designed something like a reference: Instructors are encouraged to supplement this book with their own experiences and with visits from guest speakers. Additional instructional material, available on the book's Website (www.abacon.com/gurak), includes examples, worksheets, model presentations, and a student bulletin board.

Chapter Overview

This book assumes that many students have already taken an introductory public speaking class at an undergraduate level or have given presentations at work or for other classes. Yet even with these experiences, most students find that they cannot remember even the most basic organizational principles and have gotten severely out of practice. Therefore, the first three parts of this book focus on basic skills and concepts, including four basic types of presentations relevant to technical communication. The last two parts introduce advanced material specific to issues of science, technology, and the public and to the use of digital technology, copyright, and visual communication.

Each part begins with an overview, presents each chapter, and ends with a word of advice from a presentation professional. This advice (Presenting . . .) is intended to give students a connection between classroom experience and the presentation experiences of working professionals. Instructors are encouraged to invite guest speakers to class as appropriate.

Part One: Presenting You, Presenting Your Message

Part One begins with the basics. Chapter 1 describes oral presentations specific to science and technology. Chapter 2 provides an understanding of why presenters become anxious and explains how to overcome nervousness. Chapter 3 takes up the subjects of how to project a confident personal character (ethos); how to rely on memory; and how to use voice, body language, and gesture appropriately (delivery). Finally, Chapter 4 offers other techniques for easing nervousness and becoming a more practiced presenter. Even if students are comfortable speaking in public, it is helpful to review this material.

Part One concludes with a word of advice from Saul Carliner, a past international president of the Society for Technical Communication and currently a professor and consultant.

Part Two: Audience, Purpose, Beginnings, Endings

Part Two teaches students a basic framework for creating effective presentations. Chapter 5 notes that presenters must be familiar with the audience and their level of knowledge, their inclination toward the subject, and other demographic characteristics. Chapter 6 explains that students must also be aware of the purpose of the presentation: Are they there to persuade? To teach an audience how to perform a task? To inform? In Chapter 7, students learn the importance of strong introductions and conclusions. Chapter 8 describes how to research the topic for a presentation, including using the web and other sources. Note that although Chapter 8 provides some suggestions on how to outline a presentation, it does not devote a great deal of space to the topic of invention per se. Given that this book is designed for upper-division undergraduates, most of these students will be familiar with how to generate and outline ideas. As with the rest of this book, instructors and students who need more examples in this area can consult the book's Website.

Part Two concludes with some thoughts from Daphne Walmer, manager for the 35-person technical communication department at Medtronic, the world's leading medical technology company specializing in implantable and interventional therapies.

Part Three: Types of Technical Presentations

The third part is organized around the various types of presentations technical communicators generally might give. Noting at the outset that these presentation types are not always exclusive (informative can sometimes be persuasive, and vice versa, for example), Chapter 9 describes informative presentations and Chapter 10, persuasive presentations. Chapter 11 discusses presentations that involve specific plans of action, and Chapter 12 teaches students about task-oriented, how-to presentations. Although students may encounter other types of presentations in their internships or on the job, these four types will provide a strong foundation for most presentations they may encounter.

The four presentation types in Part Three are intended to give instructors and students ideas and help get them started. For certain classes, it may be appropriate to focus on only one or two of these types and modify the material in the book to conform with the classroom situation. For example, for a class of engineering students, it may be appropriate for students to learn about the types of presentations they will give in their profession. For a classroom of working students from a certain company or industry, it may be best to learn the specific presentation format for this organization. Or, instructors may have a presentation format that they prefer over the ones offered here. The information in Part Three is general enough that it can be modified for this purpose.

Part Three concludes with some thoughts by Kevin Kinneavy, a technology trainer and manager for Minnesota Education Technology Alliance, that provides technology leadership, training, and support services to schools and businesses throughout Minnesota.

Part Four: Science, Technology, and Non-Expert Audiences

Although this entire book is designed around the idea that technical presentations require special skills, the fourth part in particular offers some very specific concepts and techniques to help students as they work with increasingly difficult technical or scientific material. Chapter 13 discusses the relationship among the technical communicator, the public, and science or technology information—specifically, this chapter teaches advanced techniques for making complex information enjoyable and compelling to an audience. Chapter 14 uses two theories from rhetoric—genre switching and stasis theory—to help students understand how to shift science and technology from the expert realm to the realm of the public. Chapter 15 continues this rhetorical discussion by teaching students how to use analogy and metaphor in their oral presentations. Finally, Chapter 16 discusses the differences between visual and verbal communication.

Part Four concludes with some thoughts from Peggy Durbin, a team leader in technical communication at Los Alamos National Laboratory. Before her position in management, she was a technical writer-editor at the Laboratory for eleven years.

Part Five: Presentations and Technologies

Finally, Part Five discusses presentations in the digital realm. Chapter 17 examines both the positive and negative aspects of using presentation software (such as Microsoft PowerPoint, Lotus Freehand, and Adobe Persuasion). At first glance, it may seem odd that the section on using presentation software is not covered until the final part of the book. Yet unless students have the basic skills and understanding of what makes an effective scientific or technical presentation, software won't help. In fact, software might even make a presentation worse if the presenter doesn't understand audience, purpose, presentation type, or the other concepts presented earlier in the text. If students have access to a computer and presentation software, they can practice using presentation software while working with this chapter. If students don't have access, this chapter can serve to provide them with guidelines for when they inevitably encounter computer presentation software. Chapter 18 looks at other useful presentation technologies, including overhead projectors and flip charts. Chapter 19 discusses legal issues of copyright and fair use, which affect oral presentations in our digital age. Finally, Chapter 20 teaches students some basic concepts about privacy and censorship in relation to oral presentations in technical communication.

Part Five concludes with some ideas from Lisa Kattan, a lawyer interested in intellectual property and technology who studied scientific and technical communication before going to law school.

Additional Resources: Companion Website

In today's information-rich, globally linked world, it's critical for communicators to have the skills necessary for presenting complex technical information in a personal, professional, and accessible manner to a variety of audiences. This book combines theory, practice, technology, and exercises in a way that will provide hands-on skills and also long-term principles. Good technical communicators need to become experts at making information usable to a wide audience; this book will provide practical and theoretical information toward that goal. In addition, the companion Website to this book, available at **www.abacon.com/gurak** offers an excellent supplementary resource for teachers and students. This site contains samples of audience analysis worksheets, sample presentations, PowerPoint presentations, examples and worksheets, links to other useful sites, and more.

Acknowledgments

I appreciate the efforts and support of all who were involved in this project. First and foremost, I wish to thank Professor Sam Dragga of Texas Tech University for encouraging me to take something that had existed for many years as an idea in my head and turn that idea into something that can be used by the entire technical communication community. Thank you also to Eben Ludlow of Allyn and Bacon for his support and encouragement of this project. Thank you to the reviewers of this first edition, who gave the first draft a close reading and offered excellent suggestions. The reviewers were Bernadette Longo, Clemson University; Libby Miles, University of Rhode Island; Carolyn Plumb, University of Washington; and Kristin R. Woolever, Northeastern University. Special thanks to Kirk St. Amant for his assistance with the international communication exercises, to Linda Clemens and Carol Felts for their excellent editorial assistance, and to John Logie for his work on the book's Website. Finally, I am grateful to my students at the University of Minnesota for all they have taught me about the art of oral presentations.

PART ONE

Presenting You, Presenting Your Message

Part One teaches you how to make complex technical and scientific information interesting, useful, and accessible to a wide audience, and to do so orally through your speaking skills, talents, and interest in the audience. Oral presentations can be one of the most effective ways to communicate. You are right there with your audience. You can judge their mood and their interest. You can answer questions and provide information. And unlike writing, every presentation is a live performance—an adventure with your audience as you explore new topics and concepts. To prepare for the task, you need some basics. Part One will help you understand your role as a technical communicator giving an oral presentation. It will also give you tips and techniques for dealing with nervousness, using your personal credibility, and strengthening your power of memory and delivery.

CHAPTER

1 Oral Presentations in the Realm of Science and Technology

CHAPTER OVERVIEW

This chapter will provide you with a general sense of the *what* and *why* of this book; in other words, what this book means by the phrase "technical communication" and why oral presentations are so critical in technical communication. This chapter covers the following topics:

- Who Are Technical Communicators?
- The Responsibility of Technical Communicators to the Public
- Technical Writing versus Technical Presentations
- Being a Good Listener
- Oral Presentations for Technical Communication
- Using Technologies to Give Technical Presentations

Who Are Technical Communicators?

Many people play the role of technical communicator. For some, this is their career and vocation. In industry, their job titles might include technical writer, information designer, information developer, publications specialist, science writer, technical editor, or instructional developer. In all cases, their job is to make technical information accessible to a wide range of audiences. In the computer industry, for example, technical communicators are the ones who write and design the manuals and quick reference material that come with a computer. They also write, design, and code online help and other support and information screens that are built into software. Other fields, such as biomedicine, pharmaceuticals, agri-business, manufacturing, and banking, employ technical communicators, too. These professionals write and design information that is in line with end user needs, conforms to any industry or regulatory standards, and accurately informs the reader or listener about the technical topic.

Scientists and engineers, though not full-time communicators, often play the role of technical communicator as well. Often, a scientific or technical expert is asked to present expert knowledge to a non-expert audience. For example, a biologist might be asked to provide her opinion about the environmental impact of a proposed neighborhood wetlands project. An atmospheric scientist might need to speak before Congress to discuss long-term policies toward global warming. A computer engineer might be required to write a summary about computers and privacy for a local community newspaper. In all of these instances, the expert is playing the role of a technical communicator.

As the world grows increasingly complex in terms of new discoveries and technologies, many people will play the role of technical communicator from time to time. This role brings with it a special relationship between communicator and general public.

The Responsibility of Technical Communicators to the Public

As a technical communicator, you have a unique responsibility to the public. You provide a link between the world of experts and non-experts; between complex technical information and easy-to-use information. Your job is to make technologies and technical information interesting, enjoyable, and accessible—and in line with your audience's needs. Because you connect the world of the expert and the public, you are responsible for how people come to understand and use new technologies. You may communicate in many forms—in writing (brochures, documentation), via new technologies (online help, Web pages), and orally (training sessions, other presentations).

Because your role as technical communicator is so important, it's especially critical to be the most effective communicator you can be. Oral presentations are one of many important ways to interact with the public; your skill at giving excellent presentations will enhance the special relationship you have with nontechnical audiences.

Part of this special relationship involves your ability to help people *make informed choices* about serious science, technology, health, and legal issues. Let's say, for example, that a new drug suddenly becomes available, and that this drug can cure a major disease. Like most drugs, however, this one is not without side effects, one of which includes possible damage to the optic nerve resulting in loss of vision. How can a non-expert make a wise decision about whether or not to use this new treatment? Scientific articles from medical journals are not written for the general public—what most people need is information presented in simple terms that answers the most commonly asked questions. In other words, the information must be crafted by someone who understands both the medical side and the people side. A skilled technical communicator can do just that, thus making it far easier for people to make informed choices.

Another part of a technical communicator's responsibility is to help citizens participate in the democratic process. In a democracy, citizens are expected to be aware of pending legislative issues and to *participate in the democratic process,* either by voting or by contacting one's representatives in government. In other words, democracies only work when citizens participate. But in this age of highly technical topics, how can average citizens truly understand topics well enough to be involved? Recent congressional debates over encryption, a mathematical algorithm that keeps cellular telephone conversations private, have been in the news. But unless the listener or reader is a computer expert, these debates are difficult to follow. Here again, technical communicators play an important role in making this sort of information accessible to non-expert audiences. This concept is related to *freedom of speech,* something central to democratic forms of government. When people understand a topic, they are more able to exercise this important First Amendment right by contacting legislators, expressing opinions on the issue, and informing others.

Technical communicators play an important *ethical* role, too. Many of today's complex topics have an ethical component. Consider genetic testing, for example. Whereas the scientific side focuses on how to understand genetics and how to map genetic structures, the ethical side asks questions that focus on people and applications: How will this technology affect my ability to obtain health insurance? Do I want to know if I have a gene that predisposes me to a certain disease? Should my children know before they have children? Technical communicators, who understand the science and technology along with the ethical side, can make these issues easier to understand.

Finally, when you present information and ideas that you care about, you participate in what one expert in public speaking calls "the joy of sharing" (Thompson, 1998, p. 10). When you share ideas with an audience and do so enthusiastically, you share something only you can give—your concern, insight, and personal perspective on a topic that you consider important.

In the end, the responsibility of technical communicators to the public is an important one with many facets. By learning to give excellent oral presentations, you'll enhance this important responsibility.

Technical Writing versus Technical Presentations

Almost all technical communicators have taken at least one course in technical writing; most have taken several. Writing has traditionally been the focus in technical communication academic programs and on the job. Technical communicators learn to write clear, accurate prose that makes information accessible and usable. To do their job well, technical communicators must be especially focused on the audience and purpose for a given piece of information. (These concepts are discussed in Chapters 5 and 6.) Communicators also need to be concerned with the visual layout of the document, the amount of time readers will have to absorb the information, the size of the final document, and more.

FYI

Issues and Technologies in the Public Eye

As the twenty-first century unfolds, many technical and scientific topics loom large in the public's mind. As a technical communicator, you can help the public understand these topics by giving effective oral presentations. Some of the topics you may encounter include the following. As you read this list, think of what topics might appeal to you.

- Genetic engineering
- Computer privacy
- Internet commerce
- Reproductive technologies
- Global warming
- New drugs and cures for diseases
- Pollution and electric vehicles
- Space travel
- Definitions of life

In the same fashion, effective technical presentations are very much focused on the needs of a specific audience and a specific set of purposes. Technical presentations need to be clear, accurate, and accessible. Like technical documents, which often have specific page limitations, technical presentations are usually constrained by a time limit.

But unlike written documents, oral presentations are far more interactive. Face-to-face communication is arguably the richest form, because the speaker can obtain immediate feedback from the audience, and because the audience can ask questions. Also, the nonverbal cues during a face-to-face encounter—cues such as vocal inflection, hand gestures, body posture, facial expressions—make presentations far more complex and capable of sending far more information.

In addition, oral presentations are usually (unless prerecorded) live performances. Because of this real-time feature, the speaker only has one chance to get it right. With written documents, writers create drafts, revise, and revise again until producing the final product. In oral presentations, any revising takes place before the presentation—the presentation itself is like the final version of a written document, with no chance to make any changes. The burden is on the speaker to know the material, be well prepared, and organize and present the material in the most effective, understandable form possible for that given audience.

The terms from Kaufer and Carley (1993) presented in the FYI feature can help explain the nature of oral presentations. Live oral presentations are synchronous, nonfixed, less durable than print, and, unless broadcast over the Internet or television, have less reach than print. In an oral presentation, the focus is very much on the moment—on you, your message, your personality, and your connection to the audience.

FYI

Face-to-Face versus Written Communication

Technical presentations are in some ways similar to technical writing but in other ways very different. Kaufer and Carley (1993) offer a useful system for understanding the differences between written and oral communication. After you read this list, think of other differences between writing and speaking. When is writing a more appropriate approach to a communication situation? When is an oral presentation the best choice?

Sychronicity involves whether a communicative transaction is real time. As Kaufer and Carley note, "face-to-face communication, oration, and telephone conversations" are synchronous. So are real-time Internet chats or video conferencing (p. 100). Writing, on the other hand, is asynchronous; that is, it allows communication between many people across distance. The sychronicity involved in face-to-face communication (like an oral presentation) allows you to have a far richer form of interaction with your audience.

Fixity is "the degree to which communication technology enables the communication to be retransmitted without change" (p. 100). Print is the most traditionally fixed form; printed pages maintain the same information no matter who reads them. Online printed material, such as Web pages, are less fixed and more fluid. Oral communication is the least fixed: Presentations are constructed as the speaker talks and each presentation is different every time it is given.

Durability is "the length of time the communication is available for communicative transactions." "Print," say Kaufer and Carley, "made communications more durable" (p. 102) in part because printed material can be distributed over and over again. Oral communication, on the other hand, vanishes once it has been completed. Even if someone tapes or video records an oral presentation, the real live presentation itself, including that very audience and those specific dynamics, can never be duplicated. Yet with this lack of durability comes the power of speaking directly to your audience.

Multiplicity involves "the number of partners with whom one can communicate at the same time" (p. 103). Print, the Internet, television, and radio all have what Kaufer and Carley call "high multiplicity" (p. 103), because these technologies allow communication to many people at the same time. Traditional oral communication has had a medium level multiplicity when delivered to a large audience but a low level when compared with print or TV. Today, oral communication can be delivered widely depending on the technology involved.

Being a Good Listener

Part of being a good communicator involves being a good listener. Along with effective skills at presenting technical information, you'll need good skills at listening to your audience. As just mentioned, oral presentations offer a situation far richer than written communication, because you can interact with your audience. Good listening skills let you know if you have structured the information at a level that is too complex or too simple. By listening closely, you obtain immediate feedback about the audience's point of view on a subject. Also, when audiences ask questions, they provide you with important insight into what they don't understand and why. All of this feedback can be useful as you redesign your information and as you prepare for your next presentation. Being a good listener not only involves listening *to* your audience, it also includes learning to listen when you are *in* the audience.

Even though you may hear what someone is saying, that does not necessarily mean that you are listening. To become a good listener, you need to practice active listening; that is, "make a conscious effort to both hear and understand the speaker's entire message" (Lewis, 1997). Often, when you listen to a message, your mind is concerned with other things; what one expert calls "filters." These filters can include your previous experience or expectations about a topic, your relationship to the speaker or audience, your personal history with the subject, and your emotional state at the time (1997). In order to shift from passive listening (hearing) to active listening, practice the following guidelines:

- Suspend your judgment about the topic. You may have a well-formed opinion about the topic or about an audience member's viewpoint, but do your best to set your opinion aside and truly listen.
- Focus on what the person is saying. If you are an audience member, pay close attention to the speaker's main points, persuasive techniques, argument structures, and so on.
- Restate an audience member's question. If you are a presenter and you are not sure what an audience member is asking, restate his or her question in slightly different terms until you are sure that you understand.

Oral Presentations for Technical Communication

Two key factors in any technical communication presentation are situations and purposes. As mentioned earlier, situations vary greatly across job titles, companies, and professions. Different professions, companies, and classes require slightly different types of presentations. Yet despite these contextual differences, it is possible to define some basic presentation types. Once you have mastered these basic types, you will be well prepared to give presentations in a variety of settings.

Technical communicators often need to give presentations that *inform* an audience about a topic, product, or idea. They may also need to *persuade* a group about one particular point of view. Sometimes, such presentations involve a specific *action plan or strategy* to solve a problem or create a new approach. Most communicators at one time or another will be involved in presentations that train

SCENARIOS

Typical Technical Communication Presentations

The following scenarios illustrate two possible situations a technical communicator could encounter.

Scenario One: Guidelines for Translation
Meredith Green is a technical communicator for a large computer company. Specifically, she is a technical editor, and her job involves overseeing the translation of documents from English into several other languages. She must be sure the English materials are written so they can be easily translated, and until now, she has been following some very general rules of thumb about this process. Recently, she designed a set of guidelines that writers can follow to help them write easily translatable English. Meredith prepares a thirty-minute presentation on how to use her guidelines. Her presentation is aimed at other technical writers in the company. Her job is to inform them about the new guidelines and to persuade them to use these guidelines.

Scenario Two: Wetland Restoration in an Urban Community
Chris Brannigan is a wildlife biologist who teaches at a major research university and is an expert on wetlands and biodiversity. Chris lives in an urban neighborhood with lots of lakes. Recently, the city council has been considering the restoration of a series of wetlands in order to help maintain clean lakes. The public is concerned about this restoration, because the land in question is currently a popular children's park. The city council asks Chris, as both a scientist and a neighbor, to give a twenty-minute informative presentation at its next meeting.

---

or explain *how to perform a task.* And in any of these cases, presentations may be given alone or as a *group;* also, technical communicators sometimes *prepare presentations for others* to deliver. This chapter's Scenario presents descriptions of two of these types of technical communication presentations. As you continue your study with this book, you will encounter additional examples of these and other types of presentations.

Using Technologies to Give Technical Presentations

Many people feel that the easy-to-use presentation software products, such as Microsoft PowerPoint or Lotus Freelance, make the job of technical presentations a no brainer. Nothing could be further from the truth, however. Although presentation software, Web pages, and other technologies do allow you to create powerful, complex, and easy-to-follow presentations, they are of no help whatsoever if you do not understand the basics. Audience, purpose, your role as communicator, and

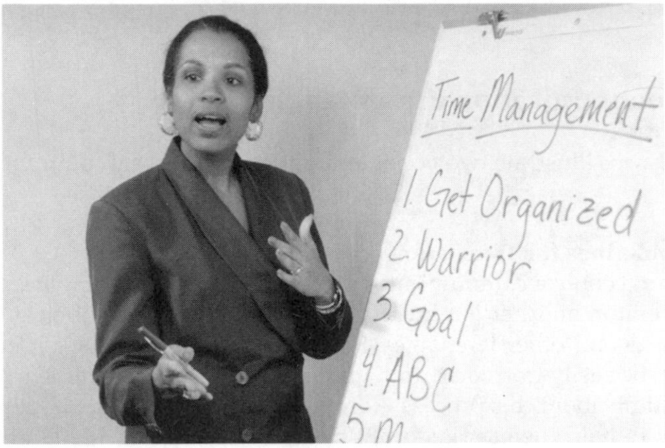

FIGURE 1.1 Oral presentations are an important part of a technical communicator's responsibility.

a strong understanding of the subject matter are all critical elements in effective technical presentations. Once you have developed a solid foundation in these areas, however, presentation technologies can be great tools. You can incorporate diagrams, photos, sound, color, animation, and more. Most technical communicators use presentation software, and often with excellent results. The Web, too, is becoming a place where you can create and store presentations, not only so you can use them again and again, but so that others who can't attend your talk can view your material. An effective technical presentation makes skilled use of digital technologies. This topic is discussed in far greater detail in Part Five.

In Summary: Getting Started

To begin your adventure in technical presentations, start with the basics. The rest of Part One (Chapters 2–4) will present information and exercises to help you with some of the most basic skills you'll need: skills in overcoming nervousness, in developing your personal character and credibility, in employing effective delivery and good use of your memory, and in generally becoming comfortable with yourself as a speaker (see Figure 1.1). Once you have these skills, you can move on and begin thinking about the audience and purpose for your presentation. Then, you'll be ready to give it a try!

QUESTIONS / EXERCISES / ASSIGNMENTS

1. List several scientific or technical topics that are familiar, interesting, or seem important for the future. Under each topic, list the key elements that are important for clearly understanding this subject. Then list situations when you might be required to present this material.

2. Listen to a presentation on a scientific or technical topic (you can often hear these sort of talks on public radio and television, CSPAN, the Discovery Channel, and other sites). Notice the topics that are presented and the ways in which the presenters help focus their topics for a non-expert audience.

3. In this chapter, you learned about several ways in which oral technical presentations differ from technical writing. Can you think of any others? How do these differences affect the ways in which presenters prepare their material? When is one more appropriate than another?

4. Interview a scientific or technical professional to get a sense of what role presentations play in his or her career. Share your findings with others in class via email.

Presentations and Cyberspace. Search the Web and identify sites for two or three upcoming academic conferences in a scientific or technical discipline that interests you. Review the information at each site and develop descriptions of the types of presentations scholars will be giving at each conference.

Presentations and Teamwork. Join with two or three other students whose scientific or technical specialty is similar to yours. In your team, list as many topics as possible that you as technical communicators may need to explain to the general public. Identify the topics that you believe will be the most challenging to present, and discuss the reasons those topics may be difficult.

Presentations and International Communication. Identify three products or industries that you feel will be important to your future career, and then determine what three nations are either the largest producers or consumers of that product or have key offices or facilities related to that industry. With one or two other students, discuss what types of jobs you might have in these industries and what sort of oral presentations you might give.

Presentations and Your Profession. Interview a professor in your field who teaches undergraduates. Ask the professor to explain what he or she does to ensure that the undergraduates understand the technical information presented in lectures. Or, if you are using this book as part of a class, interview your instructor and ask your instructor to explain about the types of presentations she or he gives at conferences, as a consultant, or in other situations.

REFERENCES

Kaufer, D. S., & Carley, K. M. (1993). *Communication at a distance: The influence of print on sociocultural organization and change.* Hillsdale, NJ: Erlbaum.

Lewis, J. (1997). Learn to listen. National Seminars Group. Available at www.natsem.com/9706.html.

Thompson, W. D. (1998). *Speaking for profit and pleasure: Making the platform work for you.* Boston: Allyn & Bacon.

CHAPTER

2 Dealing with Nervousness

CHAPTER OVERVIEW

For many people, the idea of giving a presentation in front of a group is cause for much nervousness and anxiety. This chapter will analyze speaking anxiety and help you understand the component parts that often create this anxiety. This chapter will also provide you with some helpful suggestions and tangible items you can do to prevent nervousness. This chapter covers the following topics:

- What Is Speaking Anxiety?
- Everyone Experiences It
- How Your Body Reacts to Anxiety
- How to Overcome Anxiety

What Is Speaking Anxiety?

Speaking anxiety is a general term used to describe the feelings of nervousness and fear that you may feel in response to giving an oral presentation. Some people experience this anxiety at the very thought of having to speak; others experience it directly before getting up to begin their presentation. Many surveys, both formal and informal, report similar information: Americans rank speaking before a group as one of their biggest fears. Though no one is sure why, this high rate of speaking anxiety is probably related to the earlier discussion about the differences between technical writing and oral presentations. In writing, no one is actually looking at you, just at your words on a page. And if you make a mistake, you can move the cursor back over that section and correct the error. The writing process involves many rough drafts before the final draft, all of which provide time to correct errors. But in oral presentations, the action is live, and you are the main focus. Any mistake, mispronunciation, or other problem is real time, and you can't correct it. The embarrassment factor is far higher. Another possible reason is that whereas people spend most of their lives writing (reports, letters, birthday cards, and so on), they spend very little time speaking in public. Because people don't have the experience, they fear that they might fail.

Everyone Experiences It

No matter the number of times or the amount of skill with which a person gives presentations, everyone occasionally experiences speech anxiety. It's a perfectly natural phenomenon—it's live, and you are in front of people. Even very experienced, highly entertaining speakers can relate stories where they suddenly became nervous before a presentation, perhaps because someone of significance was in the audience (their mother, their boss) or because the event was extremely important (an award ceremony). Or, for no reason in particular, the adrenaline just begins to flow. Don't make it harder on yourself by worrying about being worried. Remember that it can happen to anyone and won't happen every time. You can drastically reduce your chances of experiencing this anxiety, as we'll discuss in a moment.

How Your Body Reacts to Anxiety

People experience a variety of physical symptoms when they become anxious about having to give a presentation. These can range from sweaty palms to increased heart rates to fully flushed faces to total memory loss. For each person, this experience can change given the particular situation. A presentation in front of a limited number of coworkers in a small conference room is often far less anxiety-producing than a presentation in a big lecture hall. Physical symptoms are often a result of adrenaline, a hormone produced by the body in times of stress and fear. It's often called the fight-or-flight hormone, because it is usually produced when a person (or animal) is presented with a situation that requires immediate defense. In many presentation situations, you might prefer flight, but that is usually not an option! You can control the amount of adrenaline your body produces, and thus control your nervous reactions, by following a number of simple, yet often ignored, guidelines. The following sections describe these guidelines for controlling speech anxiety.

How to Overcome Anxiety

You can work on two areas in order to overcome speech anxiety. First, you can change your state of mind. The power of the mind is amazing, and you can literally talk yourself into a whole new outlook and new physical state. Second, you can take certain concrete actions in terms of how you prepare, organize, and deliver your presentation.

Change Your State of Mind

Your Audience Can't Tell Whether You Are Nervous. Often, when people are nervous about an oral presentation, they worry that the audience will be able to tell. It's very common after a presentation to hear the speaker say, "I was so nervous" and to hear the audience say, "You'd never have known!" Your inner state is barely visible to the audience. So, even if you feel somewhat nervous or anxious, remember that the audience is unlikely to know about your anxiety, and you will probably do very well.

Visualize Yourself as Confident. If you feel anxious, you then begin to lose confidence. And, as you lose confidence, your anxiety grows! You can stop this process right in its tracks by changing your thinking from one of nervousness to one of confidence. Close your eyes and imagine yourself confidently walking up to the front of the room. You know your material and feel confident. Your audience is looking forward to hearing you. If you visualize yourself as confident, you will feel that way.

Think Positive Thoughts. Along with visualizing yourself as confident, you can think other positive thoughts, too. Think about the best presentation you ever gave. Think about a time when you felt extremely confident and comfortable. Think about how much you enjoy your subject matter and how exciting it is to talk about it. You can also think more broadly, about times when you were on vacation or just relaxing, as a way to settle your mind and put a positive spin on your presentation.

Make Eye Contact. If you make eye contact with your audience before you start speaking, you will see that they are nothing more than people, just like you. And chances are, they are friendly people. Look at them for a moment and smile. It will change your state of mind.

Think of Your Audience as Supportive Colleagues. As one author has noted, the audience is "on your side" (Fujishin, 1997, p. 35). Your audience *wants* you to do a good job. They've come to hear you, and they are excited to learn more about your subject. So they want you to do well. Also, everyone in the audience has at one time or another been a presenter, so they know how much work you've put into your presentation and recognize that you might be a bit nervous. Think of them as supportive colleagues who want you to succeed.

Be Enthusiastic. As you are giving your presentation, be enthusiastic about your subject. Remember the discussion in Chapter 1 about the special role of the technical communicator. You are an expert at conveying complex scientific and technical material—material that is often fascinating for an audience. A presentation about black holes in space, for example, can be delivered with an enthusiasm for the wonder of outer space exploration. Your enthusiastic view will change your anxiety into high, positive energy.

Be Optimistic. Before, during, and after your presentation, be optimistic. Remind yourself that your presentation will go exceptionally well. As you present, remind yourself about what a great job you are doing. And at the end, give yourself a mental pat on the back for doing it!

Take Concrete Actions

Harness Your High Adrenaline Level. The same high level of adrenaline that is due to anxiety and causes physical symptoms like sweaty palms can also be used to make you an enthusiastic, energetic speaker. Utilize your high energy for positive results by giving the audience a great big smile and then opening with an enthusiastic introduction.

Be Extremely Well Prepared. As one author has noted, one of the biggest reasons that people are apprehensive about giving oral presentations is that they simply don't know how to communicate effectively (Richmond & McCroskey, 1998, p. 97). One key to effective communication is to be well prepared. The more carefully you prepare for your presentation, the less nervous you will be. If you know the material and have spent time researching the topic, organizing your presentation, and analyzing your audience (topics this book will return to in Part Two), you will feel confident and perhaps even excited to give the presentation.

Have an Interesting and Well-Memorized Introduction. Many people find this guideline to be one of the most effective ways of reducing nervousness. Write an interesting introduction, and be sure you have it memorized. Before you begin, take a nice deep breath and smile at the audience. Then, give your introduction. You'll be off to a great start, and your nervousness will often simply disappear.

Have an Interesting and Well-Memorized Conclusion. The same advice holds true for the conclusion. If your concluding remarks are also committed to memory, you have a clear place to end the presentation. Knowing your introduction and your conclusion provides you with a solid framework for the presentation, and this framework will help you avoid being nervous.

Organize the Body of Your Presentation. Between the well-memorized introduction and conclusion should be a well-organized body to the presentation. If your material is organized, you won't stray into topics you don't know or find yourself wandering into a line of thinking that might throw you. So be sure to be organized.

Select an Interesting and Important Topic. You are less nervous when you present material that you find interesting and important. Select something that matters to you—a topic that you care about and that is enjoyable to talk about.

Know Your Subject. Not only should you be enthusiastic about your topic, you should also know it. Even experienced presenters will become anxious if they are asked to talk about something they don't really know or understand. So whenever you have a choice, select a subject that you know well.

Know Your Audience and Purpose. When it comes to nervousness, the more you understand the audience and purpose for your presentation, the better. If you really feel in tune with the audience and their needs and interests, you will not view them as potentially hostile or as a faceless group of people. Instead, you will view them as people with interests, needs, and concerns, and as such, you will feel more as if you are talking with them rather than giving a performance. The same is true about purpose. The better you understand the purpose of the presentation (Am I selling a concept? Informing them? Explaining how to do something?), the more confident you will be about your material.

Practice, Practice, Practice. It's critical to practice your presentation, especially if you are still learning to become a good presenter. Even experienced presenters spend time rehearsing their material. If you can, practice in front of a group of colleagues or friends, and ask them for critical feedback: Can they hear you in the back of the room? Can they follow your line of reasoning? Do they find the presentation interesting? Don't overpractice to the point of exhaustion, but do run through your material several times or until you feel confident.

Breathe. Breathing deeply is an oldy but goody when it comes to nerves and public presentations. Taking several slow, deep breaths before your presentation (and while you are preparing, if necessary) will help settle your mind and calm your nerves. Also, before you start your introduction, take one final deep breath, look up, and smile at the audience. This act will create a sense of calm and get you off to a good start.

Relax Your Muscles. Before your presentation, or during your practice sessions, pay attention to your muscles. Are they tensed up? Pay particular attention to the muscles around your face, neck, and upper back. Relax these muscles as you breath deeply.

Be Well Rested and Physically Prepared. Get a good night's rest before the day of the presentation. If you normally run or work out, don't skip this: Exercise helps create endorphins, which help you relax. Be sure you've eaten and drunk enough water, so that you are physically prepared for your presentation.

Schedule Your Presentation for When You Are at Your Peak. You may not have as much choice as you'd like, but if possible, pick a presentation time that best fits your body clock. If you aren't a morning person, try to avoid an 8:00 A.M. time slot. Also, if you can, avoid giving presentations directly after lunch, as audiences often get sleepy right after eating!

Prepare Interesting and Organized Visual Aids. Overhead transparencies, slides, flip charts, computer presentations: All of these visual aids can be great at helping with nervousness, because suddenly people's eyes are not just on you, but on your slides, too. Of course, all the visual aids in the world won't help if you're not prepared and don't have the basics in place and can, in fact, make you even more nervous: There's nothing worse than being unprepared *and* not being able to find the correct transparency! But, when prepared, presenters often find that using visual material suddenly makes them feel far less anxious.

Have a Backup Plan for Any Technologies. Another way to overcome anxiety is to have a backup plan. What if the computer won't work? What if the bulb goes out on the overhead projector or the slide projector? When using technology, always bring handouts or have a contingency plan (more about this in Chapters 17 and 18).

Don't Stress If You Feel Less Than Perfect. If you've done a great job preparing, you will probably do a good job presenting. Don't add to your stress by striving for an unattainable goal, and don't mentally penalize yourself if you feel things are not going as well as you'd like. Emphasize the positive and remind yourself that you are doing a great job!

Do More Reading and Writing in Areas of Science and Technology. You'll be far more confident and comfortable as a presenter if you are knowledgeable about science and technology topics generally. In other words, read newspapers and magazines, watch educational television programs, and stay current about topics in your field and in the world. As you learn more about a topic, you will increase your vocabulary and your understanding of the specifics. The broader your knowledge base, the more comfortable you will be answering questions and engaging your audience. For instance, assume you are interested in weather patterns. If you watch the local news each night and pay attention to the technical terms (wind sheer, high pressure systems, jet stream), you will begin to increase your understanding of the topic.

Observe Other Presenters. As you learn more about the art of giving presentations, you'll find yourself listening critically to other presenters. Cultivate this critical listening skill, and pay attention to how other presenters do their job. Look for items they do well, and also notice items where they might have improved. For example, you may begin to notice that certain presenters seem very confident and comfortable. They move around the room with ease. They know their topic well. Their voices are clear and easy to understand. They use well-designed graphics to explain their ideas. Model yourself after people whose presentations are examples of excellence.

In Summary: Be Positive

Remember, being nervous or anxious about your presentation is natural, and everyone experiences it from time to time. Use the power of your mind to create a positive state for yourself. Be prepared, know your subject, know your introduction

CHECKLIST

Overcoming Presentation Anxiety

As you prepare for any presentation, remember the following items:

- Harness your high adrenaline level.
- Be extremely well prepared.
- Have an interesting and well-memorized introduction.
- Have an interesting and well-memorized conclusion.
- Make sure the body of the presentation is organized.
- Select an interesting and important topic.
- Know your subject.
- Know your audience and purpose.
- Practice, practice, practice.
- Breathe.
- Relax your muscles.
- Be well rested and physically prepared.
- Schedule your presentation for when you are at your peak.
- Prepare interesting and organized visual aids.
- Have a backup plan for any technologies.
- Don't stress if you feel less than perfect.
- Do more reading and writing in areas of science and technology.
- Observe other presenters.

---

and conclusion, and be well rested and ready to go. Your expertise as a person who works with scientific or technical knowledge puts you in a special position as a communicator, and now is your time to show everyone how talented and skilled you are.

The rest of this book will provide you with a set of skills and concepts that you can use to become an effective and confident oral communicator. So don't be nervous—be enthusiastic about your abilities.

QUESTIONS / EXERCISES / ASSIGNMENTS

1. Identify a past situation when you've been nervous about giving a presentation. Isolate as many individual factors as you can as to why you were nervous in that situation. Next to each item, list steps you can take to overcome these anxiety-producing items.

2. If you are not a particularly nervous speaker, ask yourself why this might be. What factors in your personality, speaking style, or organizational habits help you?

3. Stand up, balance your posture, and take a series of slow, deep breaths. Breathe in through your nose, then exhale through your mouth. Notice the muscles in your

face and neck. Relax these. Throughout the next few days, pay attention to your breathing and muscle tension. In stressful daily situations, practice deep breathing and muscle relaxation.

4. Attend a presentation and make notes on the presenter's overall tone. Did he or she appear relaxed? What things did the presenter do or not do well? Think about the kind of presenter you would like to be.

Presentations and Cyberspace. Using search engines, find useful articles on the Web that focus on strategies and tactics speakers can use to reduce and harness nervousness. Create a list that supplements the checklist presented in this chapter (be sure to cite your sources), and share the list with your class.

Presentations and Teamwork. With another student, create a list of the specific things people are afraid will happen when they speak. Create a master list of the anxiety-inducing events that the groups in your class have listed. Then, working again in pairs, create an equally long list of the specific actions a speaker can take to reduce the likelihood that those events will occur. Share that list with your class; in addition, decide which actions you will use to increase your speaking comfort.

Presentations and International Communication. Imagine that you are scheduled to travel to England to conduct a training workshop, and the attendees will represent countries throughout Europe. What aspects of this presentation might make you anxious? What specific steps can you take to alleviate your anxiety?

Presentations and Your Profession. Obtain and use a resource (e.g., book, audiotape, videotape) that provides information about visualizing success. As suggested by your resource, practice visualizing yourself giving a successful presentation to your work group. Plan how you will use this process to help you give effective presentations.

REFERENCES

Fujishin, R. (1997). *The natural speaker* (2nd ed.). Boston: Allyn & Bacon.
Richmond, V. P., & McCroskey, J. C. (1998). *Communication: Apprehension, avoidance, and effectiveness* (5th ed.). Boston: Allyn & Bacon.

CHAPTER

3 Ethos, Memory, and Delivery

CHAPTER OVERVIEW

The art of giving oral presentations is rooted in the study of rhetoric, an ancient art that still provides many key concepts that will help you become an excellent presenter. This chapter explains some basic concepts from rhetoric and illustrates how these concepts can help enhance your speaking abilities and make you a more effective and believable presenter. Of the key concepts in rhetoric, ethos, memory, and delivery are three of the most important ones for any presenter; therefore, this chapter discusses these three in detail. Throughout the rest of the text, you will draw on this chapter's explanations of rhetoric as you advance in your study of presentation skills.

As with most aspects of oral presentations, items in this chapter are not to be thought of as rigid rules. All presentations must be guided by the audience and purpose of the talk, including whether you are speaking to an international audience. For certain rhetorical concepts, such as delivery, issues of international communication are especially significant, and these issues will be discussed here. This chapter covers the following topics:

- Rhetoric as a Framework for Oral Presentations
- The Classical Rhetorical Canons
- Ethos: Your Appeal Based on Character and Credibility
- Memory: Using Your Innate Abilities
- Delivery: Using Your Body, Voice, and Technology

Rhetoric as a Framework for Oral Presentations

The art of rhetoric in Western culture dates back more than 2,000 years, to the days when Greek civilization was beginning to struggle with how to govern itself. In those times, a new form of democratic government arose. Citizens could speak and represent themselves in court and in the governing bodies of their communities. In order to perform this duty effectively, Greek citizens needed to learn how to become effective orators. The more effective a speech, the more easily the speaker could defend a claim in court or make an argument in front of the senate. It became clear, then, that it was important to understand the technicalities of how to make an effective presentation.

In response to this need, the ancient philosopher Aristotle developed a body of work that described how to understand and create effective speeches. Aristotle's system of rhetoric continues to provide a useful framework for communication today. For both technical writing and oral presentations, Aristotle's system provides a set of concepts and tools that are used widely to describe and create effective communication.

This system comprises two interconnected parts: the canons and the appeals. Throughout this book, you will refer to and use these concepts as you create specific oral presentations. The rest of this chapter briefly explains the entire system but focuses on three features: ethos, memory, and delivery.

The Classical Rhetorical Canons

Five main concepts, called canons, form the classical system of rhetoric: invention, arrangement, style, memory, and delivery. Each canon works with the others to create an effective, audience-centered presentation.

Invention

Invention is the aspect of a presentation where you plan what you are going to say and literally invent your argument. That is, before you can begin to create an effective presentation, you need to determine how to approach the topic. Will you use a logical approach? A more emotional approach? A combination of both? Most presentations use both, but some focus more in one direction than another. In deciding how to invent the argument of a presentation, most people draw on one or several of what are called the three *appeals:* ethos, logos, and pathos. Ethos, which is discussed later in this chapter, is an appeal to the audience based on your character and credibility. Logos is the type of logical argument you use, and pathos is an appeal to the audience's emotions. All three appeals work together, but sometimes, one is more appropriate than another. For example, if you were giving a presentation about the problems with a toxic waste site in your community, you would probably appeal based on a logical argument (logos) and also on your character as a speaker (ethos). But pathos could also play an important role in your presentation, because you might find it most effective to appeal to the audience's emotions of fear and concern for toxic waste in their neighborhood and around their children.

Arrangement

Arrangement is simply the way in which you organize and structure (or arrange) your presentation. Most presentations begin with some sort of introduction, continue with a body, and end with a conclusion. The introduction is very important in terms of setting audience expectations and creating your initial impression with the audience. For the body of any presentation, you must also choose how to arrange your material. Do you take a top-down approach, where you begin with the conclusion and then explain the details, or do you choose a bottom-up approach, where you provide details and lead your audience toward the summary? Do you present your material chronologically, in a problem-solving format, or based on cause and effect? Finally, your conclusion is the place where you can reemphasize important points and leave a final impression. In Part Three, you will learn about the various ways to arrange oral presentations based on the presentation's type and purpose.

Style

For many people in the United States the concept of a communication style may not have much meaning. The United States tends to be a casual culture, and often, when speaking in front of a group, U.S. citizens maintain the same casualness that they use with friends. Yet style is an important consideration in an oral presentation: If a situation calls for a formal style, but you come prepared with a more casual presentation, you probably won't make a good impression on the audience. Style involves word choice, tone, and attitude; although style is not always associated with technical communication, every kind of presentation, including technical, conveys a particular style (Jones, 1998, p. 3–5). For Aristotle, style also involved the use of metaphor (trans. 1991, p. 1405a), a powerful technique for technical communication that is discussed in Chapter 14. For most technical communication presentations, an appropriate style is one that is formal, professional, and respectful but also demonstrates respect for the audience and the importance of the situation; or, put another way, "combines a certain degree of formality with the best attributes of good conversation" (Lucas, 1998, p. 292).

Memory

Memory is the ability to use your brain's innate capabilities to retain information so that you can recall items when you need them. During Aristotle's time in ancient Greece, people communicated primarily through oral communication (speaking, reciting epic stories and poems, theater). They delivered large amounts of information, such as long epic stories or legal arguments, reciting these from memory and completely without notes (MacDowell, 1978, p. 250). The practice of using memory was also strong in the Middle Ages, and throughout the world, in various cultures at various times, humans have used their memory the way contemporary Westerners now use computers, handheld digital calendars, sticky notes, and other tools. In order to be an effective presenter, you will need to rediscover the ancient art of memorizing. Although it's usually not advisable to memorize an entire presentation word for word, it's very effective and important to have the introduction, conclusion, and main points memorized and ready to go. More on memory in a moment.

Delivery

Delivery, rhetoric's fifth canon, involves how you physically and vocally project yourself and your presentation. Delivery involves your physical gestures (such as hand and arm movements), vocal inflections, facial expressions, eye contact, and other nonverbal types of communication. As discussed in a moment, delivery is important, because your physical state conveys your character and confidence to an audience. The rest of this chapter will focus on the appeal of ethos and the two canons of memory and delivery.

Ethos: Your Appeal Based on Character and Credibility

Aristotle gave careful thought to what makes a good presenter. Times have not changed all that much, even after more than 2,000 years. He noted that "There is persuasion through character whenever the speech is spoken in such a way as to make the speaker worthy of credence" (trans. 1991, p. 1356a).

Picture the following scenario, based on the last time you attended a lecture or presentation. You were in a room, seated with many other people, waiting for the presentation to begin. Soon, the presenter came through the door; perhaps it was someone you've never seen before. She moved toward the front of the room, arranged her material, then began her presentation. If you can, recall how you felt after only the first few minutes of the presentation. What was your initial impression of the presenter: Was she trustworthy? Could you understand her presentation? Did she make you feel interested in the subject matter? Did you think of her as a nice person? Competent? Now, if you can, recall how you felt about the person at the end of the presentation. Overall, what kind of impression did this person make on you?

If you are like most people, you had an immediate reaction to the presenter from the moment she entered the room, and you continued to construct this person's character and credibility as the presentation progressed. If you did not feel the person to be trustworthy or honest, for whatever reasons, chances are that you didn't listen carefully to the presentation, nor did you take the person's message seriously. And later, if someone asked you how you enjoyed the presentation, you might easily have said, "I just didn't care for the speaker," even if you thought the message was interesting or important.

This projection of character and credibility is known in classical rhetoric as the speaker's *ethos*. As mentioned earlier in this chapter, ethos is one of the three appeals of the classical system. Along with logos and pathos, ethos is part of how an audience determines whether or not to accept the presenter's message. Yet unlike logos or pathos, ethos is projected from the very moment the presenter enters the room. And the presenter's ethos is extremely powerful: If the presenter appears to be unlikable, his or her message will not be heard.

For Aristotle, ethos was extremely important; he called it "the controlling factor in persuasion" (trans. 1991, p. 1356a). Ethos is still of great importance in today's communication situations. The moment you walk in the room, smile (or not), and look at the audience, you begin to project a certain character. What you wear, whether you are on time, how well (or not) you are prepared: These and many other factors have an impact on the audience's concept of you as a person. And, as Aristotle and many other teachers since him have noted, who you are is important to an audience.

The power of ethos is especially important in a technical or scientific presentation, where you may be presenting complicated or controversial material. For audience members to be truly open to listening to the technical details or hearing your side of the controversy, they must feel that you are trustworthy. Even more, at some level, the audience should find you likable—audiences find it easier to listen to someone they like. A speaker who consistently uses sexist or racist language, for example, will probably be far less likable than one who is careful about word choice. A speaker who is late and has kept an audience waiting will also create a bad impression.

You have control over many factors that affect your ethos. Here are several of them.

Understand Your Audience

The more you understand the needs, values, and interests of your audience, the more closely you can relate your information to themes and topics they care about. And by relating your presentation to the audience, you do what is sometimes called bridge building: You build a bridge of common understanding between yourself and the audience. Audiences relate best to a presenter who speaks directly to them and their needs. By learning as much as possible about your audience and conveying that understanding, you establish a strong link between yourself and the audience.

Be Prepared

The more organized and prepared you are, the more the audience will accept you as a credible presenter. If you come to the presentation with your material well planned, your presentation slides or computer display ready to go, and your handouts nicely copied and arranged, your audience will see that you are taking the situation seriously and professionally. Presenters who are sloppy or who lose their place while speaking ("Sorry. Wait just a minute while I find the right overhead") quickly lose their connection with the audience.

Establish Credibility during Your Introduction

The introduction to your presentation provides a perfect place for you to state your authority about a subject. Let's say, for example, that you are giving a presentation to your department about how to use certain features of a new software product. If, during your introduction, you state that you've used this product for several years and have had special training in the new features, your audience will learn that you are an expert and should be listened to. Or, if you indicate that you have a degree in wildlife biology at the outset of a presentation about restoring lakes and wetlands, you will have quickly and easily established your authority on that topic. Of course, the rest of your presentation needs to be well organized and researched in order for that authority to stay in place! But the introduction of your presentation is the perfect place to indicate your knowledge and credibility about a subject. Chapter 7 will discuss the importance of the introduction further.

Be Interested and Enthusiastic

By being an interested, energetic, and enthusiastic presenter, you'll invite the audience to see you as someone who truly cares about the subject. And when audience members sense that a presenter cares, they respond by viewing you as credible and competent. This response translates into positive ethos for the presenter. So, when you can, select topics that you care about and that have meaning for you. Even if you are assigned a topic that is less than your favorite subject, find a way to make it interesting for you—if it's interesting for you, your audience will find you more credible and believable. Interest and enthusiasm are especially important parts of a technical presentation. Often, the material might seem overwhelming or hard to understand to your audience, but your mood will put them in a position where they find you exciting and interesting.

Be Sincere

Although humor and sarcasm sometimes work in specific cases (more on that in a moment), sincerity is always your best bet. It's usually easy for an audience to sense when a presenter is not being sincere. Even when a presenter may not be aware of it, audiences sense insincerity through the presenter's body language, tone, and word choice. In the same fashion, audiences easily sense when a topic is serious and important to the presenter. Your sincerity will help make you a more believable speaker.

Be Sensitive to Cultural and Age Differences

Audiences are rarely homogeneous; depending on the situation, your audience will probably contain a mix of people from different cultures and age groups. Learn as much as you can about your audience in advance, and make sure your presentation is sensitive to any special needs. As Chapter 5 will discuss, a hand gesture that might be appropriate for one culture could be insulting to another. For older populations, you'll need to be sure the type on your visual aids is large enough, because people's eyesight changes with age. Again, your sensitivity to these and other audience issues will help establish you as a credible, caring presenter.

Be on Time

If you want to gain the audience's confidence right from the outset, be on time. There is nothing more irritating to an audience than to be kept waiting, and the longer they wait, the more your credibility decreases. Show respect for their busy schedules by being ready to begin at the stated time. If you are scheduled to speak at 2:00, for example, you should be ready to start *speaking* at that time. You should not be fiddling with your computer, chatting with someone, or trying to see how the overhead projector works. Get to the room early for these preparations.

Be Organized

As with being on time, being organized shows the audience that you respect them and appreciate their time. If you are disorganized, you convey an unprofessional ethos. Your message will get lost in the commotion of you trying to find the slide you misplaced or looking through your briefcase for a pen. Also, your presentation itself should be well organized, because if people cannot follow what you are saying, they'll lose respect for you and your message. An organized presenter conveys a professional ethos.

Be a Good Listener

A big part of being a good presenter involves learning to listen. Audiences are not just static groups waiting to be handed information. They are thinking people who have questions and comments about your topic. Learn to listen carefully and with respect. Even if you do not agree with the questioner, begin your answer by indicating that you see her point. For example, you can say, "That is an excellent comment. I had never thought about it from that perspective before. On the other hand, allow me to present a different side." By showing that you actually listened to her comment, you present yourself as considerate and respectful.

Avoid Humor Unless You Know the Audience Well

Humor can be a great way to connect with an audience, but if and only if you know the audience well and can accurately predict how they will respond. What is funny to some may be very insulting to others. Some humorous items are perfectly appropriate for a certain audience and situation. For example, in a presentation designed to address how technology induces stress, the cartoon in Figure 3.1 is a great way to get started.

For an audience of people who are always sending and receiving information via many types of technology (cell phone, email, pager, fax machine), this cartoon

"In this stress test, we're going to hook you up to a fax machine, voice-mail unit, and a 56K modem."

FIGURE 3.1 Humor can help a presenter connect with the audience.
Source: ©1998 Ted Goff. Reprinted by permission.

would probably bring out some smiles. But before using it, it would be wise to try the cartoon out on a smaller group and test an audience's reaction.

Dress Appropriately

Most people have heard about dressing for success, and although it may seem silly, how you dress conveys who you are. Think about a judge who walks into the courtroom dressed in his robes: The robes convey authority, power, and respect. Similarly, how you dress for a technical presentation will make an immediate impact on the audience. Your choice of how to dress should be based on the audience and purpose for the presentation. In many high tech organizations, for example, casual dress is common, especially among software developers. If you were speaking as a fellow engineer, a formal outfit, such as a suit and tie on a man, might seem out of touch with the culture of these professionals. But if you were speaking as a sales representative, you might be expected to dress more formally. Find out what you can about the situation; if you are unfamiliar with the group, you can call ahead and inquire about the dress code.

Exercise Appropriate and Professional Delivery

How you speak, gesture, stand, and physically interact with the audience all convey your ethos. More on this in the coming section on Delivery. This chapter's Checklist summarizes ways to establish your ethos.

Ethos and Ethics

A discussion of ethos would not be complete simply by listing various items that you can employ to create a good impression. You must also recognize the relationship between ethos, authority, and ethics. Consider this: Ethos is often taken to mean the presenter's *projection* of his or her character but not of the underlying moral character of the person herself. It's easy to think of situations where a speaker may have projected a sincere, caring ethos but in reality had other motives for moving an audience to take action. According to one authority on Aristotle, the famous teacher of rhetoric meant "the character of the person, not the rhetorical presentation of that character" (Kennedy, 1991, p. 8); in other words, ethos is not just the projection of the presenter's character, it is also his or her actual moral and ethical character and values that become central to an effective and high-quality presentation. As a presenter, you are responsible not only for structuring the most effective presentation, but you are also charged with the job of knowing how you feel about the topic and of being the most honest and sincere presenter that you can be. If you are asked to give a presentation on a topic that you find morally unacceptable, would you do it? Only you can answer this question, but you should

CHECKLIST

Ways to Establish Your Ethos

As you work on establishing your ethos with an audience, keep the following items in mind:

- Understand your audience.
- Be prepared.
- Establish credibility during your introduction.
- Be interested and enthusiastic.
- Be sincere.
- Be sensitive to cultural and age differences.
- Be on time.
- Be organized.
- Be a good listener.
- Avoid humor unless you know the audience well.
- Dress appropriately.
- Exercise appropriate and professional delivery.

recognize that when you prepare and deliver a presentation, you are in a position of power, authority, and responsibility. Everyone knows all too well the dangers that come when a speaker uses his or her powers to sway an audience to bad purposes. Examples such as Hitler come immediately to mind, and these examples should serve as a reminder of the ethical choices involved in the power of ethos in oral presentations. For some teachers of rhetoric in the Roman era, a good speaker was not only an effective speaker, he (remember, all speakers were men at that time) was also someone who reflected good character—"a good man of character and courtesy" (Meador, 1983, p. 166). Your character—who you are and what you believe in—is an important part of your ethos.

Memory: Using Your Innate Abilities

Plato, Aristotle's teacher, worried about writing. He thought that writing might destroy our ability to memorize. In the Phaedrus, one of Plato's many dialogues, he described his feelings about the use of writing:

> The fact is that this invention [writing] will produce forgetfulness in the souls of those who have learned it. They will not need to exercise their memories, being able to rely on what is written, calling things to mind no longer from within themselves by their own unaided powers, but under the stimulus of external marks that are alien to themselves (Plato, trans. 1956, p. 275).

We still have these concerns today. In this age of laptop computers, voicemail, sticky notes, handheld personal organizers, and other memory devices, the innate and powerful human ability to memorize is often left untapped. Yet all the blame can't be placed on computers: Even before the digital age, pen and paper allowed people to rely less on brains and more on external devices. Plato bemoaned the invention of writing for the negative impact it would have on the use of memory. For the Greeks, memory was a crucial element in presenting a message; in legal presentations, for example, speakers created a far more credible impression when they memorized and delivered their material (MacDowell, 1978, p. 250).

The use of memory continues to be a powerful device in oral presentations, and despite how little it is used in this digital world, with a little work most people can learn to use memory effectively and for the benefit and success of oral presentations. Memory is related to ethos, because the more you know your material, the more credible and understandable you will be to your audience. Presenters who have material well organized and placed in memory will make a good impression on the audience. It is impressive to audiences to hear speakers who know the material well and do not need to turn constantly to their notes. Good use of memory is also important for you as the presenter, for it relieves you of having too many objects (such as notes, index cards, and so on) and lets you concentrate on the topic and the audience.

For many people, the power of memory has been asleep, unused to its full potential because of our written and digital culture. (Often, people can't even go to the grocery store for a few simple items without a written list.) But with the aid of some simple devices and with continued practice, you will find that your memory is a powerful tool, ready to work for you. Here are some devices you can use to increase your memory ability.

Mnemonics

These are devices intended to help you remember based on linking new material to something easy to recall: a sequence of numbers, a sentence, a phrase. For example, if you were trying to memorize rhetoric's five canons—invention, arrangement, style, memory, delivery—you might link them to the initials letters (IASMD). Or you might create a simple sentence, such as "I am starting my day." Mnemonics are fine for simple ideas that don't require you to understand the concept but merely to repeat a series of words or concepts (Coe, 1996, p. 93). In oral presentations, you can use simple mnemonics to help you remember certain key points or terms in your presentation.

Memory Based on Space

You can also associate items with particular spatial arrangements at the time you are introduced to the information. For example, if you were to enter a room of ten or more people and be introduced to each one, you might have a hard time coming up with a way to remember their names. But if you linked a person's name to the place where he or she was standing, you could probably remember the name more easily. In oral presentations, this is a good technique if you need help remembering the names of people in your audience. Also, you may wish to associate the introduction and conclusion (where you generally will always want to speak from memory) with some sort of spatial memory device: perhaps the room in your house where you memorized what you were going to say or something in that room, like a clock. You can train yourself to think of that item and associate it with your presentation material.

Linking to a Familiar Idea

Often, you can help yourself remember a new or complex idea by linking it to something with which you are familiar. If you are seeking to understand and explain how a computer organizes information, you might mentally compare an electronic file system to an old-fashioned file cabinet. A file cabinet has drawers, and each drawer contains items related to a specific topic. Each drawer is then subdivided into folders. If you can find a particularly useful metaphor, it will not only help you remember the concept, it will help your audience, too.

Memory Joggers

Sometimes called ticklers, memory joggers are physical devices that you can use to help recall an entire idea. One example would be sticky notes. You may put one on your computer with the word "kids," and whereas this word might not mean something to anyone else in your office, it might immediately remind you that you need to call your kids this afternoon and see if they have any homework. Computer presentations, slides, and overheads can be very effective memory joggers: A bulleted list of items is usually all you need to remind yourself of what you wanted to talk about. If you have practiced and know your material, you generally do not need any additional notes beyond these shorthand items. In technical presentations, where you are often dealing with highly specialized terms and concepts, memory joggers can help.

Another aspect to consider is your audience's memory. When people read information, they can always turn back a few pages if they forget something. But with an oral presentation, you have a responsibility to organize your material so that the audience can remember your topic, main points, and overall argument. You do this by using advance organizers, designing clear overheads and visual aids, and reminding your audience where you are headed as you advance through the presentation. These topics will be covered in more detail in Part Three.

Delivery: Using Your Body, Voice, and Technology

A recent ad for a computer projection device gives this advice about presentations: "Let's face it. You are what you present" (Toshiba, 1998).

These words were written to describe a new, high tech computer presentation system. Yet they could also easily describe that which does not involve bits and bytes, but rather something far more basic: your physical presentation. "You are what you present," at its most basic level, means that your character, credibility, and message cannot be separated from how you look, speak, gesture, stand, and so on. In classical rhetoric, these features were considered under the fifth canon of delivery, which involves the *bodily* part of your presentation: how you physically project yourself and your message. Delivery includes gestures, vocal inflections, facial expressions, eye contact, and other nonverbal communication.

Delivery is important, because your physical state conveys your character and confidence to an audience. Delivery is obviously closely linked to ethos; your character and credibility are created not only by your message but also by you and how you look and act toward your audience.

There are a number of aspects to good delivery. As you gain experience and practice in oral presentations, you will find a combination of these features that works best for you. The best presenters are those who have found a delivery style that is natural but professional.

Voice

You may not ever have stopped to consider all the various components that make up your voice. There is tone, pitch, the rate of your speech, and how well you articulate.

There is also volume: how loud or softly you speak. All of these features combine to create the overall vocal quality, and presenters shift these features depending on audience and situation. When you talk with a group of friends, for example, you may speak quickly, use lots of contractions, slur certain words, and interrupt. When you speak to a child, you may speak more slowly and use words more carefully. And when you speak to a group of professionals at work, you probably assume a professional delivery style, using words carefully and speaking clearly. It's important to become aware of your natural speaking habits and consider what sort of vocal qualities you'll need to practice in order to be an effective presenter. If you always say "um" or "OK" at the end of sentences, for example, you'll want to work on correcting this distracting habit. If you tend to speak very softly, you'll need to practice projecting your voice. One expert suggests that there are three main factors you can concentrate on to improve vocal quality: proper posture, relaxed neck and shoulder muscles, and breath support (deep breaths give you the air you need to speak fully and clearly) (Hillman, 1999, p. 91). Also, in presentations involving international audiences, you'll need to learn about vocal qualities that are appropriate: One expert (Axtell, 1991) notes that in France, loud conversations are to be avoided (p. 136) and that in Poland, people tend to speak softly (p. 147).

Facial Expressions

Smiles, frowns, enthusiastic glances, looks of surprise, and other expressions are generally considered to be outward expressions of a person's emotional state. When you smile, you convey happiness, and when you frown, you convey anger or dissatisfaction. A large part of a presenter's delivery style is reflected in his face. If you are enthusiastic about your subject and happy to be giving your talk, it will show, and your audience will share in these feelings. Your facial expressions can bring excitement and energy to your subject matter, which is important in technical presentations, where material might appear to be intimidating or difficult. For international audiences, although many facial expressions are universal, certain expressions do differ from culture to culture—for example, according to Axtell (1991), winking one eye signifies a shared secret among Americans and Europeans, but this same expression may be seen as rude in Hong Kong (p. 64).

Eye Contact

How and how often you make eye contact with your audience is another crucial part of delivery. As with facial expressions, eye contact is culturally based. In certain Asian cultures, for example, it is considered impolite to stare straight into someone's eyes; in other cultures, such as parts of the United States, people who don't look you in the eyes are often considered untrustworthy. For most U.S. audiences, however, eye contact is a sign that you are interested in your audience and wish to engage them directly. In large groups, you must make sure you look at the entire audience. It's easy to make eye contact with one friendly person in the front of the room and then continue to only look at that person. In technical presentations, audiences are counting on you to help them understand complex information, so give the whole group your attention.

Posture

Your posture conveys your presence. If you are slouched over with your head bent down, you send a signal of being nervous and uninterested in your audience. If you keep your hands in your pockets, you appear unprofessional, and your body is often forced into a slouching position. One corporate speech trainer describes what she calls the "forbidden postures": postures that distance you from your audience and make you appear nervous (Woodall, 1997). In general, it's best if you stand straight and tall with your hands at your side (see Figure 3.2). Using your hands to change overheads or operate the computer gives you something to do with your hands and usually keeps you in a good position—but be sure to move around and not block your audience's view.

FIGURE 3.2 Forbidden postures convey nervousness and lack of audience awareness; good posture projects confidence.

Source: Woodall, Marian K. (1997). *Presentations That Get Results.* Lake Oswego, OR: Professional Business Communications. Reprinted by permission.

Gestures

The relationship between gesture and speech is very interesting. Some people, for example, are natural gesturers: They simply cannot talk without using their hands. Others rarely gesture while speaking. In oral presentations, it's best to determine your natural style of gesture, then learn to what extent your style is distracting (or not) to an audience. Don't try to stop gesturing, and don't try to add more gestures than you normally would. When you practice your presentations, get feedback from people and adjust accordingly. (Most people can probably remember at least one speaker who gestured so much and with such enthusiasm that they found themselves watching that person's hands at the expense of listening to the message.)

Along with differences in personal style, gesture use also differs by culture. A gesture of friendliness in one culture might be an insult in another; for instance, the common habit in some cultures of standing very close or even touching a person while you speak would be unacceptable in other cultures (Axtell, 1991; Morris, 1994). For international audiences, presenters have an additional task of determining what constitutes an appropriate set of gestures.

Delivery as Medium

Recently, scholars of rhetoric have come to consider delivery as more than physical presence. In the electronic age, the concept of delivery must also include the medium through which the presentation is delivered (Welch, 1990). In ancient times, it was the physical body alone that delivered the presentation, but today it is a combination of physical selves and technologies. Television, radio, the Internet, computer presentation software, and other technologies thus join the list of items to consider with delivery. This electronic aspect of delivery is addressed in detail in Part Five.

In Summary: Ethos, Memory, Delivery

The ancient art of rhetoric provides some useful concepts and tools for becoming an effective oral communicator of technical information. The five canons (invention, arrangement, style, memory, delivery) and the three appeals (logos, ethos, pathos) offer a framework for understanding how to construct and deliver a presentation. Specifically, the concepts of ethos, memory, and delivery are especially critical for a presenter, because these three concepts work together to create an initial impression with an audience and convey character and credibility.

QUESTIONS / EXERCISES / ASSIGNMENTS

1. In order to understand the interaction of ethos and presentations, watch a speaker on TV (CSPAN) or attend a political speech, campus lecture, or other presentation. Characterize that person based on what you saw and heard. Was the person trustworthy? Interesting? Sincere? Discuss how and why you came to these conclusions.

2. For the next week, try some aerobic exercises for your memory. For example, use the technique of mnemonics to go grocery shopping without a list. Memorize people's names by associating their names with their locations in a room. Prepare for a meeting but don't bring notes; memorize what you will say by remembering just the bulleted items.

3. Find your own style. Draft a short description of yourself, your interests, and a technical issue that you find interesting and know something about. In front of a mirror, practice giving a short talk about this subject (one minute). Don't be concerned yet about how you organize your material: Just talk. As an actor might, try on various styles: a professional style; a conversational style; a speaking-to-children style. Discover what kind of style feels comfortable and natural to you. If you can, videotape yourself giving a short talk—perhaps a description of your home or something else that is familiar. Watch this tape and notice your style and delivery.

Presentations and Cyberspace. On the Web, locate an academic site that presents information about the classical system of rhetoric (The Forest of Rhetoric is one excellent site; find it at http://humanities.byu.edu/rhetoric/silva.htm). Choose one of the five canons and study the information about that canon at the site you have selected.

Presentations and Teamwork. Form a team of two to three students and perform the following exercise in delivery. Have each person give a short informal presentation, with no visual aids or other items, on a topic that's recently been in the news or is of interest to him or her. Have another team member tape this presentation; all team members should listen carefully to the presenter's speaking style, vocal inflection, and other delivery habits. Play back the tape recording and provide feedback on voice, posture, body language, and other features.

Presentations and International Communication. Identify how communicators from other cultures establish ethos. You may accomplish this in many ways. You might interview a consultant who specializes in helping U.S. citizens prepare to work effectively in other cultures by teaching them how to establish and maintain their credibility in other cultures. Or, you might research this topic on the Web or read a book or several credible articles on this topic. Share your findings with your class.

Presentations and Your Profession. After practicing the chapter's memory devices during your daily routines, attend a meeting where you are likely to know few or no people (for example, a local association meeting of professionalss in your field). Use your favorite memory devices to learn and remember the names of fifteen people at that meeting; test yourself each day for a week after the meeting by reciting those names aloud.

REFERENCES

Aristotle. (1991). *On rhetoric: A theory of civic discourse* (G. A. Kennedy, Trans.). New York: Oxford University Press.

Axtell, R. E. (1991). *Gestures: The do's and taboos of body language around the world.* New York: Wiley.

Coe, M. (1996). *Human factors for technical communication.* New York: Wiley.

Hauser, G. A. (1986). *Introduction to rhetorical theory.* Prospect Heights, IL: Waveland.
Hillman, R. (1999). *Delivering dynamic presentations: Using your voice and body for impact.* Boston: Allyn & Bacon.
Jones, D. (1998). *Technical writing style.* Boston: Allyn & Bacon.
Lucas, S. E. (1998). *The art of public speaking.* Boston: McGraw-Hill.
MacDowell, D. M. (1978). *The law in classical Athens.* New York: Cornell University Press.
Meador, P. A. J. (1983). Quintilian and the "Institutio oratoria." In J. J. Murphy (Eds.), *A synoptic history of classical rhetoric* (pp. 151–176). Davis, CA: Hermagoras Press.
Morris, D. (1994). *Bodytalk: A world guide to gestures.* London: Jonathan Cape.
Plato. (1956). *Phaedrus.* (W. C. Helmbold & W. G. Rabinowitz, Trans.). New York: Macmillan.
Toshiba Corporation. (1998, June). Toshiba's advanced TLP-511 3-D projector dramatically enhances every image. *World Traveler,* p. A-12.
Welch, K. E. (1990). Electrifying classical rhetoric: Ancient media, modern technology, and contemporary composition. *Journal of Advanced Composition, 10*(1), 22–38.
Woodall, M. K. (1997). *Presentations that get results: 14 reasons yours may not.* Lake Oswego, OR: Professional Business Communications.

CHAPTER

4 Other Techniques to Build Confidence

CHAPTER OVERVIEW

This chapter provides additional information on how to improve your confidence and become comfortable as a presenter. This chapter covers the following topics:

- Join a Local Speechmaking Organization
- Give Presentations to Children
- Present to Small Groups
- Try Your Ideas in Writing
- Read Science and Technology Written for General Audiences
- Pay Attention to Museum Exhibits
- Attend Presentations and Be a Critic

Join a Local Speechmaking Organization

One effective way to increase your presentation skills is to join a local organization such as Toastmasters International or another speechmaking club. Although some of their techniques may not be specialized enough for technical communication, and some of their advice may not completely parallel what you'll learn in this book, there is nothing wrong with learning from a different perspective. These organizations are usually focused on giving speeches, not presentations, and on management and business settings, not technical ones. But technical communicators often give presentations in management settings; plus, any chance you get to practice, receive feedback from an audience, and critique other speakers will help improve your own presentation abilities. These groups also offer support and assistance if you have any presentation habits you'd like to work on.

Give Presentations to Children

An excellent way to gain confidence and experience in giving presentations is to speak to groups of children. If you are nervous about getting up in front of groups, you'll find children to be far less intimidating than adults. Also, children are generally enthusiastic about any topic when the material is presented to them in an exciting fashion, so you'll have a chance to practice crafting your message into one that is delivered with enthusiasm and interest. In some ways, children resemble lay adult audiences: In both cases, audiences are not familiar with overly technical language or jargon. By presenting to children, you'll also be performing an important civic duty—giving back to your local school or community. Children respond well to graphics and visual information, too, so you'll be able to test ideas for other presentations. Finally, you'll be helping educate the next generation about important scientific or technical issues.

Present to Small Groups

Small, somewhat informal groups can often seem less intimidating than large rooms of seemingly faceless people. By speaking to small groups, you will be able to see everyone in the room and will soon realize that your audience is friendly and interested. Also, small group presentations are often given where you know people: work, school, or a community organization. For example, the technical departments of many companies often have brown-bag lunch presentations, at which people eat lunch around a conference table while listening to a presentation. These sorts of opportunities will give you practice and help you increase your confidence.

Try Your Ideas in Writing

Writing and speaking are inherently connected. When you write down your ideas, you get a chance to see them move from unorganized thoughts in your head to words, titles, and tangible concepts. This move from your brain to hard copy characterizes the rhetorical canon of invention, discussed in the previous chapter. Your ideas are invented as you write them down, make changes, revise, and work through your thoughts.

Even though you are planning an oral presentation, not a written document, it's often very useful to write down your ideas before you even begin preparing the presentation. Naturally, at some point in the preparation process, you'll probably create an outline (more on this in Part Two). But even before you outline, do some brainstorming on paper. Write a short paragraph describing your presentation topic: why you like this topic, what you know about it, what items you still need to research. When you discover that one idea does not logically flow from the next, revise your paragraph so that it makes sense. Review your writing to see if you consistently use any jargon or technical language. The act of writing down your ideas will help you get started and will give you confidence.

Read Science and Technology Written for General Audiences

How well a person speaks and writes is to some extent related to how much and what kinds of materials that person reads. As a technical communicator, you are skilled at understanding scientific and technical concepts and making these concepts interesting, understandable, and useful for a variety of audiences. Another group of professionals who are also skilled in this way are science and technology journalists. As you'll learn in Part Four, these journalists must understand complex technical topics and be able to express them clearly. Read science articles in the newspaper; the *New York Times* has an especially good science section on Tuesdays. Read magazines such as *Scientific American, Discover, Omni, Science,* and *Nature.* Look up words you do not know, and push yourself to understand topics that may seem complicated or difficult. Be especially in tune with topics that are related to your area of interest. If you are a technical communicator in a software organization, for example, read about the latest computing advances and controversies. If you are in medical communication, read as much as possible about new medical discoveries and technologies. You'll build your vocabulary and your store of knowledge, and these tools will increase your confidence in front of an audience.

Pay Attention to Museum Exhibits

Museum curators have always been adept at communicating technical information to a wide audience. Pay attention to how science and technology exhibits are organized, and you'll observe some helpful techniques (use of visuals and metaphors, for example). You'll also teach yourself something new; as with reading, the more you know, the more confident and effective you'll be as a presenter.

Attend Presentations and Be a Critic

Teachers of rhetoric and oratory have known since ancient times that along with learning rules and guidelines, effective speakers become effective by watching others. Attend lots of presentations, and take mental notes about what aspects you liked and didn't like. Be a critic: Think about how you responded to the speaker, how certain computer or slide presentations worked, and what you learned from the talk. Even without really trying, you'll begin to model your own approach on certain presentation styles and techniques that you observe in others.

In Summary: Other Techniques to Build Your Confidence

There are many ways you can gain confidence and become comfortable as a presenter. These include joining a speechmaking club, presenting to children and small groups, using writing to try out your ideas, reading science and technology articles, paying attention to museum exhibits, and attending presentations given by others. These activities will enhance your skills, no matter what type of presenter you are.

QUESTIONS / EXERCISES / ASSIGNMENTS

1. Locate a professional speaking association in your community and check into its services. Attend a meeting if you can and find out more about its opportunities and events.
2. Volunteer to give a talk to the local elementary school or at your public library's children's section. Pick a topic that involves something you care about and think children will find interesting.
3. If you have a job or internship, offer to give a brown-bag lunch presentation at work. If you don't work, offer to give a talk to your dorm or a student club on campus. Keep it short and simple, and use it as a time to practice your posture, eye contact, and other delivery skills.
4. For the next two weeks, increase your normal reading habits by including new items on scientific and technical ideas. Make notes while you read about words or concepts that are new to you, and look these up in a dictionary or other source. Observe how science and technology journalists make complex topics seem simple and interesting.

Presentations and Cyberspace. Connect to the Website for Toastmasters International at www.toastmasters.org/ and learn more about this organization. Check out their "10 Tips For Successful Public Speaking" at www.toastmasters.org/ tips.htm. If you wish, attend a local meeting.

Presentations and Teamwork. With several other students, attend one or more local presentations and critique the speaker(s), use of visuals, and other items. Write down your observations and discuss them with your teammates. Pay particular attention to items you would like to emulate.

Presentations and International Communication. Determine when you would want to use a translator for giving a presentation to an audience from a different culture. How would you work with this translator (e.g., where would the translator stand during the presentation, would he or she receive a copy of the speech in advance, would you want the translator to be seen or only heard)? What are some questions or pointers you would want to go over with the translator prior to the presentation?

Presentations and Your Profession. List several projects you are doing or have recently completed in your field; identify some that might be interesting to elementary school students. Arrange to give a presentation to a class at a local elementary school. (It will probably be a good idea to meet with the teacher several days before your presentation to learn more about the group of students, explain what you plan to do and say, and to solicit the teacher's suggestions for ensuring the effectiveness of your presentation.)

REFERENCES

Koch, A. (1998). *Speaking with a purpose.* Boston: Allyn & Bacon.

Woodall, M. K. (1997). *Presentations that get results: 14 reasons your may not.* Lake Oswego, OR: Professional Business Communications.

PRESENTING . . .

Saul Carliner

Saul Carliner is a professor and consultant who travels around the world giving seminars, lectures, and technical presentations. He is also a past international president of the Society for Technical Communication. Here are his thoughts about Part One, Presenting You, Presenting Your Message.

In some ways, speaking is who I am. I love sharing information with people who need to know it and nothing excites me more than sparking excitement about that information in an audience. Although technical writing offers an opportunity to share information with people who need to know it, only technical presentations and seminars let me immediately see whether I have sparked excitement in an audience. One of the things about my presentations that audiences say they like is the passion I show on the podium. What surprises people, however, is that I get nervous before every presentation I give. The concern is a natural one. Each time I give a presentation, I speak to a new audience and I wonder: Did I fully understand who they are? Have I expressed the information in a way that they can connect with, and that they ultimately find meaningful?

Even if the content of a presentation for two audiences is the same, the audiences are not. In some cases, the differences are bold, like the difference between doctors and lawyers. In other cases, the differences are subtle, like the difference between technical communicators in Minnesota and those in Silicon Valley. These subtle differences are often harder to detect, but when you uncover them, you can relate to the audience in a far more powerful way. For example, a large majority of technical communicators in Minnesota work in the financial and health care industries; a large majority in Silicon Valley work in the computer industry. The two groups work for different types of companies and on different types of projects. I change my examples in the two areas to provide ones that are more relevant to the audience.

I've also learned that some people come into certain types of presentations with preconceived notions and some advance work can resolve inappropriate perceptions. For example, I teach a seminar about designing Websites to people who have never designed a Website. Although the course description is clear that the seminar is intended for inexperienced designers and does not explain how to use HTML authoring tools, such as FrontPage, some participants had extensive experience in Web page design and expected to learn how to use authoring tools.

I also believe speakers have a responsibility to make themselves understood, so when people participate in a workshop with incorrect perceptions, the speaker must work with the audience to address the issue. So I began sending a pre-class questionnaire to all enrolled participants asking them what they expected to learn. If a participant said that they were expecting to learn how to use FrontPage, I would contact them and tell them that this workshop did not do that. (The client for whom

(continued)

PRESENTING. . . Continued

I taught the course insisted that training about tools be covered in another class, otherwise I would have changed the workshop to meet the audience's requests.) If I learned that a participant had a lot of experience designing Web pages, I would alert them that they might not learn anything new in the class. After I began distributing the pre-class surveys, evaluations of the course improved because students' perceptions matched the course description. I also noticed, too, that after I began distributing the pre-class questionnaire, students left the class with a higher level of enthusiasm about designing Websites. So distributing the pre-class questionnaire helped me achieve success on one of my personal measurement scales—the "spark of excitement" scale.

PART TWO

Audience, Purpose, Beginnings, Endings

Part Two discusses four key items for creating successful presentations. First, you must understand your audience and create a presentation that they will find interesting, useful, and understandable. Second, you must understand the purpose, or context, of your presentation: Why are you giving this talk, anyway? Then, you must create a presentation that has a strong foundation: a solid introduction and a well-crafted conclusion. Finally, you must plan and craft the body of the presentation, organizing it carefully and conducting research as necessary.

No matter what type of situation you may be involved with, these four key items are critical to any good presentation. An understanding of audience, purpose, introductions, and conclusions will set up a solid framework for your entire presentation.

CHAPTER

5 Know Your Audience

CHAPTER OVERVIEW

One of the most central concepts for any sort of technical communication, written or spoken, is a solid understanding of your audience. By knowing the values, needs, interests, and concerns of those who will attend your presentation, you can design a presentation that is suited especially to their specific situation. In addition, when you understand your audience and relate your ideas to their world, you present yourself as a concerned individual who has taken the time to connect your ideas to theirs. This chapter covers the following topics:

- What Is "Audience"?
- Audience Types
- Important Audience Features
- International and Cultural Issues
- Changing to Meet Audience Needs
- Secondary Audiences
- Audience Analysis Worksheet
- How to Obtain Information about Your Audience

What Is "Audience"?

In everyday language, "audience" is often used to describe a group of people who sit quietly, listening to a concert or watching a movie or play. This common usage connotes a very passive understanding of audience, in that movie or concert audiences are not generally seen as active participants. At first glance, oral presentations appear to be similar to movies or concerts in that way: A speaker stands in front of a room, dispensing information, and an audience sits and takes it all in.

In technical communication, however, the concept of "audience" is far more active than what the original term connotes. Audiences of technical documents, such as computer documentation, are actively engaged in the process of reading and interpreting the material. These readers want to perform a task, for example, and as they read the material, they make notes, ask themselves questions, and move back and forth from the documentation to the computer, trying things out. In perhaps an even more explicit way, audiences for technical presentations are very active. Although they may be polite and quiet during your talk, they are constantly forming opinions of you and your topic. You and your audience regularly exchange nonverbal cues, such as yawns or smiles. And when your presentation is complete, your audience becomes an active part of the process, asking questions and creating a dialogue among everyone.

Unfortunately, many presenters view their audiences in the traditional, movie-going, passive way. However, even movie or concert audiences are not really passive, because they are forming opinions of the movie as it unfolds. And in technical communication, where concepts and language can be somewhat difficult, understanding your audience as an active participant is one of the most critical elements for effective presentations. If you do not understand your audience's level of knowledge about a subject, for example, you may create a presentation that is either too complex or too simple. If you do not understand your audience's position on a topic, you may seek to persuade a group that does not need persuading, or you may use the wrong argument for that particular group.

In order to understand your audience, you can perform an *audience analysis.* This process involves finding out as much as possible about your audience *before* you even begin to plan your presentation. Once you begin to know and understand the needs, interest, and other features of your audience, you can design an interesting, exciting presentation that will effectively convey your message.

Audience Types

Audiences for technical presentations can vary according to the specific situation. For example, if you are giving a presentation about groundwater contamination for your local citizen advisory board, your audience might consist of adults with mixed educational and technical backgrounds. If you are presenting on how to use a new in-house software product, your audience might be technical staff at your company. Each presentation requires you to perform a careful analysis of your audience so you can design your material to reflect a specific audience's level of understanding and interest. Knowing your audience and designing a carefully crafted presentation is the key to effective technical communication.

Often, audiences for technical presentations fall into one of several categories: business, technical, school, or community. These categories are not exclusive; sometimes, an audience will comprise a mixture of these groupings. In addition, people play different roles in different settings. For example, a person who is a manager at work and functions as such during business meetings shifts into the role of parent at a school meeting or the role of consumer at a presentation about a new product. Your job as a presenter is to determine what roles different audience members play at the time and specific setting of your presentation.

The following categories of audiences describe typical attendees and items that often interest them.

In an Organization. In a business or organizational setting, audiences can be made up of professionals with various responsibilities.

- Managers: meeting objectives for their units; creating effective working conditions for their staff; costs; long-term projections and trends
- Executives: controlling costs; corporate goals and missions; forecasting long-term market projections and trends
- Support staff: specifics related to their job functions (e.g., how a computer change might affect order processing)
- Employees: day-to-day tasks involved in producing products or services; job security; keeping abreast of long-term market outlooks
- Contractors: possible projects with this company; maintaining a professional and productive relationship
- Corporate attorneys: legal and ethical ramifications for the organization
- Sales representatives: information to help them compete; meet customer needs; meet sale objectives; earn a good commission

In a Technical Setting. Although technical settings often overlap with organizational ones, it is useful to think specifically about audience types for settings where your audience will be composed primarily of technical professionals.

- Scientists: research and data; how a research study was conducted; statistical features of a study; how terms are defined and used
- Engineers: research, data, and applications of theory to product design; efficiency and usefulness of product or service; time involved in research and development
- Research assistants: research and data; relationship of material to possible graduate research project or thesis
- Lab technicians: how information will relate to specific laboratory tasks
- Technical support staff: how information will affect day-to-day production and service/support tasks

At School. At school, you may give presentations in the classroom or elsewhere within the college or university environment. Your audience may consist of people with the following roles.

- Other students: information related to school, career opportunities, recreation and hobbies, campus activities
- Faculty and instructors: how well you integrate classroom concepts into your presentation; how well you present your material; your understanding of the subject matter

- Administrators (deans, department chairpersons): how your ideas may be of value to the campus community; costs and sources of funding for your idea or project
- The public: learning more about what is being studied and researched at a university
- Corporate representative: industry-university relationships; knowing how classroom material will apply on the job

In Your Community. If you give a presentation in your community, you will often be speaking to a mixed group whose common interest revolves around the community event in question.

- Homeowners: how information relates to property, neighborhood, taxes
- Business owners: how information relates to business, customers, taxes, sales
- Parents: how information relates to children, schools, after-school activities, playgrounds and recreation areas, health matters
- Children: how information relates to school, afterschool activities, playgrounds and recreation areas
- Administrators: all community concerns; costs; political considerations; long-term plans

The "General Audience"

Although the phrase "general audience" is often used to describe those people who will be listening to a presentation, this idea can be problematic. Technical communicators understand that the more they know about their audience, the more carefully they can craft a presentation designed to fit this audience's needs and interests. Yet if you think of an audience as general, you may stop trying to understand them as unique; thus, you may make the mistake of designing your information for some vague group of people who probably do not exist anywhere except in your imagination.

No audience is ever general, but many times, audiences are mixtures of a wide variety of people with different educational backgrounds and experiences who are assuming various corporate, organizational, and personal roles. For instance, assume you are a computer professional, and you've been asked to give a presentation at the local library brown-bag lunch series. Your topic is high-definition television (HDTV). The librarian indicates that attendees tend to be a mixture of business people on their lunch hour, some college students, retired people from the neighborhood, and an occasional person from the mayor's office. As you can see, you have a mixed audience of adults with differing levels of technical and business experience, varying ages, and mixed levels of interest. Because the presentation is informal , audience members are probably assuming a role other than their role at work—a role as interested citizen trying to eat lunch while listening.

Designing presentations for mixed audiences is more difficult than designing for more homogeneous audiences, but it can be done. As with the more specific audiences just described, your job would be to design a presentation that comes as close as possible to meeting the overall needs of this audience by designing an appealing introduction, choosing appropriate language, and using other techniques discussed throughout the book. The next section provides some tools and guidelines for analyzing an audience.

Important Audience Features

When it comes to understanding your audience, you begin by first understanding what type of audience you will be speaking to. But these types are rather general concepts, and, as just noted, audiences are often diverse. To understand your audience more specifically, you can begin to isolate some of the unique features of the group you will be speaking to. As you read the following pages, notice how you will need to adjust various components of your presentation to reflect characteristics of the audience. It is not enough to know your audience—you must also know how to adapt your presentation in response to those characteristics.

Demographic Features

Some of these features are *fixed demographic items* that are often easy to assess and respond to.

Age. In general, people of different age groups relate to material in slightly different ways. There is much talk about middle-agers, twenty-somethings, Generation X-ers, and so on, and although these categories include some stereotyping, they also point out that people understand material based on their life conditions. A metaphor about World War II, for example, might be more useful for people who lived through it than for younger people who are not readily familiar with the conditions and symbols of that era. In addition, age also affects attention span: Children can sit for far shorter periods than adults. Finally, age plays a role in sight and hearing, too. Older audiences might appreciate type sizes (on your overhead transparencies or flip charts, and so forth) that are easy to read, for example.

Gender. Years ago, it was common to use male pronouns (he, his) and words that only represented men (fireman, mailman) to represent all people. Today, in order to represent the population in its entirety, you must use language that is gender fair. Gender-fair language is especially important in technical presentations: Although the world is slowly changing, it's still a fact that women are underrepresented in the science and technology fields, so you don't want to use language that will enhance cultural biases that all engineers, scientists, and technical experts are men. This chapter's Checklist presents several guidelines for avoiding gender-biased presentations.

CHECKLIST

Creating Gender-Fair Presentations

The following guidelines can help you create gender-fair presentations.

Avoid using male pronouns (he, his) to represent a generic person. Use the plural instead. For example, instead of saying "When a doctor is on duty, he must always be available," say "When doctors are on duty, they must always be available." In cases when a singular pronoun must be used (when you are truly referring just to an example of one), use "he or she." Watch for parellilism: Do not use a singular noun and a plural pronoun. For example, "When a doctor is on duty, they must always be available" is not correct, because "a doctor" is singular and "they" is plural. This lack of parallelism is common in oral presentations, because often presenters will start a sentence with a singular noun ("a doctor") but then, faced with the choice of a pronoun, choose "they" to be gender neutral. Avoid this lack of parallelism, if possible.

Alternate "she" with "he." Vary your choice of gender pronouns. This technique can be distracting for the listener, however: Suddenly, your audience is listening for which pronoun you will choose rather than the content of your presentation.

Avoid using job titles that contain the word "man." Unless the job is exclusively male, try to use non-gender-specific titles. For example, say "firefighter" instead of "fireman" or "postal carrier" instead of "mailman."

Use visual examples that are representative. When creating visuals, especially in the traditionally biased science and technology fields, be sure to use examples that show both men and women in the lab or at work.

Educational Level. Knowing the audience's educational background will help you choose appropriate language and content. Grade-school children require a basic level of language and examples that relate to their world of understanding. High school, college, on-the-job training, and regular adult activities such as reading and watching television provide a wide range of background and reference information for these audiences. Audiences with graduate or specialized training (such as law or medical school) will be familiar with specific terms and concepts from their field. Knowing the audience's educational background will help you design a presentation that is accessible to your listeners.

Experience with the Topic. How much do your audience members know about your topic? If they are familiar with the subject matter, you will not need to spend time defining terms and explaining lots of background material. On the other hand, if they are not aware of the topic at all, you'll need to begin your presentation with a clear statement of the issue and then spend time explaining important terms and concepts. Somewhere in the middle of these two extremes (lots of background or no background whatsoever) are audiences who know a little bit about the subject but would like to learn more. Your material must be suited to whatever level is appropriate.

Attitudes toward Science and Technology. Along with experience and knowledge about a subject, audiences also bring their attitudes, biases, and personal experiences toward the subject. On a scientific topic such as cloning, for example, audiences may know a bit about the subject and may have strong opinions about it, too. Some audience members may feel that cloning is ethically questionable; others may think cloning is a major medical breakthrough. Even if you don't agree with audience opinion, you'll need to know and understand their attitudes in order to create a message that they will listen to. (More on persuasion and persuasive presentations in Chapter 10).

Context-Dependent Features

Some features of audience members are more *context dependent;* that is, they will vary given the specific situation and purpose of the presentation (Chapter 6 describes *purpose* and *context* in more detail).

Role(s) within the Organization. Depending on the situation, certain audience members may have certain roles. For example, in a presentation to a software development team, some audience members may be managers, and others may be programmers, interface designers, or technical writers. Each member's role in the organization will impact how he or she listens to your topic. Sometimes, an audience member's role within the organization will encourage that person to ask you certain types of questions—he or she may not be particularly interested in your response but rather is trying to impress someone else in the audience (his or her manager, for example) or to show off in front of the group (Lawson, 1999, p. 147).

Decision-Making Power. Not everyone in an audience is able to have the final say on a topic. If you are speaking to an organization, it may be the manager or vice president who has final word over what decision is made. Or it may be a team of people. Especially if you are explicitly trying to convince or persuade an audience, you need to determine in advance who the decision makers are so you can pay particular attention to their attitudes and questions.

Motives. Most times, audiences attend presentations with a particular set of motives about your topic and the context of the presentation. They may want to learn more about a new product, for example, so they can impress their boss or excel on the job. Or, audience members who are students may be motivated to learn more about a subject so they can increase their knowledge base and also perform well in class. Sometimes, in training or how-to presentations, audience members come with the desire to learn how to perform a specific task or set of tasks. The more you know about audience motives, the more you can craft your information to suit their needs.

Use of Information. You should learn all you can about how audience members will use the information from your presentation. Will they rely on the information to perform a task? Make decisions? Prepare a report? Do they need to learn *about* something or learn to *do* something? You must determine in advance what audience members expect to know or do after your presentation so you can structure it to meet their needs.

Group Features

Groups of people together operate differently than individuals. Therefore, it is important to understand your audience as a group.

Group Ethos. We've all heard the phrase "The sum is greater than its parts." A similar idea holds true for groups of people: Although the sum may not be *greater,* it is different. As individuals, each audience member has a unique perspective and character, or ethos. But when individuals come together to form an audience, they exert a group ethos. Ask a comedian or actor to comment on how the audience affects his or her performance. If the audience does not laugh when expected or is shuffling feet and shifting in their chairs, the performer will be able to sense that and adapt his or her performance to this group ethos.

Room Size. It is critical to know the size of the room in advance of your presentation. A small room allows you to get to know your audience members more personally and lets you use handouts and a variety of visuals and graphics; a large lecture hall means that you won't have much or any one-on-one contact with your audience, and, although all visuals should always be readable, regardless of room size, large rooms mean that you *must* use large fonts and easily readable graphics.

Room Layout. Along with room size, you should learn what you can about the room layout. Will you be in a conference room, with audience members seated around a table? Or will you be in a more traditional, classroom-style room, where you speak from a lectern at the front while the audience sits theater style in rows? The layout and arrangement of the room are important factors in analyzing your audience and how they will relate to you.

International and Cultural Issues

Even within a relatively homogeneous situation, such as a group of managers for a specific company, audiences can be formed by people from a variety of cultural backgrounds. This cultural diversity is especially true in today's global marketplace, where technologies such as video conferencing, real-time chats, and conference calls allow people to meet (virtually, that is) across vast physical distances essentially at the same time. Even within the same geographic region (such as a part of the United States), you cannot assume that your audience members will have similar cultural backgrounds. Therefore, part of your audience analysis must include attention to international and cultural issues.

Learning what you need to know about an international or intercultural audience can be time-consuming and can defy what seems obvious. Facial expressions, gestures, forms of personal address, humor, computer representations, and many other items that seem natural and innocuous to you can easily be interpreted in ways that would surprise you. For example, slapping the fist of one hand into the palm of the other hand has no specific meaning in North America but is usually considered an insult in France, Spain, and South America (Morris, 1994, p. 74). Color, too, has different meanings in different cultures. And the way in which instructions are given can be different, too, depending on the culture. In American English, for example, technical writers often use the direct, imperative style ("Turn on the computer.") In Japan, although instructions and technical material may also be written in the imperative, such material may also be interspersed with a more polite, tentative, or honorific style (Kohl et al., 1993).

There are many more factors that you need to take into account when considering international audiences. The topic itself could (and does) take up an entire book. You can learn more about international communication by reading the books mentioned in the FYI feature. You can also contact people in your company who do a good deal of corporate travel and ask them for advice on a presentation to an international audience.

FYI

International Audiences

You can learn more about how to design presentations for international audiences by taking a course in international or intercultural communication. Many technical communication programs have such a course; these courses may also be offered by the Speech Communication department. In addition, some companies give seminars in communicating to international audiences. The following books will also provide you with useful information:

Hoft, N. L. (1995). *International technical communication: How to export information about high technology.* New York: Wiley.

Lustig, M. W., & Koester, J. (1999). *Intercultural competence: Interpersonal communication across cultures.* New York: Longman.

Changing to Meet Audience Needs

Even the best attempts at audience analysis sometimes are not good enough. Often, you simply do not have time to send out a survey or even talk with someone in the audience. Or, even after doing what appeared to be a thorough audience analysis, you discover that your material is too technical, not technical enough, or not in the right order.

A good presenter becomes skilled at adapting on the spot to meet the needs of the audience. For example, a nutritionist was scheduled to talk to a group about managing diet and exercise to prevent the development of atherosclerosis due to elevated cholesterol levels. The nurse who scheduled the presentation assured the nutritionist that the audience members had learned from their doctors about the types of cholesterol levels. Yet, five minutes into the presentation, an audience member interrupted: "So," he asked, "what's LDL and HDL? I have plaque in my arteries? We don't know what you are talking about!" The nutritionist knew immediately that he had to incorporate some additional information in order to meet the needs of his audience—he had to adapt.

When adapting to your audience needs, you should consider your own ethical stance on the issue at hand. In the example of the nutritionist, it was important to adapt in order to make the information understandable to the audience members. But what if you are giving a more persuasive-style presentation, and you realize that the only way the audience will accept your argument is if you pretend to have more in common with their views than you actually do. Is it ethical to pretend in this way? Probably not. Pretending or lying is not the same as adapting to an audience; pretending to agree with something you do not is a shift in character from a credible, honest speaker to a dishonest one. If an audience does not agree with you, use other strategies to establish places where you do agree (more in Chapter 10). But lying or pretending is never a good idea—honest presenters are always more credible, believable, and ethical.

Secondary Audiences

Sometimes there are audiences for presentations who never attend the presentation and may not be in the forefront of your mind as you prepare your material. Yet many audience members will leave your presentation with new ideas and information that they wish to share. They may circulate a memo or email message to others in the organization giving an overview of your presentation, or they may post a message on the company's Intranet (internal Web page server) so that others can learn from the presentation. Because not everyone in the organization can attend a presentation, copies of your handouts may be circulated, also.

The people who see your material and learn about your presentation after the fact can be considered *secondary audiences.* Unlike your primary audience (the people who actually attended your presentation), secondary audiences cannot ask questions or see your presentation material firsthand. Instead, they will rely on the summaries of others plus any information you choose to leave behind.

If you discover that there will be a secondary audience, and you wish to have your information conveyed as clearly as possible, provide sources where people can obtain more information. Bring handouts, create a Web page and distribute the URL, or provide your email address.

Audience Analysis Worksheet

For each presentation situation, you should customize an audience analysis worksheet based on the unique features and audience characteristics for that

Audience Analysis Worksheet

Audience Type. In general, what type of audience will I be speaking to?

- ☐ Organizational
- ☐ Technical
- ☐ School
- ☐ Community
- ☐ Other (define)

How will this affect the way I design and deliver my presentation?

Audience Features. What are some demographic and other features about my audience?

- ☐ Age range
- ☐ Gender
- ☐ Education level
- ☐ Experience with topic
- ☐ Attitudes toward topic
- ☐ Role within organization
- ☐ Decision-making power
- ☐ Motives
- ☐ How audience will use information

How will this affect the way I design and deliver my presentation?

Group Issues. What issues about my audience as a group are important for me to know?

- ☐ Group ethos
- ☐ Room size
- ☐ Room layout

How will this affect the way I design and deliver my presentation?

International and Cultural Issues. What international issues must I be concerned with for this presentation? How will this affect the way I design and deliver my presentation?

Secondary Audiences. Who are the potential secondary audiences and how are they likely to obtain information about this presentation? How will this affect the way I design and deliver my presentation?

presentation. The worksheet shown here is just an example of one that you might use. In the next chapter, you will append this worksheet and add information about the presentation's purpose. In later chapters, as you prepare presentations, you will use this worksheet again.

How to Obtain Information about Your Audience

To conduct a proper audience analysis, you need to obtain the most accurate information you can. Sometimes, you are able to speak directly with some audience members and find out what you need to know. Other times, you may only have access to the person who invited you to speak or to a manager or other representative from the group. In still other cases, you won't actually be able to speak to anyone from the audience and will need to conduct your analysis on a group that most closely matches your real audience. The following table presents possible information-gathering strategies.

Who Is Available	Your Strategy
Real audience members	Interview as many people as possible; be sure to speak with as diverse a group as possible to avoid getting a limited point of view.
Manager or other representative of the organization	Interview that person. Ask if there are others you can speak with. Ask about the range of possible audience members to avoid getting a limited point of view.
No one from the actual audience or organization	Learn all you can about the organization. If possible, interview other people who have presented before this audience. Select people who are a close match for your real audience members and interview these people instead.

Sometimes you will have very little opportunity to conduct an audience analysis. You may find that you are pressed for time and that no one from the audience or organization can help you. In these cases, you must try your best to construct in your mind a picture of your audience. Drawing on all the information that you have available, envision your audience and all of their characteristics. Perform an audience analysis based on your image of the audience, and ask someone who resembles a typical audience member to review your notes and give you feedback.

Consider the nutritionist described earlier. If he was envisioning his audience, he might ask himself the following questions:

- After patients hear medical information from health care providers, how well do they usually understand it? How much do they usually remember?
- How many nonmedical people that I know really understand the differences between types of cholesterol?
- Patients with elevated cholesterol usually feel just fine. How motivated are they to make lifestyle changes to treat a disease with no apparent symptoms?

By answering these and other questions, the nutritionist can include appropriate information, use diagrams, and be encouraging and motivational—thereby giving a presentation that meets the needs of his audience.

Be sure to take advantage of the latest Internet technology, too, to perform your audience analysis. Email messages or mailing lists, for example, allow you to reach hundreds of people with a few simple keystrokes, and these tools allow recipients to answer at their convenience. You may be able to distribute a survey or questionnaire to potential audience members via the Internet.

In Summary: Know Your Audience

Although computer technology, cool graphics, and Internet connections may be the latest trends, truly exceptional technical presentations always have one item in common: They are easy to understand, and they speak to the audience. Knowing as much as possible about your audience allows you to create a presentation that is interesting, useful, and important to listeners. An audience analysis is the key to gaining this understanding.

In the next chapter, you'll learn about another pivotal point for technical presentations—*purpose*. As you will see, audience and purpose are closely linked.

QUESTIONS / EXERCISES / ASSIGNMENTS

1. Take a few minutes to write a short paragraph about a topic with which you are very familiar. Now, consider this topic with two different audiences in mind: middle-school children and college-educated, mixed-background adults. Make a list of the changes in language, approach, and content you would make for each audience.

2. Create an audience analysis worksheet for a presentation about the topic in question 1. In a group of three to four students, take turns asking the group the questions on the sheet. Once each student has completed the audience analysis for the group, take turns discussing how the information you learned from the analysis would help you in creating a presentation.

3. Customize the audience analysis sheet in this chapter for a specific presentation (an electronic version is available on the companion Web page to this book).

Presentations and Cyberspace. Search the Web for information about intercultural audiences and international communication. Along with the items discussed in this chapter, create a list of features that you must pay attention to when creating presentations for international audiences. In particular, think about how you would discuss a particular technical topic in this setting.

Presentations and Teamwork. Identify a fairly controversial technical or scientific topic that interests you, and outline the points you would make in an oral presentation about the topic. Present the points to a small group of students in your class, and, as a group, discuss any aspects of your presentation that were unclear, unconvincing, or had gaps. If you had done an audience analysis before preparing the outline, what questions would have provided relevant information and enabled you to construct an outline that better met the needs of your audience?

Presentations and International Communication. In a high-context culture, the way in which a message is presented is often just as important or more important than what is actually said or written. In a low-context culture, what is said or written is often more important than the way in which that message is presented. Using these definitions and doing some additional research (library, Web), identify one high-context and one low-context culture. Report your findings to the class, and explain how you would approach audience analysis and oral presentations when you know an audience will include people from low- or high-context cultures.

Presentations and Your Profession. Focus on a current job, or one you recently held, and think of an oral presentation you might realistically make in that setting. Using the guidelines in this chapter, analyze and characterize your audience. For each audience feature that you identify, define specific characteristics your presentation should have to reflect and accommodate that feature (e.g., the audience is completely familiar with the topic and the work you have been doing, therefore you will provide very little background information).

REFERENCES

Frank, F. W., & Treichler, P. (1989). *Language, gender, and professional writing: Theoretical approaches and guidelines for nonsexist usage.* New York: Modern Language Association.

Hoft, N. L. (1995). *International technical communication: How to export information about high technology.* New York: Wiley.

Kohl, J. R., Barclay, R. O., Pinelli, T. E., Keene, M. L., & Kennedy, J. M. (1993). The impact of language and culture on technical communication in Japan. *Technical Communication, 40*(1), 62–73.

Lawson, K. (1999). *Involving your audience: Making it active.* Boston: Allyn & Bacon.

Lustig, M. W., & Koester, J. (1999). *Intercultural competence: Interpersonal communication across cultures.* New York: Longman.

Morris, D. (1994). *Bodytalk: A world guide to gestures.* London: Jonathan Cape.

CHAPTER

6 Know Your Purpose

CHAPTER OVERVIEW

Along with understanding your audience, you also need to know as much as possible about the *purpose* for your presentation. Is your presentation intended to persuade people? To inform them? To solicit funding? All of the above? Most presentations have several purposes, and the more you understand these reasons for your talk, the better you will succeed. This chapter covers the following topics:

- Why Are You Giving This Presentation, Anyway?
- The Situation and Context
- Types of Presentations in Technical Communication
- Audience and Purpose Worksheets
- Purposes, Purposes, Purposes

Why Are You Giving This Presentation, Anyway?

The bottom line on determining the purpose for your presentation is to ask yourself a few questions. Why, exactly, are you giving this presentation? What should your audience *know* and/or be able to *do* after hearing your presentation? What would you like to achieve overall? And, what does your audience expect? You need to answer these and other questions carefully and with as much accuracy as possible if you intend to create and deliver an effective presentation. As one experienced presenter has noted, "purpose controls content"—in other words, the purpose of the presentation (along with audience considerations) controls what material you'll include, and what material you'll leave out (Perlman, 1998, p. 2).

In technical communication, many presentations fall into two categories: those that inform and those that argue or persuade (Houp et al., 1998, p. 14). At a general level, these two types are useful places for understanding your presentation's purpose. Yet "inform" and "persuade" often overlap, and each category can contain many subcategories. For example, it is almost impossible simply to inform without doing some persuading. The simple choice of terms and way in which a presenter arranges and presents material reflects a point of view. In addition, informative presentations may have a variety of subpurposes: to teach, to create community awareness, to update an audience's existing knowledge, and so on. The same is true for persuasive presentations. Rather than view these categories as discrete, a good presenter knows that presentations often have several purposes, and that these purposes depend on the particular situation, or context. Figure 6.1 illustrates the concept of purpose as a range from presentations that inform to those that persuade. It also lists some specific purposes of technical presentations.

As you can see, there are many ways in which a presenter might inform or persuade, and the line is not always clear. For example, a presentation designed to convince an audience to take action must be both informative and persuasive, because you'd probably need to provide the audience with some background information before making your argument. A presentation designed to teach or explain a new technical concept is not only informative but also persuasive, in that you will be presenting your particular view of the concept.

The best approach, therefore, is to be as specific as possible. Often, you have some idea of why you were asked to give a presentation. Perhaps you are an expert on an aspect of using the Internet, for example, and you are asked to speak at work on the subject of online privacy. You know after talking to your manager that she wants you to inform your coworkers about the latest happenings in privacy and cyberspace. But you also learn that some troubling questions have been brewing among management: Should workers be allowed to use the Internet at work for personal Web surfing? How much should and can the company monitor employees' time on the Internet? And, how safe is the Internet for online commerce? You discover that the company would like to open a dialogue among employees to

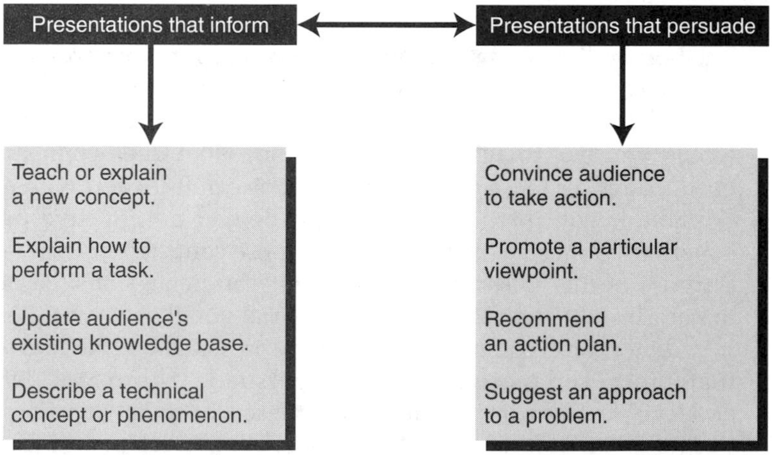
Presentations that inform
Presentations that persuade
Teach or explain a new concept.
Explain how to perform a task.
Update audience's existing knowledge base.
Describe a technical concept or phenomenon.
Convince audience to take action.
Promote a particular viewpoint.
Recommend an action plan.
Suggest an approach to a problem.

FIGURE 6.1 The range of presentations, from informative to persuasive.

establish fair and reasonable company policies. So, your presentation is not only meant to inform, it's meant to encourage people to learn more about these issues and to participate in the process of devising company policy.

In a situation such as the one just described, or for any presentation, you should spend time writing out a statement of purpose. The simplest way to write such a statement is to begin with the phrase "The purpose of my presentation is to ___(verb)___." Then, go beyond the first sentence to be even more specific about the many goals and objectives of your presentation. For the online privacy presentation, your statement of purpose might be the following:

> The purpose of my presentation is to educate employees about the state of affairs in online privacy. A secondary, more specific purpose is to encourage employees to learn as much as possible and to get involved with company planning efforts.

This statement and other information about the presentation's purpose should be incorporated into your audience analysis worksheet.

The Situation and Context

Part of understanding purpose involves understanding the situation and context in which you will give a presentation. When it comes to context, a presentation in front of a class is very different from a presentation at work or one in front of a professional association. In the classroom, the context involves a dynamic between you, other students, and your instructor. You want to make a good impression on your fellow students, and you want to earn a good grade. At work, you may be presenting in front of a manager from another department where you'd like to apply for a position. Or, your presentation may be on a topic that is particularly sensitive or politically difficult. In front of a professional association, the context may involve highlighting your contributions to the association at the same time you explain or inform the group about your particular topic.

Here's just one example: You are a technical communicator with a software company, and your unit has been working on a controversial new online help system. You and your team believe in this system and have put many long, hard hours into designing it. You are asked to give a presentation that highlights the new system for a group of customers. Although you know that the customers support your online help system, you also know that your manager thinks it's the wrong approach. Both the customers and your manager will be in the audience. Politically, you know that this puts you in a difficult situation.

This situation requires you to make some specific choices. How informative will you be? How much will you try persuading your manager as you inform the customers? Can you use this opportunity to change her mind while giving a thorough presentation of the system's new features? These are decisions you must make in advance, or your presentation will have no coherence and will not seem to have a clearly defined purpose.

Types of Presentations in Technical Communication

Sometimes, the overall purpose of a presentation is predefined by a standard presentation type. For example, many organizations have brown-bag lunches, where presentations are expected to be informative, casual, and brief. A prescribed presentation type automatically sets up certain expectations for you and your audience in terms of the presentation's purpose. Based on a survey of practicing technical communicators, certain presentation types appear to be quite common. These types include seminar presentations, training sessions, conference presentations, panel or roundtable discussions, group presentations, marketing or sales presentations, design reviews, and press conferences (Hager & Scheiber, 1997, pp. 13–14). Part of the purpose of a roundtable discussion, for example, involves a back-and-forth discussion format, whereas a conference presentation may require a more traditional stand-up-and-deliver approach. So you'll need to know as much as you can about the specific presentation type, if there is any involved.

Audience and Purpose Worksheets

Based on the information just discussed, the audience analysis worksheet can now be expanded to include items about purpose and context.

Audience and Purpose Worksheet

Audience Type. In general, what type of audience will I be speaking to?

- ☐ Organizational
- ☐ Technical
- ☐ School
- ☐ Community
- ☐ Other (define)

How will this affect the way I design and deliver my presentation?

Audience Features. What are some demographic and other features about my audience?

- ☐ Age range
- ☐ Gender
- ☐ Educational level
- ☐ Experience with topic
- ☐ Attitudes toward topic
- ☐ Role within organization
- ☐ Decision-making power
- ☐ Motives
- ☐ How audience will use information

How will this affect the way I design and deliver my presentation?

Group Issues. What issues about my audience as a group are important for me to know?

☐ Group ethos ☐ Room layout
☐ Room size

How will this affect the way I design and deliver my presentation?

International and Cultural Issues. What international issues must I be concerned with for this presentation? How will this affect the way I design and deliver my presentation?

Secondary Audiences. Who are the potential secondary audiences and how are they likely to obtain information about this presentation? How will this affect the way I design and deliver my presentation?

Purpose Statement

☐ What is the primary purpose of my presentation?
The purpose of my presentation is . . .

☐ What are the secondary purposes of my presentation?
Other purposes include . . .

☐ What are some features central to the context or situation of my presentation?
The political and organizational aspects of my presentation include . . .

Presentation Type. Does your presentation need to fit into a prescribed type (conference, roundtable, etc.)? If so, how does this affect your overall purpose?

Focus. Is the purpose of the presentation specific enough? Are there too many purposes?

Other Information. What other information would be useful as you plan your presentation?

Purposes, Purposes, Purposes

As one experienced presentation consultant puts it, there are two problems when it comes to defining the purpose of a presentation: Either the presenter does not have any purpose in mind, or the presenter has too many purposes (Woodall, 1997, p. 13). So far, this book has discussed the idea of defining your purpose and determining if there are any secondary purposes. But beware: Too many purposes, and you'll have a presentation that is unclear and lacks focus. As a technical communicator, you often are knowledgeable about a wide breadth of information on particular topics. Sometimes your impulse might be to share *all* of this information, in part because you find it so interesting and are enthusiastic about your topic. Yet you must keep your focus and learn to adhere to one primary purpose.

One way to limit your purposes and stay on track is to adhere strictly to the time limit for your presentation. Along with being polite and respectful of your audience, sticking to the given time limit forces you to include only the most important and relevant information. You can always give another talk on a different topic, or you can allude to the additional information but not give detail. A good technical presentation is focused and stays on point.

Figure 6.2 illustrates the primary and secondary purposes for the online privacy presentation. This number of purposes is enough, but not too much.

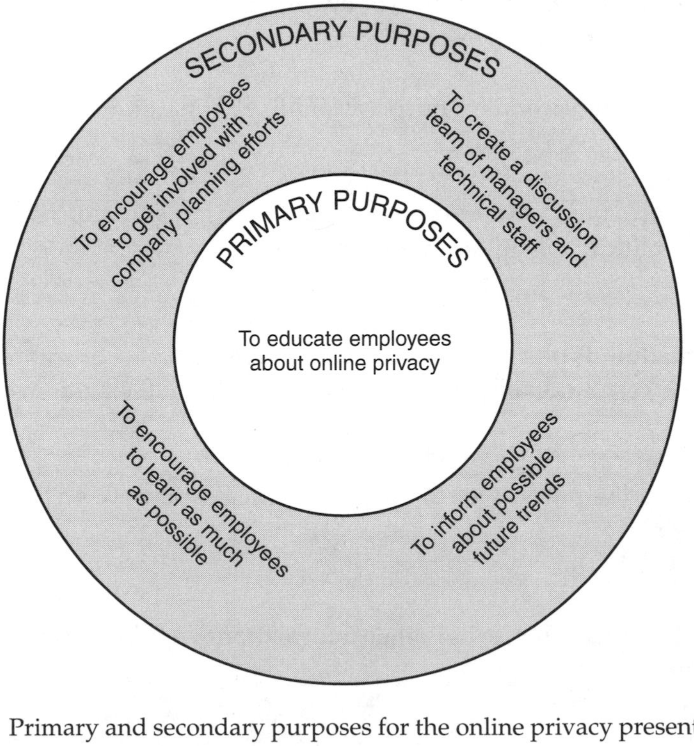

FIGURE 6.2 Primary and secondary purposes for the online privacy presentation.

In Summary: Know Your Purpose

Like audience, *purpose* is a key concept if you are to design and deliver effective oral presentations. Not only must you understand the audience members and their needs and interests, so too must you understand the context, or purpose, of the event. Why are you giving this presentation? What should people learn as a result of it? These and the other questions presented in this chapter are of central importance for you as a communicator. By using the audience and purpose worksheets and doing a careful analysis, you will prepare a presentation that fits the occasion.

QUESTIONS / EXERCISES / ASSIGNMENTS

1. Make a list of every purpose you can think of for any type of presentation you may give—as a student or in your career. Each item in your list should begin with a verb: to persuade, to convince, to inform, to challenge, to illustrate, and so on. Give your list to a classmate—either via email or on paper—and have this person collate everyone's lists into one large class list. Discuss this list in class—are any of these purposes duplicates?
2. Think of one situation where it might be difficult to determine the purpose of a presentation, and consider ways you might solve this difficulty.

Presentations and Cyberspace. In a way, Web pages are similar to oral presentations—in order to be effective, both forms of communication need to be clear about their purpose. Locate a Web page that appears to have a clear and focused sense of purpose. Write a purpose statement for that page. Then locate a Web page that lacks a clear sense of purpose. Write a statement critiquing that page. Include suggestions for what the Web master should do to modify this page.

Presentations and Teamwork. At the end of Chapter 1, you and your team identified technical topics that may be challenging to present to the general public. For each of those topics, brainstorm three possible purpose statements for presentation; in addition, describe a situation and context for each possible presentation. Evaluate each statement to be certain that it's clear and appropriate for the situation and context.

Presentations and International Communication. Contact someone whose job now requires him or her to give presentations to U.S. as well as international audiences. You may wish to contact a graduate of your college or university, a professor who teaches international communication, a colleague at work, a consultant, or someone you locate on a Website. Ask this person to describe how the contexts and purposes differ among such audiences, and how he or she prepares differently when planning these presentations.

Presentations and Your Profession. Contact a person who graduated from your major department within the past two or three years. Ask this person (in person if possible; otherwise, via email) to describe presentations he or she has given at work and to explain how the context and purpose differ from speeches the person gave while a student. If the alum has not yet given any presentations, ask about presentations he or she has seen others give at work. (The alumni office at your institution usually maintains a database of alumni who are willing to be resources for current students.)

REFERENCES

Hager, P. J., & Scheiber, H. J. (1997). *Designing and delivering scientific, technical, and managerial presentations.* New York: Wiley.

Houp, K. W., Pearsall, T. E., & Tebeaux, E. (1998). *Reporting technical information* (9th ed.). Boston: Allyn & Bacon.

Perlman, A. M. (1998). *Writing great speeches: Professional techniques you can use.* Boston: Allyn & Bacon.

Woodall, M. K. (1997). *Presentations that get results: 14 reasons yours may not.* Lake Oswego, OR: Professional Business Communications.

CHAPTER

7 The Importance of a Strong Introduction and Conclusion

CHAPTER OVERVIEW

There are many ways to arrange a presentation, depending on the audience and purpose. (Later chapters discuss the specifics of individual presentations.) But in general, all good oral presentations begin with a strong introduction and end with a strong conclusion. The introduction is where you establish your initial credibility with your audience and outline your presentation; the conclusion is where you leave a lasting impression and restate your main points. This chapter covers the following topics:

- The Importance of Introductions and Conclusions
- The Introduction
- The Conclusion
- Memorize the Introduction and Conclusion

The Importance of Introductions and Conclusions

One feature that marks effective technical communication, whether written or spoken, is that the material is well organized and easy for an audience to follow. In this age of information overload, where attention is constantly being drawn in many directions, people are busy and need information quickly and efficiently. They need to know why they are receiving information and how it will affect their lives, jobs, or day-to-day tasks. In addition, the highly technical nature of today's information makes it that much more difficult for audiences to understand and use what they read or hear. Written material must also be well organized but can usually be referenced later. Oral presentations, however, are not bound together like a book. They go directly from you to the audience and contain no indexes, tables of contents, or running heads. Therefore, your oral presentation must be carefully organized, and you must provide your audience with as many tools as possible to make the material interesting and easy to follow.

The two places to begin this task are the introduction and the conclusion of your talk. The introduction is where you introduce your material, make an impression, and outline your talk. The conclusion is where you wrap things up and restate your points. These two places in the presentation are critical. They define the rest of the presentation and are an important aspect of establishing your ethos for the entire event.

Of course, between the introduction and conclusion is the body of the presentation. We'll discuss the body at points in this chapter but will focus on it more in upcoming chapters. For now, think of your presentation as a house, which needs a strong support structure, or frame, before it can be built. The introduction and conclusion are the two major pieces of the support structure.

Unlike the support structure of a house, however, the introduction and conclusion of your presentation will need to be modified as you work on the presentation's body. This is a natural process—the way you invent and arrange your ideas in the body of the presentation will change what you need to say at the beginning and end of the talk. And before you can write the introduction and conclusion, you'll need to have done some thinking about the general topic of the presentation. In other words, creating a presentation is an iterative process; that is, it's a process whereby you are constructing your plan as you go along, moving back and forth between the introduction, body, and conclusion. Although you can't be sure about the final product until you've worked on all the parts, a basic framework of introduction/conclusion is a good place to begin.

The following figure illustrates the main parts of a presentation.

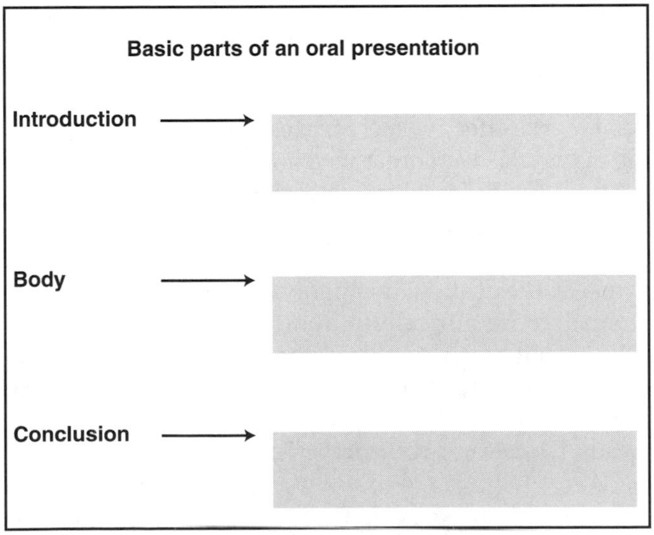

The Introduction

When you first step to the front of the room or direct people's attention to your end of the conference table to begin your presentation, you immediately set the stage for the rest of the event. The introduction could be considered the most important component of the presentation, for it's where you establish your ethos and rapport with the audience and set the tone for the rest of the presentation. In fact, a recent study found that in presentations with strong introductions, audiences listened more closely, had stronger confidence in the presenter, and understood the presentation more thoroughly (Andeweg et al., 1998). Therefore, you want to create an introduction that gets things off to a good start.

There are several key elements to a strong introduction. Although these elements may vary depending on the particular circumstance, in general, an effective introduction will include the characteristics described on the following pages.

Capture Your Audience's Attention

Your first job in any presentation is to capture the attention of your audience. As a technical communicator, you are becoming skilled at making scientific and technical topics understandable, interesting, and enjoyable for your audience, and the introduction to your presentation is where you can arouse people's natural curiosity and capture their attention. Even if an audience is keenly interested in your topic, you still need to get their attention at the outset. There are many ways, depending on the audience and purpose of your presentation, to focus an audience's attention.

1. *Begin with a story.* You may never have noticed before, but newspaper and magazine articles about even the most serious subjects often begin with stories: tales of individuals or families, towns, or companies. These stories draw the reader into the material by using a narrative format. They make the reader want to know more. Effective presentations often use the same technique. They begin with a story that stirs the imagination and draws the audience into the material. For example, a presentation about cloning might begin this way:

> Missy, an eleven-year-old collie-husky mix, recently boarded an aircraft bound for College Station, Texas, where she'll make pet history. Based on messages sent across the Internet, Missy's owners located scientists who were willing to make their favorite dog the first pet ever to be cloned.

This story based on a 1998 Associated Press article, captures your attention and makes you naturally curious and interested to learn more. It puts a local, personal face on what might otherwise be a general and intimidating topic (cloning). A storytelling opening is appropriate when you want an audience to become involved in the topic of your presentation, but it may not be the most appropriate for a formal or academic presentation, such as a scientific conference paper.

2. *Draw upon a recent event.* The story about Missy the dog was, at the time of this writing, a very recent event. The daily news is filled with stories about science and technology, stories people may have seen or read about in the media. Use such recent events to capture your audience's attention and ground your topic in something your audience can relate to and is familiar with. Obviously, you can't always draw upon a recent event—for some topics, there is no current event to link to. But for other topics, a current event will be a natural opener.

3. *Connect with something your audience knows or cares about.* Another way to capture your audience's attention is to connect your material with concepts and ideas that they know and care about. For example, if you were speaking to an audience familiar with cloning and some of its ethical or social controversies (employees of a genetics lab, scientists, or biology students, for example), you might use the Missy story this way:

> Should cloning be available on a pay-per-pet basis? Researchers at one university seem to say "yes." Recently, an anonymous couple donated $2.3 million to a Texas university to have their collie-husky mix, Missy, cloned into several new Missy pups.

In this version, the story of Missy and her potential cloning is set up as an ethical question, something that this audience would care about. It's always important to link your introduction to issues of concern for your audience.

4. *Ask questions that are relevant or compelling for your audience.* An interesting technique included in the previous example is the use of what is often called a rhetorical question (not the best term, because all questions are rhetorical in that all questions are part of language use). It is a question that either is not immediately answered or is asked and answered by the presenter. It is used to frame an issue, draw in an audience, and set the tone for the presentation to follow. Sometimes, presenters will use a series of such questions, for example:

> Should cloning be available on a pay-per-pet basis? Or should the government be more closely regulating this new technique?

Often, when performing your audience and purpose analysis, you'll create a list of questions that your audience might ask—questions about items they don't understand or that are controversial. You can use these questions to form your introduction. But be careful not to ask too many questions in a row, or you will lose the impact.

5. *Relate a personal story or anecdote.* Another way of using the storytelling method is to tell a personal story, which helps the audience immediately connect to you and your topic. They see you standing before them, and they can relate what you are talking about to a real person. For example:

> When I was growing up, I used to help my father, a veterinarian, deliver all kinds of baby animals, from farm animals to house pets. How, I wondered, did a black cat give birth to a tabby? What caused one calf to have a star on its forehead and not another? Little did I know that, by my late 20s, scientists would be able to answer these questions and even create animals that looked exactly like one parent—that we would be discussing what we now call "cloning."

This story leads the audience into the topic of cloning by relating it to a personal memory, something most people can relate to. Everyone was a child at one time, and most were curious about the world around them. If this presentation were designed for veterinary students, it would be even more appropriate and compelling. Using a personal story is an effective way to establish your ethos. This approach may not be appropriate for highly technical settings, such as a meeting of scientists or engineers, but it is often used when presenting to a more general audience.

6. *Compliment your audience.* Sometimes it is appropriate to compliment your audience, but only when you are sincere in doing so. If you have a sincere comment to make about your audience's abilities and talents, you will create a bond of mutual respect with them. For example, somewhere in the introduction you might say something such as:

> Obviously, all of you are concerned citizens with an interest in important matters to our community, or you would not be here today.

This brief sentence suggests that you understand and respect your audience's intelligence and interest. It's important to compliment your audience if you know that they have been left out of the discussion process on this topic, or if you know that they might hold a different opinion from the one you're going to present.

7. *Create suspense or dissonance.* Part of a good introduction often involves creating a sense of suspense or dissonance in your audience's mind. Dissonance is a feeling that things are just a bit unsettled; a dissonant chord in music, for example, is one that leaves you wishing for just one final chord or note to "settle" the sound. If you create this feeling in the beginning of your presentation, your audience will want to continue listening in order to have the problem or issue resolved. For example, a researcher talking to a general audience about some of the newest research on curing cancer might begin her speech this way:

> We used the patient's own tumor cells to prepare a vaccine, and on Monday morning we injected the patient with the preparation, but by Friday the vaccine had not shown any effect on the tumors growing in so many of his organs.

Such an introduction is likely to capture the attention of the audience and to keep their attention, because it sets up an expectation of a positive effect within three days but then indicates that this expectation was not met. You might wish to use this style of introduction if you are speaking to an audience that needs some motivation to listen to your talk; for example, if you are speaking about a complex topic to a group that does not appear to be extremely interested or does not have enough background on the subject to know why it is important. If you have information that will resolve the suspense, be sure to present it at the appropriate time near the end of your presentation.

8. *Use a quotation or familiar phrase.* We've all been to presentations that began something like "As Thomas Jefferson once said, . . . " This technique can be overused and can sometimes seem staged and insincere, so be careful about using it. But on the other hand, the right quote can be a great way to catch your audience's attention and focus your presentation. You may wish to find a quote that has made the news recently or is from someone your audience knows and trusts. Often, people use quotations to begin a more formal type of presentation.

9. *Be careful about humor.* Chapter 3 briefly discussed the use of humor and noted that presenters must be careful, because what is humorous to one person is not to another. In situations where international communication is of concern, using humor becomes even more problematic. So don't use humorous items unless you know your audience well and can accurately predict their response.

10. *Avoid annoying your audience.* As one experienced corporate presenter has noted, there are several rules of etiquette you should follow during your introduction in order to establish your ethos and avoid annoying your audience. Don't, for example, begin by complaining about your travel accommodations, the size of the room, or the microphone. And don't put yourself down by indicating how boring your presentation is going to be or how much you dislike giving presentations. Although these suggestions may seem like common sense, many presenters begin with this kind of silly banter—a bad idea for you and your audience (Perlman, 1998, p. 24).

Establish Credibility and Rapport

After you capture your audience's attention, you should establish credibility and rapport with your audience. Some of your credibility will be established the minute you begin the presentation—your ethos comes through immediately. The story or other attention-grabber you choose to tell becomes part of how your audience views you. If you start the presentation with an inappropriate comment or joke, for example, you will establish a negative ethos. But if you begin with an interesting story that relates to your audience's needs and concerns, you'll establish yourself as someone worth listening to.

Often you'll need to establish your credibility even more overtly, however. If the audience doesn't know you, and if you haven't been introduced in advance, you may need to take a moment to tell the audience who you are and why they should listen to you. For example,

> Should cloning be available on a pay-per-pet basis? Researchers at one university seem to say "yes." Recently, an anonymous couple donated $2.3 million to a Texas university to have their collie-husky mix, Missy, cloned into several new Missy pups. But should the government be more closely regulating this new technique? These and other questions are still just emerging as we face the new world of cloning.
>
> My name is Erin Greene, and I'm a graduate student here at the university. As a research assistant in genetics, I am aware of not only the scientific issues surrounding cloning but also the social and ethical ones.

Here, the presenter caught the audience's attention with a combination of questions and a story, then quickly established her credibility on the subject by introducing herself and noting her credentials to talk about the subject.

Preview Your Presentation

Finally, you must provide your audience a road map, or preview, of your presentation. You are about to take your audience on a long trip through information and ideas. Like any trip, it will be far more efficient if audience members have a road map and know where they're going. Skilled technical communicators know that audiences create schema, or templates, in their minds as they read or listen to technical information. These templates help guide audiences through the material and let them know what is coming and where they are in the master plan.

After catching your audience's attention and establishing your credibility, you must preview the main points of your presentation before moving into the body of the material. Here's one way this might be done:

> Should cloning be available on a pay-per-pet basis? Researchers at one university seem to say "yes." Recently, an anonymous couple donated \$2.3 million a Texas university to have their collie-husky mix, Missy, cloned into several new Missy pups. But should the government be more closely regulating this new technique? These and other questions are still just emerging as we face the new world of cloning.
>
> My name is Erin Greene, and I'm a graduate student here at the university. As a research assistant in genetics, I am aware of not only the scientific issues surrounding cloning but also the social and ethical ones.
>
> Today, I'd like to discuss the complex issues, both scientific and social, surrounding cloning. Specifically, I'll cover the following topics: what cloning is, where we are in the science of cloning, what possible social consequences might arise, and how we can educate ourselves as this new field moves forward.

If you'll be taking audience questions at the end of the presentation, you might also preview this by including a phrase such as "At the end of my presentation, I'll be glad to take your questions and comments." (Chapter 9 provides information about taking audience questions.) Sometimes, if you're trying to make a specific point, you might also preview the purpose of your presentation at this stage: "My purpose is to convince you that . . . " or "My purpose is to inform you about. . . ." You have now caught your audience's attention, established your credibility, and introduced the main points, structure, and possibly the purpose of your presentation. Your audience now will expect you to cover these points in the exact order, without deviation, that you stated in your introduction. So the body of your presentation will contain four items:

- what cloning is
- where we are in the science of cloning
- what possible social consequences might arise
- how we can educate ourselves as this new field moves forward

(More about the body of your presentation in the next chapter.)

The following diagram illustrates these parts of an introduction.

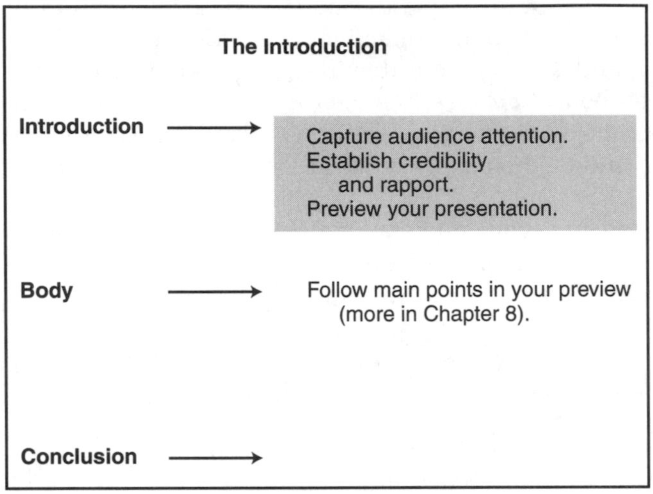

The Conclusion

After the body of your presentation comes the conclusion. You should construct the conclusion at the same time you construct the introduction. By having both of these pieces in place first, you automatically create a solid organizational structure for the body of your presentation. As noted earlier, you will have to do some thinking about the body of the presentation (see Chapter 8) before you can write the conclusion.

Like the introduction, the conclusion is a segment that people remember. It is your final chance to make an impression, reinforce your argument, and remind your audience about the important points. The conclusion puts a nice finishing cap on your presentation and should not be neglected. All too often, a presenter will give an excellent introduction and a great presentation but then fall flat at the end, saying something such as "Well, that's all I have for you today." Work as hard on the conclusion as you do on the introduction.

One author suggests that you "design your finish first and your start second" (D'Arcy, 1992, p. 71). Although this technique may not work for everyone, it is not a bad suggestion, in that it implies that you should think about your conclusion before you design your introduction. If you know how you want to conclude and what central points you want to get across at the end, you'll be very clear about the entire presentation.

Even Aristotle, more than 2,000 years ago, recognized that a good conclusion should accomplish four tasks: It should put the audience in favor of the presenter's position and against any opposing positions, remind the audience about the main subject, give the audience an emotional jolt, and remind the audience of the main points. Although you may need to adapt the following suggestions for a given audience and purpose, you will find that these guidelines will help you construct an effective conclusion.

1. *Let a clear transition statement lead into your conclusion.* The most common transition statement in this regard is "In conclusion. . . ." These words signal to your audience that you are moving from the body of the presentation into your closing comments. Although "in conclusion" may seem rather clichéd, it is better than nothing—in technical communication, audiences need signals and transitions to help them know where they are located on the road map of the presentation. There are many ways to signal your conclusion; you may wish to try "Now let me end with a few final ideas"; or, simply, "Finally, . . . ," or a question, such as "So, where does this leave us?" (Transitions are discussed in more detail in the next chapter.)

Another way to make a transition to your conclusion is to return to the story, anecdote, or quotation used during your introduction. By returning to the beginning, you'll provide a clear signal that you are winding up. For example, on the cloning presentation, you might say

> So, whatever happened to Missy the dog? Are there now a litter of Missy-like cloned puppies?

and then move on to finish your presentation.

2. *Restate the main points of your presentation.* After signaling your conclusion, you should remind the audience of where they've just been. Restate the main points of your presentation, but do so succinctly and without too much redundancy. You may begin with something as simple as

> Now that you know what cloning is and where the science stands at this point, you can make some decisions about the social consequences and how you can educate yourself for the future.

This statement reminds the audience of what they've just heard, helping to sharpen their focus on the main themes of the presentation. Remember that unlike technical writing, oral presentations (even ones where you provide handouts) *must* have a clear organizational pattern, because the audience is relying on their ears and their mind, not a book, to help guide them. By reminding them of what you've just covered, you help refresh their memory and get them ready for the final points of your conclusion.

3. *Make an appeal for action.* Now, after you have carefully made your case and explained your ideas, you can use the conclusion to appeal for action. Especially if your purpose is to persuade your audience, the conclusion is the place to suggest what actions the audience can take.

4. *Provide resources for further information.* Your audience may wish to continue learning about your topic, especially if you've given an enthusiastic and interesting presentation. If appropriate for the audience and purpose of the presentation, be sure to provide avenues where your audience can learn more—phone numbers, email addresses, and URLs of relevant Websites. You can either put this information on a slide or overhead (more on this in Part Five), or you can distribute handouts.

5. ***Do not*** *introduce new ideas.* Sometimes, when a presenter has done a particularly fine job with a presentation and is feeling relieved to be at the end of the talk, he or she will make the fatal mistake of talking about some new aspect of the topic—something that the presenter did not include in the introduction or discuss in the body of the presentation. For example, the speaker discussing the cloning of Missy the dog might make the mistake of saying in the conclusion:

> If people would just sign organ donor cards, scientists would have no need to pursue cloning research.

The accuracy or inaccuracy of such a statement is not the issue. The problem is that by including the statement the speaker is introducing an entirely new topic that was not part of the presentation—and doing so is very unsettling to the audience. Listeners are startled, and many wonder if they somehow missed an important part of the speech. Or they wonder why you said something so abruptly and did not elaborate. Remember that good technical communication follows a road map, making the material easy for the audience to follow. Stick with your original map.

The following diagram illustrates the main parts of both the introduction and the conclusion to a presentation.

The Conclusion

Introduction	→	Capture audience attention. Establish credibility and rapport. Preview your presentation.
Body	→	Follow main points in your preview (more in Chapter 8).
Conclusion	→	Provide clear transition statement into conclusion. Restate main points. Appeal for action. Provide resources for further information. Do not introduce new ideas.

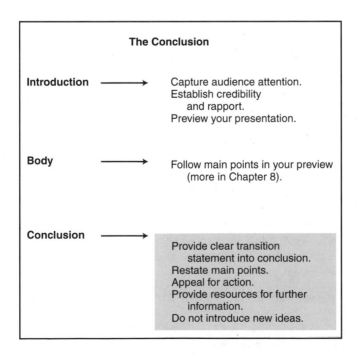

Memorize the Introduction and Conclusion

Remember the previous chapter's discussion of memory? It was noted that having material well memorized makes a good impression on your audience. It also helps you feel more confident and shows the audience that you have sincerely worked on the presentation and thus respect them and their time. It is critical that you have a well-memorized introduction and conclusion. Having these two sections memorized and ready to go provides a solid structure for the rest of the presentation.

Yet you do not need to write out the entire introduction and memorize it word for word. This technique is sometimes used in formal speeches but is rarely effective in professional presentations. You want to aim for a style that is polished and professional yet natural; a word for word memorization can sound too stuffy and insincere. Also, memorizing word for word sets you up for potential failure: If you forget one word, you lose your place in the introduction or conclusion.

The most effective approach, then, is for you to memorize the outline of your introduction and conclusion, and to do so using some of the mnemonic techniques discussed in Chapter 3. Examine the introduction of the cloning presentation on page 75.

> Should cloning be available on a pay-per-pet basis? Researchers at one university seem to say "yes." Recently, an anonymous couple donated $2.3 million to a Texas university to have their collie-husky mix, Missy, cloned into several new Missy pups. But should the government be more closely regulating this new technique? These and other questions are still just emerging as we face the new world of cloning.
>
> My name is Erin Greene, and I'm a graduate student here at the university. As a research assistant in genetics, I am aware of not only the scientific issues surrounding cloning but also the social and ethical ones.
>
> Today, I'd like to discuss the complex issues, both scientific and social, surrounding cloning. Specifically, I'll cover the following topics: what cloning is, where we are in the science of cloning, what possible social consequences might arise, and how we can educate ourselves as this new field moves forward.

To memorize this introduction, break it up into the key points, along with certain phrases you want to use:

1. **Missy** story/pay-per-pet basis
2. Should **government** regulate?
3. My **name** and position as researcher
4. Preview: cloning **definition**
   cloning **update**
   social consequences
   educate ourselves

Boldface or highlight the key words in each point that will help trigger that idea for you. Then, practice until you are confident that you can deliver an interesting introduction without hesitating or searching for words or ideas. Use the same technique for the conclusion.

If you use overheads or presentation software, you will probably have a slide for item 4 (preview of main points), and the slide will guide you through that portion of the introduction. Visual aids will help you with some aspects of memory, but you should be able to work without the technology too. (Slides and other visual materials are discussed in Part Five.)

In Summary: Strong Introductions and Conclusions

The introduction and conclusion are critical elements for a presentation. They provide a stable framework for the entire body of the presentation, and they help the audience follow your main points and central argument. Sometimes, introductions are governed by the conventions of a specific situation; for example, at the National Press Club, every speaker is introduced with a short biographical statement. In these cases, it's not necessary to introduce yourself or make overt statements about your credentials. However, the guidelines in this chapter provide a framework that is consistent with good principles of technical communication: They help the audience follow your material and make the information accessible.

The next chapter discusses the body of a presentation and how to research the content.

QUESTIONS / EXERCISES / ASSIGNMENTS

1. Attend a presentation, speech, or lecture, or watch one on television. Pay careful attention to the structure of the presentation, especially the introduction and the conclusion. From the introduction, what kind of ethos did the presenter create? Was it clear what the presentation would cover? Did you feel compelled and interested in the topic? If not, why? Make similar notes about the conclusion and describe how you might have adjusted the introduction and conclusion to be more effective.

2. Skim through several magazines and notice which stories grab your attention. Make a list of the items that caught your interest: the headlines, graphics, initial paragraph of information, and other features. Consider how you might use similar features in the introduction of a presentation.

Presentations and Cyberspace. Locate the texts of two or three presentations given at professional or academic conferences, and analyze the introductions and conclusions. How did each presenter introduce and conclude the speech? Were the introductions and conclusions effective? If not, revise them to incorporate, as appropriate, techniques you studied in this chapter.

Presentations and Teamwork. From the list of topics your team worked with at the end of Chapter 6, identify one that intrigues everyone on your team. Have each team member select a different method for capturing the attention of an audience and, for the same topic, prepare an introduction using that method. Listen to and critique each team member's introduction.

Presentations and International Communication. In a high-context culture, the way in which a message is presented is often just as important or more important than what is actually said or written. In a low-context culture, what is said or written is often more important than the way in which that message is presented. How could these context expectations affect the way in which you would word introductions and conclusions for different cultural audiences? In your response, consider directness, formality, the presentation of opinions, and the uses and presentations of examples.

Presentations and Your Profession. Describe a presentation that you might realistically give in your profession—the topic, purpose, context, and content. For that presentation, prepare two different introductions and matching conclusions. Explain the presentation to your class and give both sets of introductions and conclusions. Ask them to identify the set they prefer, and to explain their choice.

REFERENCES

Andeweg, B. A., de Jong, J. C., & Hoeken, H. (1998). May I have your attention? Exordial techniques in informative oral presentations. *Technical Communication Quarterly, 7*(3), 271–284.

Aristotle. (1991). *On rhetoric: A theory of civic discourse* (G. A. Kennedy, Trans.). New York: Oxford University Press.

Associated Press. (1998, August 26). Owners put up millions in an attempt to clone their one-of-a-kind pooch. *Minneapolis Star-Tribune,* p. A-1, A-17.

D'Arcy, Jan. (1992). *Technically speaking: Proven ways to make your next presentation a success.* New York: AMACOM.

Perlman, A. M. (1998). *Writing great speeches: Professional techniques you can use.* Boston: Allyn & Bacon.

CHAPTER

8 The Body of Your Presentation and How to Find Information

CHAPTER OVERVIEW

Once you've designed an effective introduction and conclusion, you can work on the body of your presentation. The body is the main section of content, and it must be well organized and well researched in order for your presentation to be clear, interesting, and understandable for your audience. This chapter covers the following topics:

- Finding Information
- Organizing the Material
- Using an Outline
- Previewing the Material for Your Audience
- Citing Material in Your Presentation
- Providing Handouts
- Being Ready to Adapt

Finding Information

Chapter 2 discussed a way to make you less nervous, and that is to select a topic with which you are familiar, comfortable, and enthusiastic. This is always a good guideline, yet sometimes you are asked to give a presentation on a topic that is new to you. The amount of familiarity and background you have with a topic will impact how much research you need to perform. Obviously, topics that you are an expert in require less research. Nonetheless, it is extremely important that you research your topic: There is always new information or a new point of view, especially in the changing world of science and technology. A poorly researched presentation, like a poorly researched report, paper, or any other form of communication, won't be effective. But a presentation that's backed up with solid evidence, well-researched facts, and cutting-edge information is effective and impressive.

Research Methods

Once you have selected a topic for your presentation, you can research this topic in many ways.

Using the Library. Despite the rising popularity of the Internet and the Web, libraries still remain powerhouses of information. Well before Web search engines, librarians were skilled not only at acquiring information but also at making this information accessible through card catalogs, indexes, and other retrieval tools. Your university or public library is an excellent place to research your presentation topic. Reference librarians are usually only too happy to direct you to the right index or other source to begin your research. Today's libraries are high tech, too: Card catalogs are often searchable via the Internet, and within the library itself you'll find computers and database services, like Lexus (for legal searches) or CD-ROMs.

Using Corporate Documents. Most large corporations have a wealth of documents that may be useful for a presentation, especially if the presentation involves that particular organization. Some large companies even have corporate libraries, where material is indexed and can be checked out, similar to a university or public library. Some corporate documents are confidential and require permission or special clearance to be used. Office correspondence, such as memos, email messages, or internal documents (like corporate style guides) may also be useful for your presentation. You may be required to obtain permission from the company's legal department or some other authority before using such materials.

Interviewing Experts. For almost any subject, it's always useful to interview experts. Even if you are something of an expert yourself, you can learn by talking with others who are extremely knowledgeable in the topic of your presentation. When it comes to science and technology, the world of information is becoming increasingly specialized, so it's rare for one person to know everything. When interviewing experts, be sure to tell them that you are doing research for a presentation, and ask if you can use their names during your talk. Be very well prepared with a list of specific questions before you contact the person—everyone is busy, and you want to show that you are respectful of this person's time. Email can be a very useful way to establish contact with someone you'd like to interview—unlike a phone call, email is much less intrusive and can be answered at the receiver's convenience. Don't send a survey or list of questions in your first email unless you know the person; send a query in which you introduce yourself and ask if the person would be willing to talk with you about your presentation.

Talking to Others in Your Organization. If your presentation is strictly based on job-related issues, your best source of additional information may be other people in the organization. Even if you are presenting on a topic in which you are expert, you can always learn something new from talking with others. You may be the technical development expert, but someone from technical marketing may have a perspective that you hadn't considered. Someone from the legal office may have information related to intellectual property or technology transfer concerns. Other teams may be able to update you on how their projects will impact your topic.

Reading Newspapers. A good way to stay generally well informed is to read several newspapers a day. You should read your local paper plus several of the national ones (*New York Times, Boston Globe, Los Angeles Times*). A convenient and inexpensive way to read national papers is to use the Web. Most major papers have Web versions that you can access quickly and skim. Some papers have special days of the week for science articles; the *New York Times,* for example, runs a regular science section every Tuesday. Bookmark or cut out stories that are relevant to your areas of interest.

Using the Web. The Web has quickly become an excellent technology for finding information. Almost any word or phrase typed into a Web search engine will usually yield more information than anyone can possibly use. That's because of some major differences between traditional publishing and Web publishing. Traditionally, books and articles, especially academic ones, are subjected to a review process. This textbook, for example, was written and then sent to several professors and technical communication professionals, who read the work, suggested changes, and corrected errors or problems. The book was then edited for these changes, and only then was it published, bound, and sold to students. Even magazine articles and newspaper stories are often subjected to this sort of gatekeeping—editorial boards, editors, and others in the organization usually see material before it goes to print.

The Web, on the other hand, does not require these steps before information is posted to a Website. Some Web-based articles and information are in fact reviewed, but much of what you find on the Web is not. It is written and put into HTML format by anyone who cares to do so—from professors with Ph.D.'s to ten-year-olds with a computer and modem. On the plus side, this form of publishing lets everyone have a voice and provides for a wealth of information. On the troublesome side, however, it requires Web users to be much more critical and cautious consumers of information. Just because something is on a Web page, even a really great looking Web page, doesn't mean that this information is credible. Your job, then, when researching on the Web, is to be very selective about what information you decide to include in your presentation. The FYI feature on the following page provides some useful suggestions for researching on the Web.

Example of a Web Search

A search on the terms "computers + privacy" using the MetaCrawler search engine yielded many different types of information. The first is an announcement for a computers and privacy conference (Figure 8.1). The second is a page that allows you to download encryption software—software that lets you encode your Internet communication so only the intended reader can open it (Figure 8.2). The third is the privacy statement of Fairfield Computers, a computer company (Figure 8.3). Obviously, each of these pages contains very different information. Narrowing

FYI

Using the Web for Research

The Web is a vast source of information from around the globe. Your first task is to find what you are looking for. To do this, you can use search engines, tools that search through many Web pages and select those that correspond with the criteria you've set. Some common search engines include:

AltaVista: www.altavista.com
Lycos: www.lycos.com
MetaCrawler: www.metacrawler.com

When these search engines find Websites that match your search criteria, they create a list of active links, or hits, from which you can access each site. You need to be very selective about how you search for material. A search on the word "computer" is probably too general, whereas a search on "computers + privacy" would narrow your search but even then, you still will need to carefully sort through each hit (see Figures 8.1, 8.2, 8.3).

As you sort through each hit, you need to determine if the material is credible. When you evaluate a Website, look for the following characteristics:

- An online version of a reputable published source (online newspaper, major media source, academic journal, professional journal, scholarly paper)
- A list of works cited
- An affiliation with a reputable educational or research institution
- Author of the site and information about how to contact her or him

If most or all of these characteristics are present, the site is likely to be credible, and you can feel confident using information from that site.

Several characteristics serve as warning signs that the site may lack credibility:

- No information about the author, works cited, or background; site is set up primarily to sell you something
- Site is suddenly is unavailable when you search for it
- Site is affiliated with an extremist group (e.g., groups who believe the Holocaust never happened)

your search terms might help, but ultimately, you must be a careful consumer of online information.

Organizing the Material

After you have researched your topic, you can choose from many different patterns to organize the body of the presentation. You should choose the organizational pattern based on the specific audience and purpose of the presentation. Often, you will intuitively know how to arrange your presentation—perhaps you've spoken to this group before, or perhaps your company always gives presentations in a certain way. But it's helpful to know what organizational patterns are possible so that when you can choose, you know the range of possibilities.

The following discussion summarizes characteristics of common organizational patterns. In Part Three, you'll learn about which patterns of organization best go with which type of presentation.

CFP **The Computers Freedom & Privacy Conference**

Computers
Freedom &
Privacy 1999
THE
GLOBAL
INTERNET

If you wish to be added to our email list for future announcements, please send mail to cfpinfo@cfp.org. If you'd like to get a printed copy of the advance program when it becomes available, be sure to include your snail mail address.

Year	Information Available
2000	**The Tenth Conference on Computers, Freedom and Privacy** See the CFP2000 Web site at http://www.cfp2000.org
1999	The Ninth Conference on Computers, Freedom and Privacy See the CFP99 Web site at http://www.cfp99.org. CFP'99 Call for Proposals
1998	The Eighth Annual Conference on Computers, Freedom and Privacy, Austin, TX See the CFP98 Web site at http://www.cfp98.org for details.
1997	The Seventh Conference on Computers, Freedom and Privacy, Burlingame, CA CFP'97 Call for Participation CFP'97 Web Brochure
1996	The Sixth Conference on Computers, Freedom and Privacy, Cambridge, MA CFP'96 Program information
1995	The Fifth Conference on Computers, Freedom and Privacy, Burlingame, CA Papers, Program, etc. (PDF) at Stanford CFP '95 Hotlist, Newsletters
1994	The Fourth Conference on Computers, Freedom and Privacy, Chicago, IL Program, Summary, 1 Transcript & Closing Speech (HTML) at CPSR

FIGURE 8.1 Results of Web Search on the Phrase "computers and privacy": www.cfp.org/.
Source: Copyright © 1998 CPSR. Used with permission.

MIT distribution site for PGP (Pretty Good Privacy)

PGP or Pretty Good (TM) Privacy is a high-security cryptographic software application that allows people to exchange messages with both privacy and authentication.

Privacy means that only those intended to receive a message can read it. By providing the ability to encrypt messages, PGP provides protection against anyone eavesdropping on the network. Even if a packet is intercepted, it will be unreadable to the snooper. *Authentication* ensures that a message appearing to be from a particular person can have originated from that person only, and that the message has not been altered. In addition to its support for messages, PGP also enables you to encrypt files stored on your computer.

MIT distributes PGP free for non-commercial use. This distribution is done in cooperation with Philip Zimmermann, the author of PGP, and with RSA Data Security, Inc., which licenses patents to the public-key encryption technology on which PGP relies.

How to obtain PGP from MIT

PGP is distributed by MIT only to US citizens within the United States.

MIT distributes PGP in both in source and in and executable only versions. PGP is available for most DOS, Macintosh, and Unix platforms. The current versions of PGP being distributed by MIT are:

- For DOS and Unix platforms, MIT has been distributing PGP version 2.6.2 since October 24, 1994.
- For the Apple Macintosh, MIT has been distributing MacPGP version 2.6 since June, 1994.

To obtain the current version of PGP from MIT via the World-Wide Web, click here.

If you do not have WWW access, you can use anonymous FTP to net-dist.mit.edu. Look in the directory pub/PGP and follow the directions in the README file.

PGP is available from MIT by WWW or FTP access only. If you do not have such access you will need to obtain PGP from another source.

Integrating PGP with mail programs

PGP is much more convenient to use in conjunction with an interface that integrates it into programs for reading and sending mail. Several such interfaces are available for popular mail programs. The ones distributed by MIT are:

- For users of **Emacs** on Unix systems, there is **Mailcrypt**, available from MIT. Click here for information.

Here are some other PGP/mail interfaces (not distributed by MIT):

- There are several PGP shells for **Windows** users. You can find out more about them here.

FIGURE 8.2 Results of Web Search on the Phrase "computers and privacy": web.mit.edu/network.pgp.html.

Source: Web page: Copyright © Massachussetts Institute of Technology. Used with permission. PGP lock image: Copyright © 1997, 1998, 1999 O'Reilly & Associates, Inc. Used with permission.

FairField Computers
1371 Water Street, Fairfield PA 17320
Phone (717) 642-0056 Fax (717) 642-0057

Home | About Us | News | Support | New PC Sales | Used PC Sales | Software | Web Design

Privacy Policy Statement
This is the web site of Fairfield Computers.

Our postal address is:
1371 Water Street
Fairfield, PA 17320

We can be reached via e-mail at webmaster@fairfieldcomputers.com
Or you can reach us by telephone at 717-642-0056 or by FAX at 717-642-0057

For each visitor to our Web page, our Web server automatically recognizes the domain but not the e-mail address.

We collect the e-mail addresses of those who communicate with us via e-mail and information volunteered by the consumer, such as survey information and/or site registrations.

The information we collect is used by us to contact consumers for marketing purposes or with with information regarding orders they have placed on-line or with information they have requested about our products.

If you do not want to receive e-mail from us in the future, please let us know by sending email to us at the above address or calling us at the above telephone number or writing to us at the above address and telling us that you do not want to receive e-mail from our company.

If you supply us with your postal address on line you will only receive the information for which you provided us your address.

We do not share any information obtained with other organizations.

Persons who supply us with their telephone numbers on-line may receive telephone contact from us with information regarding orders they have placed on-line or with information they have requested about our products.

Reminders: never forget important gift giving dates again
Email this page to a friend
Keep me posted if this page changes

TRUST·e
PRIVACY INFORMATION

Copyright 1998, 1999 Fairfield Computers

FIGURE 8.3 Results of Web Search on the Phrase "computers and privacy": www.fairfieldcomputers.com/privacy.htm.

Source: Copyright © D. Scott Barninger. Used with permission.

Chronological Organization

Chronological organization means that you organize your material based on a time sequence. Suppose, for example, that you were giving a presentation on how to use an accounting software package. Your presentation would probably be best organized around the order of steps: First, you load the program, then you log in, then you enter data, and so on. Chronological order works well with how-to presentations or training sessions, where your goal is to teach an audience how to perform a task.

For example, consider the following situation: A company has just purchased new external backup devices for employee computers. Employees are responsible for installing the device, and you've been asked to give a presentation on how to perform this installation. After your introduction, the body of your presentation would follow a chronological pattern, as suggested in this outline:

1. Remove the backup device from its packing material and locate the drive, power cable, and SCSI cable.
2. Attach the power cable to the back of the backup device.
3. Attach the SCSI cable to the back of the device.

You would continue to present the information in a step-by-step fashion. Chronological organization will be discussed in more detail in Chapter 12.

Spatial Organization

Spatial organization is effective when you are describing the physical arrangement of a system or item. If you were describing the South American rain forest and the flood cycles of the Amazon River, for example, you might describe the river and how it runs geographically across the continent. Or, if you were describing the circuitry of a biomedical device or a computer board, you would do best to describe these in terms of how they are actually laid out, thus using a spatial pattern to organize your main points. Spatial organization is useful for informative presentations.

Categorical Organization

Some types of presentation topics are automatically given to organization by category. Consider, for example, the topic of dogs. Perhaps you are an expert in animal behavior and are asked to speak to a group of new dog owners. You might usefully draw upon the already existing categories of dogs, classifying them first by type (retrievers, spaniels, toy dogs, and so on) and then by subtype (spaniels—cocker, King Charles, springer, and so on). You would then be able to discuss behavior characteristics of each subtype. Categorical organization is helpful for informative presentations, which are discussed in Chapter 9.

Problem-Solution Organization

If your presentation is focused on an issue that needs to be resolved or somehow corrected, you may wish to use a problem-solution organizational structure. First, you present the problem, then you outline various solutions. Usually you'll have one best solution in mind, so as you present other solutions, you explain why they may not work. Then, you present your solution. Issues of science and technology are often appropriate for this format, especially if you are recommending a specific action. Problem-solution patterns are best for persuasive or action plan presentations, which are discussed in Chapters 10 and 11.

Causal Organization

Causal organization means that you organize your presentation around how an item or series of items caused something else to happen. For example, if you were presentating theories of how the universe began, you might present these theories in a causal fashion: First, matter appeared, which caused something else to happen. Causal patterns of organization require clear logic—for instance, if you are going to argue that X caused Y, you must be sure that X did indeed cause Y to happen. Causal organization is useful for informative or persuasive presentations, which are discussed in Chapter 9.

Deductive Organization

Deductive organization is probably the most common type of pattern in technical communication. Presenting deductively means that you present your bottom line (conclusion, solution) first, then provide the audience with the background and information that led you to this conclusion. Deductive organization helps audiences understand and follow your material, because they know right away what your conclusion is and how the supporting material fits into a bigger scheme. An example of a deductively organized presentation might be as follows:

> You are asked to give a presentation designed to persuade the managers at your company to provide more funds for computer software. You know that most managers are in favor of this increase in spending, so you get right to the point. You begin with the statement: "My purpose today is to request increased funding for the software we need to do our jobs. I will support my request by stating three main reasons."

Deductive presentations are particularly appropriate for informative presentations, which are discussed in Chapter 9.

Inductive Organization

Inductive organization is more or less the opposite of deductive. When you argue inductively, you don't give the bottom line first. Instead, you give a general sense of the main topic, then you present specific instances leading to a conclusion. For example:

> You are asked to give a presentation designed to persuade the managers at your company to provide more funds for computer software. You know that most managers are *not* in favor of this increase in spending, so you begin with some background about the problem, and you build up toward your main point by using statistics to show how productive your unit has been. Then, you end with the statement: "My purpose today is to request increased funding for the software we need to do our jobs. I will support my request by stating three main reasons."

Inductively organized presentations can be more difficult to follow, because audiences don't know what the bottom line of the presentation really is. But inductive presentations are sometimes useful if you know the audience might not readily agree with your conclusion (such as in certain persuasive presentations), because in inductive presentations, you begin with the individual facts first, then lead the audience toward the conclusion. Unless you are sure an inductive approach is the only possible one, you should avoid it, because audiences don't like to be kept in the dark.

Using an Outline

When you organize your material using one of the patterns just discussed, you can use the same outlining method you use for writing papers. Select your main points and under these, list your subpoints. Make main points parallel in structure and equal in importance (Koch, 1998, p. 61). For example, your presentation is a persuasive one, structured in a problem-solution format. In your introduction, you indicate that you will request increased funding for software and that you'll support your request with three main reasons. Your outline might look something like this:

A. Introduction
- **1.** Cartoon about software use (capture attention)
- **2.** State name and number of years with company (establish credibility)
- **3.** Request increased funding for software. State problem. List 3 main points (overview)

B. Body
- **1.** Brief background of problem and proposed solution
- **2.** Reasons why we should follow my solution
    - **a.** Better software will increase productivity
    - **b.** Better software will allow us to hire cutting-edge workers
    - **c.** Better software will take less room on our computers

C. Conclusion
- **1.** Restate the introduction in general terms. Restate solution

2. Ask for immediate consideration
3. Offer my team to do the research
4. Thank everyone for attending and take questions

This is a simple example but should serve to remind you how to create an outline.

Previewing the Material for Your Audience

The body of your presentation is the place where you make your main points or arguments. Unlike written communication, where readers can leaf back through pages if they get confused or lose track of information, oral presentations are conveyed in real time, through your words and delivery style. It is therefore extremely important that the body of your presentation be well organized so your audience can follow your line of thinking and listen to your material with a clear sense of where they are headed. But just because you have organized the presentation clearly doesn't mean your audience will be able to follow you. You must provide your audience with a *clear road map and then stick to this road map* as you present your material.

In Chapter 7, you learned that you should state your main points during the introduction. By doing so, you will have already set out the main road map for your presentation. Now, you must follow these main points during your presentation. For example, imagine that you are creating a persuasive presentation about computer privacy. After researching the topic, you choose a problem-solution format. During the introduction, you preview the following main points:

1. The use of computers and large scale databases is changing what we can expect in terms of personal privacy. (Problem)
2. There are many examples of this change that you (the audience) may not even be aware of. (Problem)
3. We need to keep on top of privacy legislation and industry trends if we want to have any input in this rapidly changing field. (Solution)

Research indicates that people learn best when they are given an overview like this and can then read or listen to new material with this outline in mind. During the body of your presentation, your audience will expect you to follow this outline in exactly the order in which you previewed it.

Sometimes, as you research and prepare the body of your presentation, you'll discover that your main points are shifting around: You discover new information, change your viewpoint, or decide to present the material in a new order. You'll also notice that as you work on the body of the presentation, the introduction and conclusion will need to be modified. This iterative, back-and-forth process is perfectly natural: As you research and think about the material, you constantly invent new ways to structure your presentation. Don't panic. Just remember that once you've settled on the proper order, you must adjust your introduction and conclusion to reflect this structure.

Use Clear Transitions between Main Points

Transitions can be thought of as signposts along the journey of your presentation. They are words and phrases used to signal the audience that you are switching from one main point to another. You may be familiar with using transitions in technical writing, where they are also useful tools for helping audiences move through complex material. Examples of transitions include:

- First, second, third
- Next
- In addition
- Furthermore
- Now that I've talked about point A, let me describe point B

Consider how transitions might work in a presentation on computer privacy. First, the introduction:

> Here's a scene that's all too familiar today. You're checking out at the grocery store, and the cashier innocently asks for your BonusCard. You produce the card and she scans it. At home later, you happily notice the various discounts you received on your groceries by using the card. But did you know that along with giving you discounts, these cards also track all of your purchases, adding your name, address, and spending habits to a large database that can be bought, sold, and used by almost anyone?
>
> My name is Geoff Johnson, and I've been studying computer databases and personal privacy for three years now as a communication specialist at CompuSys Research Corporation. Though I'm pleased with many aspects of our newly emerging computer culture, I am also troubled by what I see as great changes in personal privacy. Today, I'd like to introduce you to these changes and discuss ways you can get involved in this important new area. In my presentation today, I'll cover three points: **A,** An overview of computers and personal privacy; **B,** examples of everyday interactions during which your privacy is compromised; and **C,** ways you can stay on top of privacy legislation and industry trends.

In this introduction, you see the key elements discussed in the previous chapter: an attention-catching section; a section establishing personal credibility; and a preview of the presentation's main points, labeled A, B, and C.

The body of your presentation should now follow this outline. First, you will address point A, followed by B, followed by C. However, you need to give your audience signals when you are switching from topic to topic. To do so, use transitions. After the introduction, for example, you might begin with:

> **First,** let's look over the history and current state of computers and personal privacy.

Once you complete this section, you end it with a transition that moves from your current point to the next point:

> **Now that** you're familiar with the current state of technology and privacy in the United States, **let's look at** examples of everyday interactions where your privacy might be compromised.

To move into your last point, you could use the transition "finally":

> **Finally,** there are ways you can stay on top of privacy legislation and industry trends.

These transitions provide clear signals to the audience about where you are in the presentation and where you are headed. They give the audience a road map, or organizational structure, that they can depend on. Instead of concentrating on where you are in the presentation, your audience can concentrate on your message. Remember, good technical communication is focused around your audience and around information that is easy to access. It's your job as the communicator to make your presentation as well organized and clear as possible.

The following diagram is based on what you learned in the last chapter but also includes details about the body of the presentation. Notice the transitions, which will help you and the audience members move from point to point.

The Body

Introduction →	Capture audience attention. Establish credibility and rapport. Preview your presentation. Point A Point B Point C
Body →	Follow main points in your preview; use transitions. First, Point A. Now that we've discussed Point A, let's discuss Point B. Finally, Point C. Provide clear transition statement into conclusion.
Conclusion →	Restate main points: Point A, Point B, Point C. Appeal for action. Provide resources for further information. Stick with original road map.

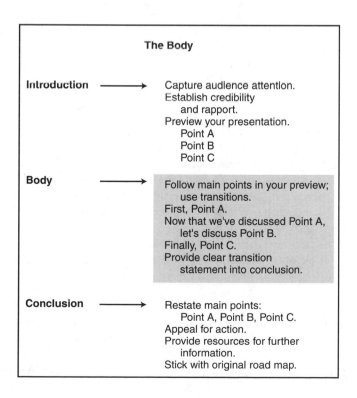

Adhere to the Allotted Time

There is nothing more unprofessional or disorganized than a presenter who ignores time constraints and exceeds the allotted time. Speaking beyond the scheduled time is disrespectful of your audience and of those who invited you to present. It is also disrespectful to any speakers who are scheduled to present after you. Always be courteous and structure your presentation to fit into the amount of time you've been given. If you're unclear about how long you should speak, make sure you ask well in advance of preparing your presentation.

When you begin preparing your presentation, you may encounter a very common problem: You have more material than you can possibly fit into a ten-, twelve-, or even twenty-minute time slot. On the one hand, that's a good sign, because it means you know a good deal about your subject and care about it. But on the other hand, you need to trim your material to make it fit into the allotted time. One way to do this is to make a careful outline, divided into main points and subpoints. First, outline your main presentation and divide by the number of minutes you have for each part. For example, in a twelve-minute presentation, you might allot one minute to the introduction and two minutes to the conclusion. That would leave you with nine minutes total for the body. If you have three main points, as in the computer privacy presentation, you then have three minutes for each main point. As you draft your material, practice each subsection to see if it's too long or too short. Then, practice the entire presentation and time yourself. Skilled technical communicators excel not only at understanding audience and purpose but also at adapting material to fit a variety of situations, from short presentations to all-day workshops.

Citing Material in Your Presentation

Based on other courses you've taken, especially writing courses, you're probably familiar with the precept of giving credit for another person's idea when you use this idea in your own work. It's unethical (and sometimes a violation of copyright—more on this in Chapter 19) to use someone else's words or ideas without giving credit. Known as plagiarism, using someone else's material without giving adequate citation is a serious offense. Most colleges and universities have strict guidelines for handling plagiarism; if you have any questions, ask your instructor.

In writing, it's not very difficult to give credit properly for someone's words or ideas. You use footnotes or in-text citations and end your paper with a Works Cited or References page. For example, a typical citation in a paper might be as follows:

> One researcher describes the Oort cloud, an area beyond Pluto that contains comets and other matter, as "the Siberia of the solar system" (Weissman, p. 84).

Later in the paper, you would find the full citation (this one is in APA style):

Works Cited

Weissman, P. R. (1998, September). The Oort cloud. *Scientific American,* pp. 84–89.

In this example, the author of the paper used Weissman's exact words. But even if you didn't use the exact words, just the idea, you would still cite the material.

Given that oral presentations are not written, how can you properly avoid plagiarism and adequately cite others' ideas? There are several ways.

Use introductory statements to preface your remarks. For example, before using material that is from another source, you can say

"According to one source, . . . "

"Based on several articles, . . . "

"According to a recent study in the *Journal of the American Medical Association, . . .* "

"To quote Bill Gates, . . . "

"As Mahatma Gandhi once said, . . . "

"Based on our latest annual report, . . . "

On your slides or overhead projector sheets, you can actually include a reference, exactly as you would in a written paper. And, at the end of your presentation, you can provide handouts with full citations, URLs, and other information related to the research of your material.

Audiences appreciate this—not only are you helping them locate additional information, you are also showing yourself to be an ethical speaker by giving credit to others.

Providing Handouts

Handouts are another excellent way to help your audience follow the structure of your presentation. Presentation software (discussed in Part Five) allows you to print your slides on paper. You can then distribute these printouts to the audience. In addition, you can also add extra material to handouts, such as URLs, book titles, and phone numbers that audience members can access for more information about your topic.

Depending on the audience and purpose, handouts are usually a good idea. In many settings, such as company presentations where this is standard practice, handouts may be expected. Conference seminar planners often ask presenters to bring handouts, or the planners offer to make handouts in advance. Handouts help people remember the presentation after it's over. In terms of helping your audience stay organized, however, the big question is not whether to use handouts but *when* to distribute them. As you can probably recall from any recent presentation you've attended, once handouts are being passed around, audience members turn their attention away from the presenter and toward the handouts. This shift in focus can be unnerving for the presenter, and it can actually distract your audience from the main message. Oral presentations are live, not written; much of the persuasive and informative power of an oral presentation comes from the real-time interactions of speaker and audience. As such, you want your audience to stay focused on you and your words as much as possible. So, if conditions permit, you should try saving handouts until the very end. Or, if you want your audience to take notes on the handouts as you go along (something that's often done in how-to or training seminars), distribute the handouts first, before starting your presentation. We'll discuss handouts and other visual aids in more detail later in the book.

Being Ready to Adapt

One of the most powerful aspects of oral presentations is that they are live. Unlike writing, where an author cannot see how every reader is responding, oral presentations provide the presenter with a real-time opportunity to be sure the information is clear and understood by the audience. As noted in the previous chapter, an excellent presenter is always able to adapt to the specific circumstance. Even if you've done a fine audience analysis and serious research, your presentation may still not be a perfect fit for a given audience. You never know until you actually begin presenting. Of course, the more carefully you analyze your audience and research the topic, the better your presentation will be. But every so often, you'll need to adapt the body of your presentation while you are speaking.

Say, for example, that your audience analysis indicated that your group was very familiar with using the Internet, the topic of your presentation. Unlike the nutritionist in the previous chapter, you have no trouble during the introduction. But as you begin the body of the presentation, you can tell from puzzled faces that almost half the audience is not at all familiar with the terms and concepts you're speaking about. A skilled presenter will make adjustments as he or she goes along. In this case, you might need to say "Before I continue, let me stop and take a moment to provide a bit of background on the Internet and how it operates." As you explain, look carefully at your audience to see how your material is registering. The audience members who didn't know these concepts beforehand will now be onboard, and you can go back to your original outline.

In this example, the problem was that your presentation was too technical or high level for the audience. The opposite can also happen; you may have prepared a presentation that is too basic or low level but discover that your audience already knows much of the material. Both cases require you to adapt.

If you pay close attention to your audience members and their expressions (do people look interested or puzzled?) and body language (are people paying attention

CHECKLIST

Adapting to Your Audience

There are several techniques you can follow to adapt a presentation to an audience. Remember, if you've done the research, your presentation will usually be a good fit. But if you notice that your audience is confused or appears to have questions, you need to make changes on the spot. Here are some ways to adapt:

- *Ask questions.* "It appears that perhaps I've gotten ahead of myself. Should I stop for a moment and explain a bit more about this aspect?"
- *Digress from your original outline.* "Before I continue, let me stop and take a moment to provide a bit of background on the Internet and how it operates."
- *Take audience questions.* "Perhaps some of you have questions at this stage. Let's take a moment and discuss these."
- *Move more quickly through certain parts of the presentation.* "It seems that most of you already know about the specific chemical structures involved in this case. Let me skip ahead to the legal aspects."

Remember not to embarass your audience by saying things like "It seems like you don't understand." Instead, be encouraging and helpful while you adapt your content to fit the situation.

or fidgeting with their pens?), you'll sense whether you need to adapt your original presentation.

Being able to adapt the body and content of your presentation on the spot takes practice, but it is a good skill to cultivate. In technical communication, where content can often be highly specialized and complex, you'll need to learn to pay careful attention to your audience and adapt as needed.

In Summary: The Body of Your Presentation

In this chapter, you learned some methods for researching and organizing the body of your presentation. The body should reflect your efforts at serious research on the topic using credible evidence, and it should be organized in a pattern that is most suitable for the audience and purpose. You should use clear transitions between main points, and you can provide your audience with handouts to give them additional information. When performing your research, remember that despite the popularity of the Web, not all Websites are created equal when it comes to the credibility of their information. Be selective about the Web material you use.

The next four chapters will look closely at four types of presentations and offer specific advice about how to structure and deliver these presentations.

QUESTIONS / EXERCISES / ASSIGNMENTS

1. Select a topic and invent an audience for it. Now think of several purposes for presentating that topic to your audience: to persuade, to educate, to solve a problem. Outline the entire presentation (introduction, body, conclusion) based on each purpose. Depending on the purpose, the body of your presentation will look very different. Pay attention to the patterns of organization you choose for each purpose.

2. Create a simple outline, using one of the organizational patterns in this chapter, for a basic presentation about a topic you know well. Outline your presentation with whatever method you use to outline a paper. In your outline, write in the transitions you will use as you move from point to point. Practice the use of transitions.

Presentations and Cyberspace. Select a topic for your first presentation. Use the Web to search for information about this topic. Use any of the available search engines (AltaVista, MetaCrawler, Lycos, etc.). With a critical eye, examine first the number of hits you receive. Of these hits, how many pages look relevant to your topic? Now click on several of the pages that look relevant. Examine these pages carefully. Who wrote the page? Is the material credible? Are the statistics and sources cited? Do you trust this source? Why? Create a list of criteria by which you can judge Web pages as credible or not.

Presentations and Teamwork. Working with one other member of your team, select one of the organizational patterns described in this chapter and prepare a presentation on a scientific or technical topic that interests both of you. Give the presentation for your team and ask them to critique your organizational pattern, considering such factors as the appropriateness of the pattern for this topic, the effectiveness of your use of the pattern, the appropriateness of specific examples you used to support each main point, and other points about which you want feedback.

Presentations and International Communication. Certain cultures have preferred patterns for organizing their presentations. In the United States, for example, it is common to begin with the bottom line first (deductive), stating your main points before beginning the presentation, whereas in other cultures, a more narrative or inductive approach, stating the specific elements and leading the audience toward a conclusion, is preferred. Through library research and interviews with international students and professionals, learn about these differences and document how you might adapt to a specific audience.

Presentations and Your Profession. Interview a professional in your field and ask about the most common types of presentations he or she gives. Ask specifically about how he or she locates and researches information and how he or she chooses the organizational pattern for the body of the talk.

REFERENCES

Koch, A. (1998). *Speaking with a purpose.* Boston: Allyn & Bacon.
Lawson, K. (1999). *Involving your audience: Making it active.* Boston: Allyn & Bacon.

PRESENTING . . .

Daphne Walmer

Daphne Walmer manages the 35-person technical communication department at Medtronic, the world's leading medical technology company specializing in implantable and interventional therapies. Here are her thoughts about Part Two, Audience, Purpose, Beginnings, Endings.

The technical writers at Medtronic rarely give formal presentations. However, I think of a presentation as oral communication done after preparation, often supplemented with visuals or handouts, the purpose of which is to inform or persuade. During project meetings, writers often provide oral status reports or explain suggestions or approaches. They educate their project teams (made up of engineers, project managers, marketing people, and regulatory people) about capabilities, processes, or trends. Their rare formal presentations might be to update the writing teams about the highlights of a seminar or customer visit, or a change, new process, or special project. As a manager, I often do presentations: to propose budgets, to explain my analysis of a situation and propose a strategy, or to request approval for a special project.

In some ways the formal presentations are the scariest, but I usually have more time to prepare for them. Just as for any type of writing, for presentations I analyze audience, purpose, and topic. While preparing, I ask representative audience members about their expectations, questions, and concerns. In fact, that is probably the most important part of preparation. For persuasive presentations, it is also important to make sure I have supporters in the room; some people even recommend delaying until you know that at least 51% of the audience members support your idea or position.

In any case, it's important to manage the audience's expectations, especially as I begin. This is easier if I have explored their expectations ahead of time. I introduce myself and briefly explain my position and function. I mention how long I will talk. Also, my introductions include what I intend to cover or what we need to accomplish. I pay attention to their reactions while I'm talking to help determine whether I'm holding their attention. If not, I may need to ask a question, adjust my pace, skip over some material, or explain something more clearly.

Despite good planning, I have in my career occasionally run into impatient audience members who jump to the end, people who ask tangential or picky questions, conversationalists, sleepers, and even hecklers. When handling a difficult audience, I find it best to listen carefully and to be polite and calm no matter what happens. It helps to think about what good teachers do in disruptive situations. Sometimes I adjust my presentation. If necessary, I promise to cover a point soon, or I ask to hold questions until the end, or to discuss it

(continued)

PRESENTING. . . Continued

individually afterward if that makes sense. Of course, I then must make sure that I in fact answer those questions.

To plan the ending, I write down exactly what I want my audience to know or do, although I don't always include it on a slide. I think about what I might leave out if I'm running short on time and need to cut to the end. I want to make sure I get a chance to ask for what I want. Also, I leave time for questions and discussion.

Throughout, I try to remember to breathe deeply, channel my nervousness into enthusiasm for the topic, engage people while I'm talking—and have fun. After all, I almost always know the material better than the audience. Usually those techniques work.

PART THREE

Types of Technical Presentations

You are now well equipped with a basic tool kit for creating and delivering effective presentations. Part Three gives you the opportunity to pull all of these pieces together—ethos, memory, delivery, audience, purpose, introductions, conclusions, presentation body, and research—and create some basic types of presentations. In this section, we'll cover four general categories of technical presentations. As noted in Chapter 1, these four categories may not exactly match the types of presentations you'll give on the job. But these types are general enough that once you've learned them, you can easily learn other types of presentations, too. Also, no type of presentation is mutually exclusive—an informative presentation is often partially persuasive, and a presentation designed to teach audiences how to do something is often informative as well.

Because almost any type of presentation can be given individually as well as in a group, each of the presentations described here is followed by an exercise on presenting in a group. Also, most presentation types include the use of effective visual communication (slides, overheads, computer displays). Although this topic will be covered in-depth in Part Five, the presentation types presented here in Part Three will touch on some basic forms of visual communication as well.

CHAPTER

9 Presentations That Inform

CHAPTER OVERVIEW

In this chapter, you will learn about presentations that inform. Informative presentations cover a range of possibilities, from conference presentations to classroom talks to design or documentation reviews. This chapter covers the following topics:

- What Are Informative Presentations?
- Types of Informative Presentations in Technical Communication
- Tips for Creating Effective Informative Presentations
- Preparing Your First Informative Presentation

What Are Informative Presentations?

According to one recent survey, the type of presentation given most frequently by scientific and technical professionals are presentations to instruct, or train, or inform (Hager & Scheiber, 1997, pp. 5–6). As the name suggests, informative presentations are presentations designed to provide the audience with information and ideas about a topic. Informative presentations can include a broad range of formats and purposes, such as conference presentations, information or product updates, design reviews, procedural information, lectures, and more. Informative presentations can address a variety of topics, too—they can present information about objects, processes, events, or concepts (Lucas, 1998, pp. 343–351). For each situation, the informative presentation will differ slightly, depending on the audience, the accepted standards for a particular presentation format or organization, the topic, and the specific purpose. But in general, informative presentations are, at their core, designed to provide useful information in a format that makes this information accessible and relevant to a given audience.

One common mistake is to think of informative presentations as simply the transfer of information from the presenter's brain into the brains of the audience. But there is never such a thing as pure information. Each presenter brings a unique perspective to a topic. The way in which a presentation is organized, the information that is selected, and the information that is left out all reflect a point of view on the part of the presenter. In other words, all presentations are partly persuasive at their core. Even the most informative presentation is persuasive in that the presenter hopes to persuade the audience to listen and accept this information. And on most scientific and technical topics, presenters have points of view, and these opinions show up throughout the presentation. Figure 6.1 presented a simpler version of Figure 9.1 to illustrate that informative and persuasive presentations are not completely distinct, but rather are part of a range. Here, you can see that there are many places along this range where presentations are more informative than they are persuasive, and vice versa.

In years past, technical communication was thought of as purely informational—that is, the object of good technical communication was for the communicator (presenter or writer) to keep her or his perspective out of things and simply get the information across. More recently, researchers in technical communication have come to realize that, as with all language, technical communication is rhetorical: It is motivated communication, designed to move people to action and always reflecting the knowledge base, viewpoint, and values of the speaker or writer. Rather than struggle to keep your point of view out of the presentation, you should recognize that there is no such thing as a purely informative mode. What you need to learn during your audience and purpose analysises is where along the continuum

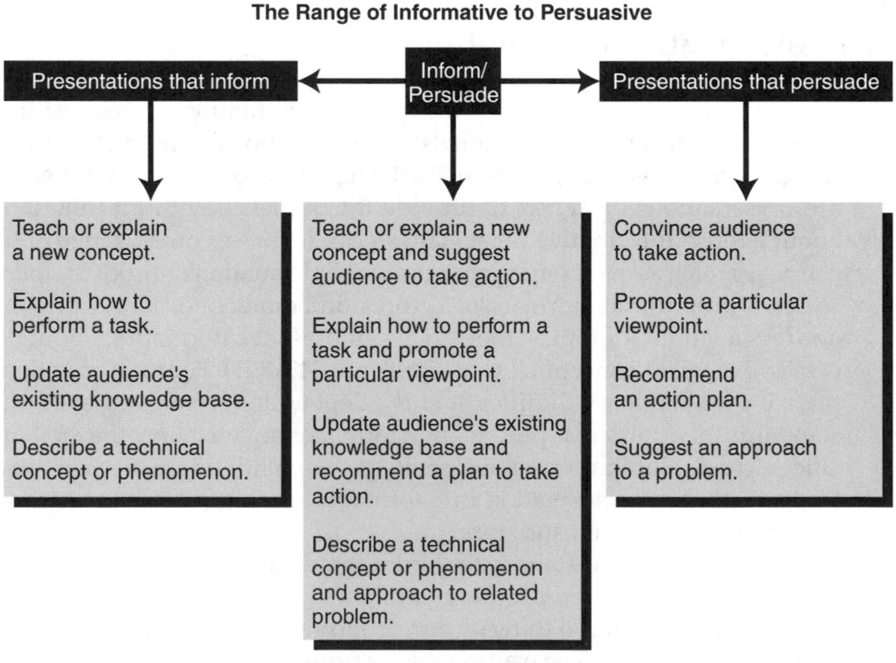

The Range of Informative to Persuasive
Presentations that inform
Inform/ Persuade
Presentations that persuade
Teach or explain a new concept.
Explain how to perform a task.
Update audience's existing knowledge base.
Describe a technical concept or phenomenon.
Teach or explain a new concept and suggest audience to take action.
Explain how to perform a task and promote a particular viewpoint.
Update audience's existing knowledge base and recommend a plan to take action.
Describe a technical concept or phenomenon and approach to related problem.
Convince audience to take action.
Promote a particular viewpoint.
Recommend an action plan.
Suggest an approach to a problem.

FIGURE 9.1 The Range of Informative to Persuasive.

your presentation should fall. Is your aim primarily informative or primarily persuasive? Is it appropriate for you to inform but also advocate your viewpoint? In this chapter, you'll learn about informative presentations. Note, however, that a presenter has a perspective on any topic; this chapter also describes ways that you can integrate your perspective appropriate to the specific presentation setting.

Types of Informative Presentations in Technical Communication

Many types of presentations in technical communication could fall under the category of informative. The following sections describe some of these types. You'll probably encounter other types of informative-style presentations throughout your career that are unique to your company, profession, or geographic location.

Conference Presentation

A professional society exists for almost every professional field—engineering, nursing, technical communication, to name a few. Engineers often belong to the Institute of Electrical and Electronics Engineers (IEEE); nurses may belong to the American Nurses Association (ANA); technical communicators to the Society for Technical Communication (STC). These organizations often hold regional, national, and international conferences, and professionals submit papers and present their ideas as part of the conference. Conference presentations are structured in a variety of formats: panels, consisting of three to four presenters, or roundtables, with five or more presenters, are two of the most common formats. Conference presentations are usually intended to be informational; professionals come together to share information and get new ideas about what's going on in their field. Each conference will have its own set of standards regarding presentation length (anywhere from fifteen to twenty minutes for a standard presentation and usually ten to twelve minutes for a roundtable), format, use of technology, and so on.

Information or Product Update

Another type of informative presentation is one designed to provide an audience with updated information about a service or product. This information may be designed for external use, such as updates for customers, or for internal use, such as updates and new information for technical staff or a sales force. On the inform-persuade scale, information or product updates would usually fall close to the inform end, in that the purpose of these presentations is to provide new information audiences need to use a product or service. For example, if you are a technical communicator or trainer with a software company, you may be required to meet with a group of customers to introduce them to your software's new features. If you are an engineer, you may be asked to explain the new version of an internal product specification to other technical specialists within your organization. Updates require you to focus on what the audience already knows about the product or service and what new information they need to know.

Customer Information Session

Similar to an information or product update but more general in terms of content, customer information sessions are designed to present customers with information about any aspect of a product, service, procedure, or organization/company. Technical communicators often have a broad understanding of an organization's mission and its products or services and are often called on to speak with customers on a variety of issues. Sometimes, customers are flown in; other times, these sessions may take place over interactive television or video conferencing. Like information or product updates, customer information sessions must be designed with a focus on audience: Are they managers? Engineers? Scientists? Technical writers? Or a mix of many types of professionals? Knowing your audience and purpose will help you focus on what kind of information is relevant for this presentation.

Design or Documentation Review

Another typically informative presentation is the design or documentation review. In these presentations, the creator of the product or documentation brings a beta version, first draft, or specification to present to others on the team. These presentations are somewhat persuasive, in that the presenter hopes the audience will accept, with minimal changes, the plan that is being presented. But reviews are primarily informational, in that they are designed to update other team or department members about the status of a project and the next phases to be accomplished. Often, the purpose of these reviews is also to solicit input from others who may have a stake in the final result but are not part of the day-to-day operations related to this project. For technical writers, for example, a documentation review is the time when writers present drafts and solicit input before the manual is produced and sent to customers. These presentations need to be well organized; often, the draft or design spec is handed out in advance, and the presentation is used to highlight the main discussion points and features.

Classroom Presentation

Either as a student, a teacher, or an invited guest speaker, you will probably give at least one classroom presentation during your professional career. The classroom is a site of learning; whether it's student to student, instructor to student, or student to instructor, the idea is that information should be presented in a way that is useful, interesting, and can be learned by those involved. Audience analysis is crucial here. How much do students know about your topic? How can you relate your topic to their needs and interests? What subjects are students majoring in, and how can you connect your topic to their backgrounds? Although in some cultures classroom presentations are given strictly in lecture mode, U.S. classrooms often are less formal and more interactive. Also, many of today's classrooms are well equipped with presentation technology, such as computers, projection devices, and slide projectors and screens.

Brown-Bag Lunches

Many organizations sponsor brown-bag lunch presentations. Employees bring their lunches and sit in a classroom or conference room while an invited speaker, often from within the company, gives a brief presentation. Topics may include employee policy updates, reports about a business trip recently taken by a colleague, or an update on technology items in the news that might affect the company. Invited speakers often give brown-bag presentations on current health care, technology, or science topics. Brown-bag presentations are usually less formal than something like a conference presentation, and they must not run over time, because employees are on their lunch hour and usually must return to work immediately following the presentation. The informality of a brown-bag presentation is often a good reason to consider using some appropriate humor, such as cartoons about workplace issues (like Scott Adams's *Dilbert* cartoons) or technology issues (like the numerous Internet cartoons that appear in many newspapers today).

Community Information Session

Technical communicators, engineers, scientists, and other science and technology experts are often asked to give presentations at community events, such as a local public library speaker's session or a junior high or high school career day. These events provide an excellent opportunity to bring the complex information of science and technology into the community.

Tips for Creating Effective Informative Presentations

Begin with a Strong Introduction

Following the guidelines presented in Chapter 7, your informative presentation should begin with a well-organized and inviting introduction. Connect your topic with something the audience knows and cares about. Make your introduction exciting and compelling; give your audience a reason to continue listening. If you've done a thorough audience and purpose analysis, you'll have a good understanding of what your audience is interested in. Make your introduction catch their attention (more on introductions in technical presentations in Chapter 13).

FIGURE 9.2 The Old-New Rule.
Source: Photography courtesy of L.L. Bean.

Follow the Old-New Rule

People learn best when you connect new information, with which they are unfamiliar, with old information that is readily understood by the audience. Think about how you might explain a computer to a small child. You'd think of things the child already understood and was familiar with, and you'd connect your description of the computer to these familiar ideas. For example, you might say "A computer is like your brain—it stores and organizes ideas and information for you." In Chapter 15, you'll learn more about using analogies and metaphors. But for now, keep the old-new rule in mind. Especially for informative presentations, in which you are introducing complex scientific or technical ideas, using something the audience already knows as a bridge to what they don't knows is a useful technique.

A flyer from L.L. Bean, shown in Figure 9.2, uses the old-new rule to introduce people to the idea of connecting to their Web page. By connecting the new concept of logging onto the Internet with the very familiar (old) idea of a log, this flyer invites people to try something technical and possibly unfamiliar. The visual is also fun to look at, and the pun (log on versus log, as in tree) makes the topic slightly humorous and less intimidating than it might otherwise be.

Be Careful about Using Technical Jargon

Almost every scientific and technical field has its own set of specialized terms. For those who know these terms, it's a useful kind of shorthand and makes communication efficient. But for others, technical jargon can be confusing and frustrating. The computer industry, for example, is notorious for using terms that sound like alphabet soup to those outside the field—RAM, ROM, SCSI, WYSIWYG, and so on. When you must use technical terms and jargon, be sure to define them clearly. Post an easy-to-read list of terms and definitions on a flip chart or overhead. Redefine the terms as you use them.

For example, in an early part of your presentation on computers to novice computer users, explain that ROM stands for Read Only Memory and that, therefore, a computer can read a CD-ROM but cannot copy files onto it. When you refer to ROM again later in your presentation, point to it on the list of definitions and remind your audience of the definition. Such repetition may seem boring to you (remember, you're an expert on the subject), but your audience will appreciate your ability to help them learn.

State Your Viewpoint Up Front

As noted earlier in this chapter, no informative presentation is completely without a point of view. In some cases, it's useful to explain your position on the topic at the very outset of the presentation, rather than to try creating an impossibly neutral impression. For example, you may be giving a presentation on the topic of global warming, which you feel is most certainly caused by human pollution and not simply by changing weather patterns. But for this presentation, you've been asked to give an informative talk on the various scientific viewpoints. You could include a short statement at the outset to convey both your viewpoint and your intent to provide as much information as possible; for example, you might say "Although many scientists and observers, myself included, believe that human pollution is the primary cause of global warming, in my presentation today I will explore both this and other points of view on the subject."

Explain Your Topic Clearly

One characteristic common to all good technical communicators, regardless of their specialty (technical writer, Web designer, trainer, scientist and part-time communicator), is their ability to make complex information not only interesting but also clear. Clarity involves many features and is always based on solid audience analysis so that your topic avoids jargon, appeals to common interests, and connects with ideas the audience needs to know. Pay attention to every piece of communication you encounter, both spoken and written, and notice which ones seem especially clear. Make notes about how and why the writer or presenter achieved this clarity. Evaluate your own level of clarity during a presentation by noticing if your audience understands you or if you are using jargon or technical language that is too complex.

Provide Adequate Background Material

For any given topic, especially complex technical ones, it's critical that you find the proper balance between too much background material, which will bore your audience, and not enough, which will leave them in the dark when you get into the details of your talk. For example, if you were giving a presentation about new research on brain chemistry and attention-deficit hyperactivity disorder, you would need to know if the audience knew anything at all about the topic. The more they understood, the less time you would need to set aside to describe the condition and the most recent research. Obviously, an audience of child psychologists at a medical conference would know more than an audience of community members at a library presentation. Your job during the audience analysis is to determine how much background is appropriate for this given presentation.

Follow an Appropriate Organizational Pattern

Review what you learned in Chapter 8 and be sure to organize your material in a pattern that is appropriate for your particular informative presentation. Informative presentations in technical communication are usually effective if they are organized in a deductive pattern with a chronological, spatial, or categorical structure. Outline your material carefully.

Be Sure Your Audience Is with You

As you go along, you should pay careful attention to your audience. Do they look confused? Bored? Does it seem that they might not understand part of your presentation? If you sense anything unusual from your audience, it's perfectly acceptable to ask them; for example, you might say "Before I go on, does anyone have any questions?" or "I get the sense that I might have covered too much just now. Is there anything I can clarify?" By inviting your audience to provide feedback, you show them your goodwill and interest in their learning experience. You also make your job easier, because you can keep their interest if you fill in the gaps in places that have confused them. Remember that oral presentations are two-way streets: Information flows from you to the audience, but the audience members are also active participants in the process. Invite their input when appropriate.

Be Excited and Enthusiastic

Remember, your enthusiasm for the topic will rub off on your audience. So be upbeat and excited (don't go overboard, however) and always be sincere, because audiences can sense when a presenter does not mean what he or she is saying. If you've selected a topic that is interesting to you, your interest level will become part of the audience's experience. Even if you are assigned a topic that's not your favorite, which can happen regularly at work, find a way to make the concepts fresh and exciting. Ask others in the organization for their input. Hunt around on the Web. Find exciting visuals to make things interesting. Informative presentations are an excellent opportunity for you to bring a new, fresh perspective to what might otherwise be a dry and unappealing technical topic.

Be Professional

The word "professional" has many meanings in many settings. Your attire, for example, is often a marker of your professionalism. In some companies today, professional attire is still appropriate for presentations, but in many firms, especially high technology ones, casual clothing is becoming more standard. If you are new to the organization and unsure about this, look around and observe others to see what the standards are. For class, ask your instructor what you should wear on the day of a presentation. Along with attire, there are several other ways to maintain a professional ethos while presenting. One way is to speak in a professional voice. What does this mean? Generally, when giving a presentation, you want to find a style that is different from everyday street talk that you use with friends but is still natural sounding for you. (Review Chapter 3, where you learned about ethos and delivery.) Also, your respect and concern for the audience reflects your professionalism, as does your handling of any conflicts that may arise during the discussion section of your presentation. Identify what you feel is your own professional style and maintain it the entire time you are speaking.

Use Effective Visual Communication

A good informative presentation usually includes the use of visual aids, such as slides, overheads, or computer projections. As noted in Part Five, these visual aids are of no help if your presentation is not well organized, well researched, in line with the needs of your audience, and suited for the specific purpose. For the most basic of presentations, however, you can use some simple visual aids to get you started. The simplest of all is the overhead projection transparency. Overhead projectors are in almost any workplace or classroom, they are easy to use, and they don't crash or suffer from other computer problems. Initially, use some simple overheads. These might include an introductory overhead showing your name and key points, an overhead for each key point, and a conclusion. In Part Five, you'll learn more advanced techniques and ways of thinking about the topic of visual communication.

Answer Questions If There Is Time

Unlike writing, oral presentations provide the opportunity for give-and-take with your audience. If it is appropriate to the format and if there is time, you will often be expected to answer audience questions. Sometimes question-and-answer (Q&A) sessions happen during the presentation itself, especially if the format is rather informal, such as a give-and-take roundtable structure. Other times, questions and discussion come at the end of the presentation. If you have a choice, you might want to use the questions-at-the-end format, because, especially if you are new at giving presentations, taking audience comments and questions during the body of your presentation can distract you. Either way, when you interact with the

CHECKLIST

Answering Audience Questions

Oral presentations, unlike written papers, allow you to interact in real time with a live audience. You need to give an excellent presentation and also be skilled at taking audience questions. Consider the following guidelines:

- Stay in form.
- Show respect for your audience.
- Don't let one or two people dominate the discussion.
- Provide pointers to additional information.
- Admit when you don't know something.
- Answer people directly.
- Restate the question if you think the audience didn't hear it.

---

audience, stay professional. Sometimes, presenters are so glad to be at the end of their talk that they will become sloppy and rather silly during the Q&A session. Stay in form and show respect for your audience. Always let an audience member get his or her entire thought out; try not to interrupt. If the comment runs counter to what you think, recognize the validity of the audience member's idea first. Transitions like "however," "on the other hand," and "but" are useful here: "I see what you mean, and I have thought of that, too. *However,* my research indicates. . . ." If an audience member seems to dominate the discussion, be polite but firm: "Thanks for your interest! Let's hear from the woman on the other side of the room who has been waiting patiently to join in." (As you learned in Chapter 5, sometimes, an audience member will ask questions to impress someone else in the audience or to show off in front of the group) (Lawson, 1999, p. 147). Provide pointers to additional information if appropriate, and, if you don't know the answer to a question, don't bluff: Instead, indicate your appreciation that the point was raised and offer to follow up later via phone or email. Also, if you think that the entire audience didn't hear the question, you can restate it. But don't do this for each and every question; it will sound rehearsed and will bore the audience.

End with a Strong Conclusion

As discussed in Chapter 7, conclude your informative presentation by making a clear transition from the body of the presentation, by restating the main informative points that you've covered, and by providing resources so your audience can obtain further information; do not introduce new material. Also, remember that you should not suddenly interject your opinion or call for action. Doing so would be more appropriate for persuasive and action presentations, discussed in the next chapters.

Preparing Your First Informative Presentation

Select a type of informative technical presentation (conference presentation, product update, design review, etc.) that is appropriate for your career or field of study. Using the techniques you learned in previous chapters, perform a brief audience and purpose analysis. Then, outline your presentation.

The following are some specifics for one possible informative presentation. You may add or modify these specifics as needed for the assignment. Use the audience and purpose worksheets from Chapters 5 and 6.

Audience. Your audience for this presentation is members of the local chapter of a professional society of which you are a member. If you are a technical communicator, this would be the local chapter of the Society for Technical Communication (STC).

Purpose. Your purpose is to inform the membership about an important and interesting topic in your field. In the field of scientific and technical communication, such topics might include:

- computer graphics
- hypertext
- online documentation
- visual communication
- technical editing
- international communication
- electronic commerce
- privacy and the Internet

Research. Find an interesting topic and research it by reading through back issues of the journal(s) and trade magazines for your field. (In technical communication, this would be the STC journal *Technical Communication.*) Also, use the library and the Web. To give your presentation a sense of balance, see if you can locate at least three sources for this presentation.

Create a careful outline of your presentation, paying special attention to the introduction and conclusion. Be sure the body is well organized. Use the outlining skills you are familiar with from basic public speaking or writing classes. Share your outline with a team of two or three other students who are also doing this assignment and provide each other with feedback.

Time. You may present your topic for 10 to 12 minutes. Practice using a timer, and be sure that you do not exceed the allotted time. If necessary, trim back or add more material.

Visuals. Although this book has not yet covered the use of visuals, at the option of your instructor, you may use the overhead projector for this presentation. Remember that you must be organized and your presentation well researched before you can use visual aids effectively. Thus, your overheads should only contain text and no graphics for this first presentation. Make sure your text is large enough to read in the back of the room (14 point or larger works well).

In Summary: Informative Presentations

Informative presentations are common in technical communication and can span a range of types, audiences, and purposes. Yet the primary goal of an informative presentation is to inform the audience about a particular topic. Informative presentations require you to have a clear understanding of the audience and purpose.

QUESTIONS / EXERCISES / ASSIGNMENTS

Select a topic about which you would feel comfortable giving an informative presentation. Without any audience/purpose analysis or research, create an outline for an informative presentation. Now plan to prepare this presentation for your class or another real audience. After an audience/purpose analysis and some research, notice in what ways your presentation's structure and content changed.

Presentations and Cyberspace. Locate the Website for a professional organization in your field (check with a professor or graduate student in your department if you have difficulty locating the site) and follow links to articles from journals or proceedings from recent conferences. Identify an informative article or speech and analyze it against the tips for informative presentations that you studied in this chapter. If you were coaching the author or presenter, what elements of the article or presentation would you identify as effective, and why? As ineffective, and why? Identify specific changes the author or speaker should make to increase the effectiveness of the article or speech.

Presentations and Teamwork. Many informative presentations are given collaboratively; that is, they are given by a team of people. If you have a job or an internship, you have probably participated in or listened to an informative presentation given by a team; as a student, you probably have worked on a team project for class. As an exercise in group-style informative presentations, form a team of two to three people from your class. Identify and discuss informative topics that might be of interest to all of you, and choose one. Design a group presentation on that topic, designating specific parts of the presentation for specific people on the team. Remember that you still must perform an audience and purpose analysis, and you must also be well organized and design your presentation with care. As you work on your group presentation, keep track of how the group interacts. Do you feel more comfortable designating one person as leader, or do you prefer to work by consensus? How will you go about dividing up the workload and the presentation itself? What items do you agree should go into the informative presentation, and what items is there disagreement on? Group presentations, although often more difficult to design, can be far more interesting than an individual presentation, because you have a combination of the thoughts and ideas of many people.

Presentations and International Communication. After giving the informative presentation described at the end of this chapter, identify a different country in which you might make an informative presentation on the same or a similar topic. Conduct research to define the audience to whom you would be speaking (e.g., professional organization, student group at a university, group of citizens) and to learn about your topic within the context of that culture. Outline the presentation as you would give it in the other country. A word of caution: Avoid the trap of comparing that country to the United States. For example, if your topic is the use of color in designing corporate offices, avoid discussing color selection according to how it differs from U.S. trends; instead, discuss the topic from the perspective of the country in which you would give the presentation. After completing your outline, list the changes you made to the content and structure and explain why you made those changes. Present this information to your class.

Presentations and Your Profession. Locate a local or national chapter of an organization related to your profession, and find a listing of the presentation topics from this group's last meeting. Of these topics, which would be easy for you to present and which would be difficult? Why?

REFERENCES

Hager, P. J., & Scheiber, H. J. (1997). *Designing and delivering scientific, technical, and managerial presentations.* New York: Wiley.

Lawson, K. (1999). *Involving your audience: Making it active.* Boston: Allyn & Bacon.

Lucas, S. E. (1998). *The art of public speaking.* Boston: McGraw-Hill.

CHAPTER

10 Presentations That Persuade and Convince

CHAPTER OVERVIEW

This chapter examines presentations designed to persuade or convince an audience. Persuasive presentations take many forms, from overtly persuasive to presentations that present various sides of an issue. This chapter covers the following topics:

- What Are Persuasive Presentations?
- Types of Persuasive Presentations in Technical Communication
- Tips for Creating Effective Persuasive Presentations
- Preparing Your First Persuasive Presentation

What Are Persuasive Presentations?

As noted in the previous chapter, no clear line separates informative presentations from presentations designed to persuade or convince an audience. Instead, technical presentations span a range from those designed to be primarily informative to those designed to be primarily persuasive. This chapter will use the term "persuasive"; recognize, however, that this category can easily shift depending on the audience and purpose. Yet even though the category is somewhat fluid, persuasive presentations do have a primary purpose that distinguishes them from others—they are intended to convince or persuade an audience to accept a particular point of view or concept. Informative presentations sometimes do this as well—by presenting a given set of ideas, informative presentations tacitly ask an audience to accept the presenter's picture about the topic. But persuasive presentations usually involve presenting a particular point of view *in contrast to other possible conclusions* about a subject. For example, in the previous chapter, you read about an informative presentation on the topic of global warming, designed to review all current theories on the subject. If this topic were addressed in a persuasive presentation, it would involve more than just an explanation of the differing theories of why the earth's temperature continues to increase. It would also require the presenter to argue for a specific theory and explain why this theory is more valid than any other.

Because persuasive presentations are usually structured as arguments, taking one side over several others, they can be somewhat more difficult to present. In today's scientific culture, arguments based on emotional appeals are considered less credible. People in Western cultures are most comfortable with what appear to be neutral presentations of fact (despite all facts representing a point of view, people still trust the informational mode more). Yet persuasive presentations most often use facts *combined with* appeals to emotion to make their case.

There are some good reasons why people feel uncomfortable with the emotional appeals used in persuasive presentations. When arguments are unbalanced in favor of only emotional reasoning, people may make uninformed decisions. History has far too many examples of leaders who were able to stir the emotions of their people and lead them to do things they might not have done if they had weighed all sides of the issue. But emotional reasoning in and of itself is no more or less dangerous than the faulty use of statistics, for example, or a logical fallacy, which may appear to be rational and logical but is actually unclear.

Effective persuasive presentations attempt to bring a balance between the logical and emotional appeals and always seek the ethical combination of arguments to make their point. One excellent example of such an approach are the advertisements for the group Mothers Against Drunk Driving (MADD). MADD combines facts, such as the number of automobile deaths per year from drunk driving, with emotional appeals, including photos or short video clips of children who have died in such accidents. The former material (statistics about death rates) appeals to people's logical side; the latter (photos of children) to the emotional side. Given the horrible outcome of drunk driving accidents, it would be hard to argue that the emotional appeals used here are unfair. They are part of the problem, and they support the argument effectively and ethically.

In Chapter 3, you read about the emotional appeals of logos, ethos, and pathos. The Checklist in this chapter summarizes these for you.

Types of Persuasive Presentations in Technical Communication

There are many types of persuasive presentations in technical communication. The following sections describe some types that you may encounter. As with all

CHECKLIST

The Three Appeals

Remember that the three rhetorical appeals work together to help you create a clear argument.

- Logos: the logical part of an argument
- Ethos: the part of an argument involving the credibility and character of the speaker
- Pathos: appeals made to the emotions of the audience

presentations, the audience, purpose, and other factors unique to your company, profession, or geographic location ultimately dictate formats, time length, and other features.

Design or Documentation Review

Although typically informative as noted in Chapter 9, design or documentation reviews can sometimes be overtly persuasive, depending on the situation. As described in the previous chapter, in these presentations the creator of the design or documentation brings a beta version, first draft, or specification to present to others on the team. Sometimes, these presentations need to be persuasive, because the engineers, technical writers, managers, and other audience members either are not in favor of the presenter's plan or do not yet have an opinion about it. In these cases, the presenter wants to convince the audience about the choice of one plan or approach over another. A technical writer, for example, might use a documentation review not only to present drafts of the documentation and solicit input but also to convince other writers to accept a new format or new online version of the material.

Technical Marketing or Sales Meetings

Most scientific or technical companies have marketing and sales departments. Unlike more generic salespeople, technical marketers must know the technical details of their company's products and services; they also must know what the customer wants and needs, and they must understand how to bring these two areas together. When technical marketers or salespeople meet with customers, they are often required to give persuasive presentations, designed to convince customers that their product or service, or a new release or new product, is right for that customer's needs. Technical marketing presentations are most successful if the presenter has a good understanding of the customer's specific situation and can provide enough technical details to convince that customer to make a decision. In these cases, presenters also must know enough about competitive products or services so they can contrast their materials with others that might be available.

Community Events

Often, everyday citizens become involved in decisions about scientific or technical projects that will affect the entire community. For example, if your community learns that a waste processing company is thinking of building an incinerator in your town, you and other citizens may decide, after researching the issues, that you are not in favor of this project. You have the opportunity to attend a public forum and give a presentation, and you decide to try to persuade the town board not to allow this incinerator to be built. Audience analysis is critical here: You must understand how the opposing side feels about the issue and why they believe as they do. Although you and your side may think of the incinerator purely in terms of environmental impact, others in the community may be interested in the tax revenue or new jobs the project could bring with it. The more you know about your audience and the views they hold, the more closely you can craft your argument to fit the situation.

Conference Presentation

Although conference presentations are often designed to inform, as discussed in the previous chapter, they can also be persuasive. When a scientist or engineer attends an international conference and presents a new theory, for example, she or he not only is providing information about the theory but also attempting to convince peers that this theory is valid and that the experiment or research data will hold up under scrutiny. Sometimes, conference presentations consist of a panel of presenters, each offering his or her perspective on an issue or problem, and each presenting a different viewpoint. Each discipline or field of study will have its own standards, and you should find out in advance about how persuasive the presentation should be.

Proposal Presentation

Many times, persuasive presentations are intended not only to convince an audience about a particular point of view but also to encourage them to take a particular action in order to solve the problem. These presentations are sometimes given after the audience has read a written proposal for the particular solution. This form of persuasive presentation, where a specific solution is proposed, is discussed in detail in the next chapter.

Tips for Creating Effective Persuasive Presentations

Begin with a Strong Introduction

Following the guidelines presented in Chapter 7, your persuasive presentation should begin with a well-organized and compelling introduction. Connect your topic with something the audience knows and cares about. Consider starting with a story, personal anecdote, or recent media item that will connect the controversy to something the audience can focus on. If you've done a thorough audience and purpose analysis, you'll have a good understanding of your audience's viewpoint on the subject. If most of your audience is somewhat in favor of your perspective, you'll have an easier time creating an introduction that connects with them. If they are not in favor, you'll need to find some kind of common ground to start your presentation. This chapter's Scenario offers some guidelines for seeking common ground with your audience.

SCENARIO

Finding Common Ground in Your Persuasive Presentation Introduction

You are trying to persuade your city council not to allow construction on a given piece of land. You know the council is in favor of building, but you feel that the environmental damage will outweigh any financial gains. How can you begin your presentation in a way that will invite your audience to see your perspective? After an audience analysis, conducted by interviewing council members and speaking to others in the community, you realize that everyone, the council and those who favor environmentalism, shares a love of the community and its many parks and open lands. You also know that those in favor of the building project are interested in bringing more revenue into town, something that most would find favorable as well. You use this common theme to introduce your presentation: "Everyone in our town would agree that our parks and well-maintained open lands are a highlight of the community. In my presentation today, I'll suggest a way we can keep this important part of our town alive while also creating a favorable environment for new business."

Make sure your introduction is very clear about what position you'll take and how and why you'll convince your audience. For example, if you are giving a presentation on the dangers of genetic engineering in certain plants, you would want to make clear in your introduction that (1) you are going to attempt to convince your audience that you are against genetic engineering in certain cases, and (2) that you will make your case by pointing to the following reasons (then state these reasons quickly before moving into the body of the presentation).

In Chapter 8, you learned about deductive and inductive organizational structures. Deductive organization means that you state your bottom line first, then provide evidence to back up your claim. Inductive organization means that you state the individual facts first, building up to your argument on a point-by-point basis. You also learned that in technical communication, the deductive approach is usually best, because audiences learn better if they know the bottom line. Yet if audiences are predisposed to disagree with you, an inductive approach might be more appropriate. This is often the case with persuasive presentations, particularly where your audience holds the opposite point of view. In these situations, you should use a modified inductive approach. Your introduction should still state the main point but should do so in a general, low-key fashion, making clear that you see both sides of the issue. The body of your presentation should vigorously prove your argument, and your conclusion should make your position very clear.

For example, in the Scenario feature, the presenter held the position that the city council should *not* build on a particular piece of land. Yet the audience, the city council, is already leaning toward building on the land. The presenter began her presentation this way:

> Good afternoon, and thank you for allowing me time to speak to you today. As you know, the piece of land located at Main and 45th Streets is a valuable resource to our community. Everyone in our town would agree that our parks and well-maintained open lands are a highlight of the community. Some see this resource as continued public park space, whereas others see the commercial value this land could bring to our community. In my presentation today, I'll suggest a way we can keep this important part of our town alive while also creating a favorable environment for new business.

In this introduction, the presenter is polite and appreciative. She establishes common ground ("Everyone in our town would agree") and recognizes both sides of the debate ("Some see this resource as continued public park space, whereas others see the commercial value this land could bring to our community.") She then previews the body of the presentation ("In my presentation today, I'll suggest a way we can keep this important part of our town alive while also creating a favorable environment for new business") but does so without giving away too much of the evidence behind her argument. Again, remember that this method is only appropriate when audiences tend to heartily disagree with you right from the start.

Be Open to Understanding All Sides of the Issue

Even though you'll probably have a clearly developed opinion about the best approach to an issue, you should maintain an open mind about all sides of the discussion. One advantage of oral presentations over written communication is that when you are interacting with people, live and in real time, you have a chance to get immediate feedback and learn from one another. Especially during the question-and-answer session, be prepared to learn something that might modify or change your perspective on the topic. Being open to new ideas is a powerful part of democratic communication; on issues of science and technology, where topics can be complex and based on many kinds of evidence, you should remain open to new viewpoints. Your ethos as a fair and interested presenter will show through, too, and will make the audience respect you, even if they disagree with your opinion on the subject.

Provide Appropriate Background Material

As with informative presentations, effective persuasive presentations must reflect a proper balance between too much background material and not enough. Before you can convince your audience, you need to be sure they have a working knowledge of the subject and are familiar with concepts and terms related to the issue. Your audience analysis should guide you in determining the right amount of background information. If your main purpose, however, is to persuade your audience, don't spend too much time on informative background topics, or you will lose the focus of your presentation. Also, be prepared to explain things as you go along if needed.

Follow an Appropriate Organizational Pattern

Review what you learned in Chapter 8, and be sure to organize your material in a pattern that is appropriate for your particular informative presentation. Persuasive presentations in technical communication are usually effective if they are organized in a deductive pattern (though sometimes, if an audience is particularly against your point of view, as noted in Chapter 8, inductive is a better choice) with a problem-solution or causal structure. Outline your material carefully.

Construct Your Argument Carefully

If you've taken a course in technical writing, logic, rhetoric, or public speaking, you may remember some of the ways in which you can construct arguments that are careful, logical, and appropriate for the situation. Persuasive presentations, more than any other type, rely on well-developed arguments that lead the audience to see your point of view.

There are many methods for constructing credible, careful, logical arguments that make sense and appeal to an audience. Most arguments contain at their core a premise; that is, an underlying concept upon which the argument rests. In rhetoric, a premise is the first part of what is called deductive reasoning. Aristotle, and others since his time, have noticed that many arguments are made based on deductive reasoning in the form of what is called a syllogism:

> Natural land areas are good for the community.
>
> My proposal is for a natural land area.
>
> Therefore, my proposal is good.

The first part of this line of reasoning ("Natural land areas are good for the community.") is called the *major premise.* In rhetorical arguments, this premise is often not stated—it is assumed between presenter and audience. Usually, presenters who know their audience choose an argument whose premise coincides with something the audience values and cares about. When the premise of the argument is unstated, the syllogism is called an *enthymeme.*

FYI

Logical Reasoning

You may remember learning about syllogistic reasoning in a math, philosophy, rhetoric, or logic class. If you have learned this material before, now might be a good time to review your notes about this form of argument. If you've never learned about syllogisims before, go to the library and look for some additional information on this topic.

Beware of Faulty Reasoning

Your argument must hold up and not fall into any of several traps known as logical fallacies. One common fallacy, for example, is a syllogism that is, in essence, backwards (Houp et al., 1998, p. 148). Instead of a valid syllogism such as

> All biologists are scientists.
>
> Mary is a biologist.
>
> Therefore, Mary is a scientist.

invalid reasoning would argue that

> All biologists are scientists.
>
> Mary is a scientist.
>
> Therefore, Mary is a biologist.

Although it may seem obvious that Mary is not necessarily a biologist simply because she is a scientist, this sort of faulty reasoning is behind many an argument. Technical communicators must be especially sure that their arguments are structured on sound logic; science and technology topics are often confusing for audiences, and an illogical argument will detract from your ability to make the material understandable to your audience. Other examples of logical fallacies are presented in the FYI feature.

Use Arguments That Make Sense for Your Profession

Most fields have lines of argument that are based on common understandings for that profession. In addition, different companies and organizations have different sets of standards that they value. When speaking to an audience with a common professional or organizational background, you can usually create an argument based on what they value (Lay et al., 1995, p. 145). For example, the engineering profession usually values efficiency, cost effectiveness, and sound design principles. If you were

FYI

Three Examples of Logical Fallacies

Ad hominem. Ad hominem fallacies are arguments that personally attack the opposition. By attacking another person instead of arguing the facts of the case, presenters try to sway an audience's attention away from the actual discussion. In this example, a presenter who said

> The chairman of the city council has been involved in corruption in the past, so how can we trust this proposal before us today?

would be engaging in an ad hominem attack.

One or the other. Often, persuasive presentations are structured so that audiences think there are only two sides to an issue, when in fact, many viewpoints exist. This fallacy, also called either-or, can easily mislead audiences. In the example about land development, the presenter may see the case as *either* the environmental approach *or* the land development one. Perhaps there are other solutions, and these should be researched and presented, too.

Red herring. Also known as a "fallacy of irrelevant thesis" (Engel, 1982, p. 137), this form of fallacy involves connecting two ideas that are not related to each other as a way of providing one's main thesis. For example, a presenter tried making a case using the following statement:

> How can we think about selling this piece of land to a corporate developer at a time when our schools are in need of additional funds?

What does school funding have to do with selling this land? The term "red herring" comes from a technique used to throw search dogs off track; an old piece of herring was used to confuse the dogs' sense of smell. In the same way, red herring fallacies are often attempts to throw the audience off course by introducing an irrelevant issue.

For more on logical fallacies, see Engel, S. M. (1982). *With good reason: An introduction to informal fallacies* (2nd ed.). New York: St. Martin's Press.

presenting an idea to a group of engineers, you would want to emphasize how your idea was the most efficient approach or one that offered the most thoroughly researched design specifications.

Research Carefully and Use Solid, Credible Evidence

As with informative presentations, carefully researched presentations are intended to persuade an audience. Pay special attention to statistical information and to counterarguments (arguments that are against, not in favor of, your position). The material you obtain through research will become the evidence for your argument. Here are several places where you can obtain evidence for your argument.

Interviews with Experts. It is always useful to obtain information from experts whenever possible. If you work for a science or high technology firm or are a student at a university, you have ready access to people who have detailed knowledge about many subjects. Information obtained from expert interviews is always a powerful way to persuade an audience.

Research Reports. For most topics, written reports are available from a variety of credible agencies. In science and engineering, published academic research papers are one way to obtain information. Government reports, such as those produced by the Environmental Protection Agency or other government bodies, are also excellent sources of evidence for your argument.

Topic-Specific Organizations. Groups that focus specifically on your area of interest almost always have information that they can provide. For example, if you were seeking to convince an audience not to smoke, the American Cancer Society would be an excellent source of information to support your claim.

Internal Corporate Documents. Most companies maintain files of important corporate documents, and many larger organizations, especially those with well-developed research and development groups, have their own internal libraries. If your persuasive presentation involves a topic unique to your company, try using corporate documents to back up your argument.

Trends among Similar Companies or Organizations. Many analysts spend time comparing various organizations to study trends among industries. For example, the use of the Internet for sales and commerce in the United States is of great interest to those seeking to invest in high technology stocks; certain industry newsletters can provide you with this information.

Statistics. In most documents and research reports in science and technical fields, you will find much use of statistics. You can use statistical information to support your case. Chapter 16 will describe how statistics can be used in many ways to support divergent viewpoints. We've all heard politicians cite the same numbers to support very different causes! A careful use of statistical information, however, creates credible evidence for your point of view.

The Web. The Web is a powerful research tool. Because almost anyone can publish just about anything on the Web, you must be careful, as noted in Chapter 8, to investigate the source of material you find on the Web. If you find information that is particularly useful for your persuasive presentation, you can often email the author of the Web document and request additional information or an informal email interview. Always balance your use of Web research with other sources.

Blend Logical and Emotional Appeals

The most powerful and persuasive presentations do not rely exclusively on either logical or emotional appeals but instead blend the two. A careful audience analysis will help you decide the appropriate mix of logic and emotion. An audience of engineers might be more moved to your position by a rational, statistics-based argument, whereas a mixed audience will often respond to a blend of the two. Remember that emotional arguments are not inherently bad: Humans are made up of rational and emotional sides, and arguments that fairly appeal to emotional instincts can be extremely effective.

Address Counterarguments

A very important technique in persuasive presentations is to address the counterarguments to your position. Put simply, counterarguments are all of the questions and "Yes, but . . . " statements that people might make once you have made your case. Think of a small child who wants to have a cookie before dinner. The parent might carefully lay out the argument against this cookie: It will spoil your appetite for dinner, you won't have room for dessert, you won't eat your vegetables. The child, usually a master of counterarguments, is prepared: It won't spoil my appetite because I didn't eat lunch and am really hungry; I always have room for dessert; I ate my vegetables last time I had a snack before dinner. If the parent had anticipated these counterarguments in advance and addressed them, the child wouldn't have been able to think of any additional reply.

This simple example should give you the idea about how to address counterarguments. It's a very powerful technique, because, after laying out your position, you beat people to the punch and answer their challenges in advance. The best way to use this technique is to find out in advance what other points of view are held by your audience. Assume you are a technical communicator, and you are preparing a persuasive presentation on why your organization should switch to a new online software tool. When conducting your audience analysis, you discover that many in the company don't want to switch because they think it will take too long to learn the new tool. Others question the expense of the new product. After presenting your argument for why you should use the new tool, you move to the next phase of the presentation.

> Now, many of you might be concerned that it will take too long to learn this new tool. I felt the same way until I did a little research. And what I learned was that, in fact, the tool's main features are almost identical to what we are using now. It took me less than half a day to get up to speed on the new tool. Well, you might say, it's too expensive. That, also, is not a real concern: In fact, the cost of the new tool includes free telephone support via a toll-free number. We currently pay thousands of dollars per year for telephone support.

Notice that the presenter acknowledged the audience's concerns ("I felt the same way . . . ") but then went on to illustrate that these concerns are minor. Addressing counterarguments in this way not only bolsters your point of view, it also shows that you've taken the time to understand your audience and their fears, concerns, and viewpoints on the topic.

Be Professional

As with informative presentations, your professionalism is part of how you establish your credibility and also show respect for your audience. From your attire to your tone of voice to the quality of your handouts and overhead displays, your professional ethos will lend support to your argument: Audiences will want to consider your point of view because it will be obvious that you put time and effort into preparing yourself and your material for their consideration.

Use Effective Visual Communication

Though the topic is covered further in Parts Four and Five, note for now that visual aids (such as slides, overheads, or computer projections) can play a vital role in an effective persuasive presentation. Of course, your argument must be well structured, and a carefully conducted audience and purpose analysis must provide the framework for the presentation—you can't rely solely on presentation software to save you. But effective visuals provide a layer of support for your argument. For a basic presentation, use an overhead projector. Create simple overheads: introduction, body, conclusion. Statistics, often difficult for people to remember, are effectively displayed in this fashion; charts and graphs, discussed later, will also help support your points.

Take Questions and Be Prepared for Other Viewpoints

A persuasive presentation is all about difference: differing points of view, different approaches to a problem, different values on a topic. The core of any democratic system involves the give-and-take of good discussion. After you've clearly presented your case, addressed possible counterarguments, and concluded with enthusiasm and force, you should, if the format allows, take questions from the audience. Be prepared to encounter points of view that you didn't anticipate, and be open to listening carefully before jumping to any conclusions. Sometimes, you may find that your viewpoint is modified by others' input—this is fine, and your audience will see you as all the more credible if they see you as open to new ideas. But don't be afraid to argue your position, too. Be respectful, but stand up for your ideas. Refer to the Answering Audience Questions Checklist in Chapter 9 for more information about questions.

Preparing Your First Persuasive Presentation

Select a type of persuasive technical presentation that is appropriate for your career or field of study, and identify an issue that is important to you and your colleagues. Using the techniques you learned in previous chapters, perform an audience and purpose analysis. Then, outline your presentation. Use the outlining skills you are familiar with from basic public speaking or writing classes. Possible topics might include:

- Using (or not using) computer graphics in presentations
- Why nuclear power is (or isn't) safe and necessary
- Why the use of bovine growth hormone to produce more milk from cows is (or isn't) safe
- Why global warming is (or isn't) a problem
- Why we need better laws about privacy and the Internet

The following are some specifics for one possible persuasive presentation. You may add or modify these specifics as needed for the assignment. Use the audience and purpose worksheets from Chapters 5 and 6.

Audience. Your audience for this presentation is your fellow students in this class. Quite possibly, your class includes students from a variety of majors: engineering, science, management, and technical communication. Although your audience's background and interests may differ, they may also have certain features in common: age range, concern with their education, interest in learning.

Purpose. Your purpose is to convince your audience about a topic that is scientific or technical, is important to you, and that lends itself to a persuasive presentation.

Research. After selecting your topic, research it by reading appropriate journals, magazines, and newspapers. Newspaper editorials often provide a good sense of how to make a logical argument, so read the newspaper editorial section for several days to get some ideas. Also, use the library and the Web. To give your presentation a sense of balance, see if you can locate at least four or five sources for this presentation; make sure you research all sides of the issue.

Plan. Create a careful outline of your presentation, paying special attention to the introduction and conclusion. Be sure the arguments you'll make during the body of the presentation are clear, logical, and that they address counterarguments. Share your outline with a team of two to three other students and provide each other with feedback.

Time. You may present your topic for ten to twelve minutes. Practice using a timer, and be sure that you do not exceed the allotted time. If necessary, trim back or add more material.

Visuals. Although this book has not yet covered the use of visuals, at the option of your instructor you may use the overhead projector for this presentation. Remember that you must be organized and your presentation must be well researched before you can use visual aids effectively. Thus, your overheads should contain only text and no graphics for this first presentation. But you may list some statistical information on your overheads if this is useful. Make sure your text is large enough to read in the back of the room (14 point or larger works well).

In Summary: Persuasive Presentations

Persuasive presentations require you to convince an audience to accept a particular point of view or concept in contrast to other possible conclusions that the audience might come to. As you learned in this chapter, persuasive presentations include a range of situations, from marketing and sales meetings to community events to conference or professional presentations. Being persuasive in technical communication involves an effective blend of emotional appeals, clear logic, appeals to audience values, and understanding of the audience's point of view.

QUESTIONS / EXERCISES / ASSIGNMENTS

1. Pay attention to persuasive discourse in every day life—television commercials, newspaper editorials, Web pages, oral presentations, political speeches. Listen for the hidden major premise—what assumptions is the writer or speaker making about the audience's values? Is the premise always appropriate for a given audience? Also, pay attention to any logical fallacies in the argument.

2. Select a persuasive presentation topic and consider it for two different audiences. Assume the first audience is generally in favor of your overall idea but has not heard the specifics. Assume the second audience is generally opposed to your idea and has also not heard any specific details. Outline your presentation for each audience. Decide what form of organization the body of the presentation should take in each case.

Presentations and Cyberspace. Locate a Website (in a scientific or technical field) that interests you and that seems intended to persuade site visitors to believe something or take a specific action (if you have difficulty locating a site, skim journals and technology sections in local and national newspapers, or ask a professor or graduate student in your major). Identify the persuasive purpose and the audience of the site, and analyze it based on the tips you studied in this chapter. Examine the construction of the argument, the use of evidence, the use of appeals, the approach to counterarguments, the level of professionalism, and the use of visual elements. Do you find any logical fallacies? If so, identify the fallacy and explain why it is a problem. Does the site achieve the intended purpose? Why or why not? Plan how you would revise the site to increase its effectiveness as a persuasive site. Discuss your analysis with your class and solicit their comments about the site and your perspective on it. If appropriate, contact the site's Web master (contact information should be located at the site) and share your analysis.

Presentations and Teamwork. Persuasive presentations can be given individually or as part of a team. Sometimes, the entire team may give the presentation, and other times team members share the research and design of the presentation and elect one member to give the presentation itself. Form a team of two to three people from your class based on a persuasive topic that is of interest to all team members. Assign each member a specific set of research tasks. Work as a group to design the presentation, and decide which team member should deliver the presentation. Remember that you still must perform an audience and purpose analysis, paying special attention to the counterarguments of your audience. As you work on your group presentation, keep track of group interaction. What process did you use to assign the research tasks? How did you select one person to deliver the presentation itself? What items do you agree should go into the persuasive presentation, and what items is there disagreement on? When you prepare a persuasive presentation with a team, you ultimately may learn more about the topic and the various points of view on the subject matter than you might learn on your own.

Presentations and International Communication. Listen to the radio, CSPAN, CNN, and other sources for speeches that individuals from other cultures give in their native countries (usually given in their native language but translated into English for broadcast purposes). Listen also to some speeches by these or similar individuals given in the United States. How did the organizational style of these speeches differ? What do these differences tell you about the cultural expectations of the other culture? What do they tell you about how that culture views U.S. culture? How can this analysis help you prepare for a presentation that you will give to members of that other culture?

Presentations and Your Profession. Interview someone in your profession or in the career you are preparing for when you graduate. Ask them to tell you about persuasive presentations that they have given: What topics were addressed? How did the audience respond? In what situations was the presenter successful in convincing the audience, and in what situations was he or she not successful? Outline your findings and give a brief presentation to your class.

REFERENCES

Engel, S. M. (1982). *With good reason: An introduction to informal fallacies* (2nd ed.). New York: St. Martin's Press.

Houp, K. W., Pearsall, T. E., & Tebeaux, E. (1998). *Reporting technical information* (9th ed.). Boston: Allyn & Bacon.

Lay, M. M., Wahlstorm, B. J. & Duin, A. H. (1995). *Technical communication.* Chicago: Irwin.

CHAPTER

11 Presentations That Offer a Strategy or Action Plan

CHAPTER OVERVIEW

This chapter examines presentations designed to convince an audience to take action. Strategy/action plan presentations are persuasive, but they are more specific than general persuasive presentations in that they invite the audience to accept a specific and well-prepared solution or action plan to solve the problem. This chapter covers the following topics:

- What Are Strategy/Action Plan Presentations?
- Types of Action Plan Presentations in Technical Communication
- Tips for Creating Effective Action Plan Presentations
- Preparing Your First Action Plan Presentation

What Are Strategy/Action Plan Presentations?

Strategy/action plan presentations (called action plan presentations throughout this chapter) are persuasive presentations designed not only to convince an audience about a particular point of view (like a persuasive presentation) but also to argue for a specific solution, approach, or strategy and to suggest how the audience can take action. These presentations often follow a problem-solution format: Here's a problem or concern, and here are ways we can solve it. Perhaps even more than general persuasive presentations, action plan presentations are usually preceded by what in rhetorical theory is known as an *exigence:* "an imperfection marked by urgency" (Bitzer, 1968, p. 6). In other words, a problem or difficulty (imperfection) arises: perhaps in a company, community, or professional organization. This problem requires solving because it is urgent; that is, there is something about the situation that requires people to consider the matter, discuss it, and hopefully reach a conclusion and take action.

Your job in an action plan presentation is to convince your audience that you understand this exigence and that you can offer a specific strategy or plan to solve the problem. Action plan presentations often come about because someone has asked for a solution: a company sends you a request for proposal (RFP) asking you to propose a solution for their technical services needs; your manager asks you and your team to suggest a solution for the company's ongoing Web server slowdowns. In these cases, the audience is already convinced of the problem—thus, you'll spend far less time arguing the general position ("We need a faster Web server") than defending the specific action plan you've chosen ("We should subcontract with a local Internet service provider"). So, although action plan presentations are persuasive, they focus on specific plans that will solve the crisis or problem.

Types of Action Plan Presentations in Technical Communication

Technical communicators will encounter many types of action plan presentations in their careers. The following partial list is meant to suggest some of the action plan presentations you may be involved with. As with all presentations, the audience, purpose, and other factors unique to your company, profession, or geographic location will dictate the formats, time length, and other features.

Government Proposal

Many science and technology companies do a great deal of business with state and federal government organizations. When these government organizations require a product or service, they issue a request for proposal, or RFP. The RFP spells out the terms of what is needed and provides a specific format that should be used when submitting the written proposal. Sometimes, if the RFP specifies it, an oral presentation is required. Vendors must submit a written proposal, but they must also give a presentation. These presentations are usually structured around guidelines provided by the government agency. In many companies, employees with the most experience in government contracts will be asked to give these presentations, because these employees are familiar with the details of what is required. Although audience and purpose analyses are important, the format and amount of information in a government proposal is restricted to the stated government guidelines for preparing proposals.

Other Proposals

Government agencies are not the only organizations that issue RFPs when they need a product or service. Perhaps even more than the government, business and other organizations may select two or three of the submitted proposals and request oral presentations from these companies. A careful understanding of audience is important here: Will the primary decision makers be attending the presentation? How many will be present? Beyond the written proposal, what specific items would they like you to focus on? These situations require an action plan approach—the

FYI

Proposals in Technical Communication

Communicators in science and engineering often find that much of their time is spent writing proposals. Proposals are a major communication form for scientists, engineers, academic institutions, and manufacturing firms and are used to solicit hardware, materials, new programs, equipment, consulting services, and other items (Woolever, 1999, p. 269). If you've taken a technical writing class, or if you've worked in industry, you've probably seen a proposal. If not, the following sources can give you more information on proposals in technical communication:

Houp, K. W., Pearsall, T. E., & Tebeaux, E. (1998). *Reporting technical information* (9th ed.). Boston: Allyn & Bacon.

Woolever, K. R. (1999). *Writing for the technical professions.* New York: Longman.

organization has approached you with a problem or area where they need help, and you are proposing a specific solution. It's important not to repeat everything from your written proposal (see the FYI feature) but instead to focus on specific items that you wish to highlight and that are better served by an oral, not written, format.

Solution to a Technical Problem

Often, an action plan presentation is designed to present a specific solution to a technical problem. This problem may be within someone else's organization, and you are presenting your solution as a company that can provide this service: This case would be similar to what's described in Other Proposals. Often, however, the problem is within your own organization, and you are presenting an action plan to your department or teammates. For example, your team has been asked to review the company's billing software. You discover that this software is running on very old computers that are difficult to use. You also learn that the older software is not compatible with any of the other client software in the company. After much research, your team determines that the best solution is to begin using new billing software that is up to date and compatible with the rest of the company's computing systems. After distributing a short report about your solution, you give an oral presentation outlining the problem, presenting your solution, and illustrating why you rejected several other possibilities.

Solution to an Organizational Problem

Some organizational problems are not merely technical ones, they involve people and the way departments or companies are structured. For example, you may learn that the problem with the billing software is not the software at all. The real problem is that employees are not adequately trained on how to use it, and your organization does not subscribe to the toll-free customer support service for this software. Thus, you devise an action plan to solve the problem—provide more training and allow everyone access to the software's toll-free support line. Again, you would outline the problem, present your solution, and show your reasoning in rejecting other possible plans. Audience analysis is key—perhaps, after performing such an analysis, you learn that last year management rejected the idea of employee access to the telephone support, citing budgetary concerns. Your job would then involve illustrating how much is actually being lost in employee downtime by not subscribing to the phone support service.

Solution to a Community Problem

Action plan presentations are also a large part of community decision making. In the previous chapter, you read about a community waste processing controversy. Citizens are against the incinerator, but the town board is favoring the idea. A general persuasive presentation would be appropriate, because it would give you and other citizens the chance to register your opinion and argue your case. However, an action plan approach might be even more effective, because, along with arguing your case, you can also present some viable alternatives that might satisfy both sides. You learn that you and other citizens are concerned about the environmental impact but that the town board likes the idea of an increased tax base and new jobs. If you can present an action plan that will address their concerns as well as yours, you have a better chance of making your case.

Tips for Creating Effective Action Plan Presentations

Presenting for Someone Else in the Organization

In many types of presentations, technical communicators, who are experts at understanding audiences and making information clear and accessible, are sometimes asked to present for someone else. Perhaps the presentation itself was generated collaboratively, as part of a team or department. Perhaps the presentation reflects the overall policy of the company: We've all seen the company spokesperson who comes on television when there is a disaster, strike, or other news to announce. Most action plans are a result of collaborative work, and therefore, in action plan presentations, communicators are often asked to present a plan that was generated by many people. Sometimes, the communicator may not enter the process until it is well under way. Several chapters back, you learned that people present well when they are very familiar with the topic. So if you are asked to give an action plan presentation that's been created by many others, be sure to do your homework and learn as much as you can about the topic and the particular solution.

Follow a Problem-Solution Format

Most action plan presentations can easily follow a problem-solution format, because their purpose is to present a solution to a particular situation, problem, or need. In many cases, your audience will already be familiar with the problem, so you won't need to spend much time setting up the background for your topic. A basic problem-solution format for an action plan presentation might look something like this:

- *Introduction:* Restate the problem. Provide background if some audience members won't be familiar with the topic.
- *Body:* Present your solution in as much detail as is appropriate for this audience/purpose. Present other solutions that you explored and rejected.
- *Conclusion:* Restate the problem and make any final claims for why your proposed action plan is the most appropriate.

Provide More than What's in the Written Proposal

As one presentation expert points out, the tendency in action plan presentations is to simply repeat all the material from the written proposal. This is not a good idea, she notes, for many reasons. By repeating your written proposal, you miss the chance to show what can only be shown in an oral setting—teamwork, interactions between people, and your genuine concern with the audience's needs. You also insult your audience, because they've probably already read part if not most of your written proposal (Woodall, 1997, p. 85). Instead of simply restating the points from your written proposal, use the oral presentation as a time to make new points, sell your credibility, show your enthusiasm, and listen to the concerns and questions of your audience. (Refer to the Answering Audience Questions checklist, in Chapter 9 for more information about questions.)

Provide Background Material If Needed

Although you shouldn't repeat what's in the written proposal, on the other hand, you need to find out if everyone has read your proposal. Often, people attend meetings to hear your ideas without reading the proposal at all, or with only having read the executive summary or main points. And even if they've read your proposal cover to cover, they may have done so weeks ago and forgotten already. Thus, depending on the situation, the presentation introduction and perhaps even the beginning portion of the body should summarize the background material to get everyone up to speed. Don't repeat your entire written proposal, but don't assume everyone has read everything either. If you can't find out this information by doing an audience analysis in advance, you can start the presentation by asking a question such as the following:

> Before I begin, how many of you had a chance to look over the material I sent out last week?

Even if everyone responds in the affirmative, be prepared to give a very brief overview. And if your audience response indicates that some members didn't read the material or can't remember it, your overview should be more thorough:

> I can see that most of you did not have time to read the entire report. Allow me to take a few moments and highlight the main points.

Follow an Appropriate Organizational Pattern

Review what you learned in Chapter 8 and be sure to organize your material in a pattern that is appropriate for your particular informative presentation. Action plan presentations in technical communication are usually effective if they are organized in a deductive pattern with a problem-solution structure. Outline your material carefully.

Address Reasons Why Other Solutions May Not Work

Similar to addressing counterarguments, discussed in the previous chapter, your action plan presentation should not only present your solution, it should also illustrate that you've thought of other possible answers, and it should explain why you've rejected these ideas. For every problem, you can usually guarantee that someone else has already been thinking about ways to solve it. You should talk to others and find out what's already been tried and what suggestions people still think might work. It's far too common in an action plan presentation for the presenter to begin, enthusiastic and ready to show off his great solution, only to have someone in the back of the room say "You know, we tried that several years ago, and it failed." So be sure to do solid research in this area. Not only will you ensure that your solution is a good one, you'll also show the audience that you have an open mind and have explored other options before making a decision.

Be Well Organized

Being well organized for an action plan presentation includes everything you've learned so far—strong introduction, body that is structured so everyone can follow you, strong conclusion. Just because action plan presentations are so well suited to a problem-solution format, you still need to be sure your material is presented in an organized fashion that the audience can follow.

Be Professional

As with the other presentations discussed thus far, professionalism is part of how you establish credibility. Being professional shows respect for your audience, too. From your attire to your tone of voice to the quality of your handouts and overhead displays, your professional ethos will lend support to your proposed solution: Audiences will be more accepting of your action plan because they will see that you spent time preparing yourself and your material.

Use Effective Visual Communication

Visual communication can be a big plus in an action plan presentation. Your written proposal often can only support certain kinds of visuals—charts, graphs, simple color images (depending on whether you have the budget to print in color). With computer-generated images (such as PowerPoint displays), color does not cost anything, and a color image of your product or of a chart or graph is a very effective way to illustrate your approach to the problem. This topic is covered in detail in Parts Four and Five, but for a basic presentation, use an overhead projector. Create simple overheads: introduction, body, conclusion, and perhaps one or two illustrations to support your action plan.

Be Open to New Ideas

Even though you and your team have worked hard on choosing a particular plan of action to solve the problem at hand, you should remain open to new ideas from your audience. Even if they've read your written proposal, sometimes it's not until they actually hear an idea being talked through that people's imaginations get stirred up; unlike written proposals, live communication between people often invokes energy and ideas. So be prepared for your audience to be critical and to make suggestions, and be open to incorporating these suggestions into your plan. Often, because you have so much invested in your particular action plan, you may not be open to new ideas on the spot. But take notes and let people know that you'll think about what they've shared. Sometimes, the next day you'll wake up and say to yourself, "Hey, that was not such a bad idea that Juan had yesterday." Sharing and collaboration are exciting aspects of oral presentations, especially ones designed to solve problems.

Bring Handouts

Although everyone in your audience may at one time have received complete copies of your proposal, be sure to bring several extra copies with you to the presentation. Also, bring a smaller, more compact version of the action plan, such as an abstract or executive summary (for more information on how to write abstracts or summaries, see Houp, Pearsall, & Tebeaux, 1998). As noted in Chapter 8, don't give handouts until the end unless you're prepared for your audience's attention to shift from you to the handout.

Preparing Your First Action Plan Presentation

Select a topic for an action plan presentation that is appropriate for your career or field of study. Using the techniques you learned in previous chapters, perform an audience and purpose analysis. Then, outline your presentation. Use the outlining skills you are familiar with from basic public speaking or writing classes.

The following are some specifics for one possible action plan presentation. You may add or modify these specifics as needed for the assignment. Use the audience/purpose worksheets from Chapters 5 and 6. Possible topics might include:

- alternatives to nuclear power
- a plan to solve a computer problem in your workplace
- a solution to the increasing incidence of hypertension in the United States
- a plan to reduce the use of toxic substances
- a plan to control mosquitoes (which can spread the deadly encephalitis virus) in your community

Audience. Your audience for this presentation is your fellow students in this class. Quite possibly, your class includes students from a variety of majors: engineering, science, management, and technical communication. Although your audience's background and interests may differ, they may also have certain features in common: age range, concern with their education, interest in learning.

Purpose. Your purpose is to convince your audience to accept your action plan or strategy for solving a problem. Your presentation may call for certain specific actions, such as signing a petition, calling congressional representatives, or making a change in management structures.

Research. Find an interesting and exciting topic that clearly lends itself to an action plan presentation. Research your topic by reading appropriate journals, magazines, and newspapers. Interview experts and also use the library and the Web. To give your presentation a sense of balance, see if you can locate at least four or five sources for this presentation; make sure you research all possible solutions to the problem.

Plan. Create a careful outline of your presentation. Pay attention to the introduction and conclusion but also work on the body, making sure that you follow a problem-solution format. Don't just present your plan: Present other possible solutions and show how yours weighs in against these others. Share your outline with a team of two to three students and give each other feedback.

Time. You may present your topic for ten to twelve minutes. Practice using a timer, and be sure that you don't exceed the allotted time. If necessary, trim back or add more material.

Visuals. You may use the overhead projector for this presentation. Your overheads should only contain text and very simple graphics (one or two at most) for this first presentation. You may also list some statistical information on your overheads if this is useful. Make sure your text is large enough to read in the back of the room (14 point or larger works well). If your instructor wishes you to use more comprehensive visuals, then you may want to skip ahead to Chapters 16–18 for more information.

In Summary: Action Plan Presentations

Action plan presentations, like persuasive presentations, invite an audience to see an issue from your point of view. But along with convincing an audience of a particular viewpoint, action plans also ask the audience to take action in order to solve a particular problem. These presentations can involve many situations, such as government or other proposals and solutions to technical, organizational, or community problems. Action plan proposals are often created by a collaborative effort among many coworkers; technical communicators or other communication specialists sometimes take the role of presenting these presentations. Most action plan presentations follow a problem-solution format; presenters should be attentive to the need to provide background information, even if the audience has received a written report in advance.

QUESTIONS / EXERCISES / ASSIGNMENTS

Presentations and Cyberspace. As you learned in this chapter, audience members don't always have time to read a proposal or report prior to attending a presentation. How could you use the Internet to assist your audience in this regard? For example, could you post the report to a Web page and provide specific links for different individuals (managers, development staff, and so on). Could you email audience members reminders or small excerpts of the report in advance? Speculate on how you might use the Internet to assist you in these and other aspects of your action plan presentation.

Presentations and Teamwork. With two or three other students in your class, identify a problem on campus or in town and develop an action plan for solving the problem. If you were to present this orally to a person or group who could decide to implement the plan, who would it be? How must you focus your presentation to reflect the characteristics of this audience?

Presentations and International Communication. When preparing an action plan presentation, you will need as much information as possible about any international members of your audience. Establish a list of Websites that can help you locate country- or culture-specific information, including the U.S. State Department (www.state.gov/), the Central Intelligence Agency (www.odci.gov/cia/publications/pubs.html), the U.S. Agency for International Development (www.info.usaid.gov/), and various embassy or government/ ministerial sites (an online list of embassy contact information can be found at www.embassy.org/embassies/index.html) related to a specific nation or culture.

Presentations and Your Profession. Identify a problem or challenge that professionals in your field currently encounter, and develop an action plan for addressing that problem or challenge. Present the plan to your class (be sure to describe the problem clearly).

REFERENCES

Bitzer, L. (1968). The rhetorical situation. *Philosophy & Rhetoric, 1,* 1–14.

Houp, K. W., Pearsall, T. E., & Tebeaux, E. (1998). *Reporting technical information* (9th ed.). Boston: Allyn & Bacon.

Woodall, M. K. (1997). *Presentations that get results: 14 reasons yours may not.* Lake Oswego, OR: Professional Business Communications.

Woolever, K. R. (1999). *Writing for the technical professions.* New York: Longman.

CHAPTER

12 Presentations That Explain How to Perform a Task

CHAPTER OVERVIEW

This chapter examines presentations designed to teach an audience how to perform a task or series of tasks. How-to presentations often include informative features but primarily focus on the steps required so audiences members can accomplish something. This chapter covers the following topics:

- What Are How-To Presentations?
- Types of How-To Presentations in Technical Communication
- Tips for Creating Effective How-To Presentations
- Preparing Your First How-To Presentation

What Are How-To Presentations?

In Chapter 9, you learned that according to a recent survey, scientific and technical professionals frequently are required to give presentations that instruct or train (Hager & Scheiber, 1997, pp. 5–6). Indeed, much of the work of a technical communicator involves explaining or teaching an audience how to do something. This feature makes perfect sense: In a world with a growing number of increasingly complex technologies, users of these technologies need to know how to operate their new televisions, VCRs, laser printers, or computers. Procedures are also more complex: Tax forms, employee benefit packages, safety instructions, and more can be confusing and difficult to understand. Often, a written manual or checklist cannot provide the necessary information. Users must also be instructed face to face in how to perform the steps needed to operate technology or complete a procedure.

This type of communication is often called task-oriented communication because the goal is to help users learn to perform a task or series of tasks. Yet even though most people recognize the need for quality task-oriented information, one expert (citing several other sources) notes that "[i]nstructing people in problem-solving strategies for complex tasks is one of the most difficult challenges in [this form of communication]" (Mirel, 1994, p. 211). Because instructing people in how to do something is both a needed and a difficult assignment, technical communicators should work carefully to design how-to presentations that help audience members use and understand the technologies in their everyday lives.

Oral presentations offer a distinct advantage over written documentation when it comes to teaching an audience how to do something. In written documentation, the technical writer has no way of knowing if the person reading the instructions actually figured out how to do the task. Even though good documentation is usually tested on a group of real users before being printed, it's impossible to account for everyone. But when explaining things in an oral presentation, you have the advantage of being able to see for yourself if the idea is catching on, and you can directly answer audience questions. (Refer to the Answering Audience Questions checklist in Chapter 9 for more information about questions.)

Just as there are a wide variety of documents that teach audiences how to do something (instructions, online help, user manuals), there are also many settings and purposes when communicators give how-to presentations. Some of these types are reviewed here.

Types of How-To Presentations in Technical Communication

Training Presentations

Technical communicators often are involved in presentations designed to teach or train audiences about a specific product, service, or procedure. The most common type of training presentation is one that teaches audiences how to use a software product. From basic word processing software to complex programs for accounting, database management, or scientific visualization, the number of software training presentations is increasing, and for good reason—most software products are complex, and a well-focused training presentation can help product users learn specific features.

Other types of training presentations involve hardware training. Although hardware has come to mean computers, it can mean almost any machine or mechanical apparatus. Technical communicators often provide training in how to use all kinds of hardware, from computers to farm equipment to biomedical devices.

Product Demonstrations

Some how-to presentations are intended not so much to teach but to demonstrate how a product functions or operates. Such how-to presentations may be part of a sales presentation, in which the communicator is using the product demonstration to convince potential customers to try the product. In a typical product demonstration, the presenter uses a real or scale model of the product to show how the actual item works. Such demonstrations can be very complex, depending on the product, and they often involve a good deal of planning, preparation, and setup time. For example, if the presentation is given at a site away from the main company location, the presenter must ensure that the product and all ancillary items are shipped in advance and arrive in good working condition.

Procedural Demonstrations

In the same fashion, some presentations are designed to demonstrate, but not thoroughly teach, how to perform a procedure. Sometimes, out of sheer practicality, these presentations are done not on the real item, but using models or computer simulations. Scientists attending a conference presentation, for example, may see a simulated demonstration of a new procedure for heart surgery. Engineers or architects studying various methods for constructing a new building might see a demonstration of possible procedures via a computer model, projected onto a large screen. Procedural demonstrations may also involve areas such as how to do your taxes or how to assemble a new lawn mower—one version of the procedure is demonstrated, giving audience members a general idea of how to perform the task for their specific need.

Tips for Creating Effective How-To Presentations

Begin with a Strong Introduction

Although this tip is true for all presentations, it plays a special role in how-to presentations. According to one expert, people learn best if you immediately grab their attention and then give a clear overview of the material that you'll be teaching (Gagné, 1985, p. 166). If you catch your audience's attention with excitement and enthusiasm, you'll be off to a good start. Then, if you present a point-by-point overview of what you'll be presenting, people will have the big picture about what to expect. They'll know how much to be prepared for, and, if you've done your audience and purpose analysis carefully, your audience will see that your presentation will cover items that they need to know.

Analyze the Tasks Your Audience Will Need to Perform

You may need to adapt your audience/purpose analysis worksheets to include a special section on the type of tasks your audience needs to perform. If your presentation is on using the new office accounting software, for example, you need to learn as much as you can about the audience. Are they accountants and thus interested in specific tasks about purchasing, invoicing, and so on? Or are they sales managers, who are mainly interested in using the new software to look up customer information and balances? You can learn this information by performing a *task analysis* as part of your overall audience analysis. Interview several potential audience members to see how they now use the system. Spend time with them as they perform the task, and take notes on what you observe. Then be sure that your presentation reflects your findings.

Follow an Appropriate Organizational Pattern

Review what you learned in Chapter 8 and be sure to organize your material in a pattern that is appropriate for your particular informative presentation. How-to presentations in technical communication are usually effective if they are organized in a deductive pattern with a chronological structure (discussed in more detail later). Outline your material carefully.

Tailor Your Presentation to the Specific Needs of That Audience

There is nothing worse for an audience than to attend a how-to presentation only to learn that its level is too low or too high. An audience that already knows the basics about word processing does not need introductory material; likewise, an audience that knows almost nothing needs you to begin with the most fundamental material. Your audience/purpose and task analysis should tell you what you need to know about your particular audience.

Determine the Correct Level of Instruction

One way to tailor your presentation to your audience is to carefully determine the level of instruction. Is the purpose of your presentation to teach every detail about how to perform the task, or is the purpose simply to overview the basic steps and let everyone practice later? How much time will you have? The answer will dictate how much you can cover.

Determine the Right Level of Steps

Once you know what level of instruction your audience needs and expects, you can determine the level of steps you'll include. To illustrate this idea, take the example of downloading software from the Web. If you were giving this presentation to someone who has never used the Web and never searched for or downloaded software, you would need to provide many levels of instruction:

1. With your computer turned on, open your Web browser.
   - **a.** Locate the Web browser icon on your desktop.
   - **b.** Double-click it.
   - **c.** Wait for the browser to open.
2. Type the URL for the site from which you want to download the software.
   - **a.** At the top of the browser, find the field labeled Location.
   - **b.** Type in the URL, including all punctuation and characters.

3. Press Enter.
4. Wait for the Web page to load.

As you can see, this level of outlining assumes an audience that really has no background with the task at hand. If you were instructing people who have downloaded software before, on the other hand, you would have fewer steps and far fewer levels, too.

1. Open your Web browser.
2. Go to the URL for the site from which you want to download the software.

Far more complex examples, such as how to use software, operate high tech equipment, or implant a cardiac pacemaker, require even greater attention to the appropriate level of steps for a particular audience.

Use Action Verbs

Notice that the previous example uses the imperative voice, or action verbs, to begin each step in the series. For U.S. audiences in particular (some cultures find imperative voice rude or inconsiderate), action verbs create an immediate sense of exactly what the person must do to accomplish the particular step. Make sure your choice of verbs is specific; for example, don't say "put" if what you want people to do is "gently place" the item. Also, be consistent in your use of verbs. If you say "put" in one step, don't switch to "place" or another verb the next time you want audiences to perform the same action.

Don't Overload the Audience with Too Many Steps

You must determine the proper level of steps, but you must also be careful not to overload the audience with too many steps. Having a clear sense of purpose will help you understand just what your audience needs and can handle in a given presentation. If you only have a short time in which to present, you'll necessarily need to limit the steps. On the other hand, even if you are giving an all-day workshop, you still need to be aware that people can only digest a finite amount of information before they become overwhelmed. Your audience and purpose analysis will help you here—if your audience is young children, you will know that they have a shorter attention span than adults. If you are frequently required to conduct extensive training or instructional presentations, you should investigate information supplied by the American Society for Training and Development (see Presentations and Cyberspace at the end of this chapter), whose research and materials can help you determine how to present an appropriate amount of information without overwhelming your audience.

Audiences usually need written support for oral presentations that involve numerous steps. Thus, you should use overhead transparencies, flip charts, and handouts. (See Chapters 16–18 for more information.)

Use an Appropriate Organizational Scheme for Explaining Steps

Probably the simplest and most familiar way to present steps in a task is the numbered list format. In this organizational pattern, you explain the steps involved in the task in sequential order. On an accompanying overhead or handout, steps are numbered along the left-hand margin. If you were instructing an audience on how to use a new software product, for example, you might explain the following steps:

1. Insert the CD into the CD-ROM drive.
2. Click the CD icon.
3. Click the Getting Started icon.
4. Wait while the software installs itself.

Besides the numbered-step approach, according to Horton (1991, p. 118–120), there are other organizational patterns you can use to present steps. Some of these include:

- Description. When a procedure is easy to remember, simply describe the steps. For example, "Turn on your computer and insert the CD."
- Checklist. If you want your audience to remember to perform certain tasks in advance or to use certain items, describe the tasks as a checklist. For example, "Please include the following items before mailing your application. . . ." Then list the tasks. It is often useful to display a visual checklist and to direct audience attention to their handouts, which should also contain the checklist.
- Action-response discussion. In this format, you state the action the user should perform followed by the response that can be expected. For example, for the action you would say "Turn on the computer" and for the response you would note that "the hard drive will begin to boot up." If you use the action-response pattern, a table (see below) would be appropriate for the presentation handout.
- Question list. If the task involves many possible conditions, and if your audience might have questions once they attempt to perform the procedures on their own, you may wish to present material in the form of questions. For example, one question might be "Do you have a Macintosh computer? If so, do X."

Sample Action-Response Table

Action	Response
Turn on computer.	Hard drive will boot up.
Insert disk.	Disk icon will appear on screen.
Double-click disk icon.	Program will begin to load.

FYI

Preparing Handouts for a How-To Presentation

How-to presentations should be accompanied by handouts so your audience will be able to perform the tasks you are explaining once they leave the presentation. Not only do handouts help audiences remember the steps involved, they also provide a place for audiences to take notes. The most basic handouts will contain a list of the steps or procedures in your presentation. For more information on preparing how-to handouts, see:

Barker, T. T. (1998). *Writing software documentation: A task-oriented approach.* Boston: Allyn & Bacon.

Horton, W. (1991). *Illustrating computer documentation: The art of presenting information graphically on paper and online.* New York: Wiley.

Houp, K. W., Pearsall, T. E., & Tebeaux, E. (1998). *Reporting technical information.* Boston: Allyn & Bacon.

Presentation handouts can follow one of the organizational patterns just described: numbered steps, descriptions, checklists, action-response tables, or lists of questions. Make your handouts consistent with whatever pattern you use in the presentation; in other words, if you present your material in a numbered format, use a handout that contains numbered lists.

Make Steps Easy to Follow

Before giving your presentation, practice in front of people similar to your expected audience members to see if your steps are understandable and easy to follow. Practicing is especially important if you are extremely familiar with the subject matter: Sometimes, what makes perfect sense to an expert means nothing to novices! If you find that certain steps are too difficult, add more levels of detail or adjust your terms.

When you practice, be sure to match your level of jargon and technical terms to your audience. As mentioned under informative presentations, technical language that is too difficult will confuse the audience; language that is too simple will bore or insult them.

Allow Ample Setup Time

If you are giving a how-to presentation that involves a lot of props (hardware and other items that you will actually demonstrate), you must provide enough time to set up the items and be sure they work. If appropriate, bring along an assistant to help you. And always be prepared to give your presentation without the props—as the old saying goes, if something can fail, it probably will. As you'll learn in Chapters 17 and 18, technologies can and do break down at the most inopportune times.

So be ready to give your presentation without any props. If you find that some aspect of your demonstration is not working, take a moment to calmly try fixing the problem. But if you can't fix it after a minute or two (at most), continue with your presentation.

When giving a demonstration of a product, remember that "less is more." Don't attempt to assemble the entire machine if all you want to show is one or two components. Also, try having some of the demonstration ready in advance: Think of cooking shows, where chefs have part of the meal prepared, so audiences don't have to wait while items are cooking. If your demonstration involves a good deal of assembly, have some pre-assembled examples, at various stages, ready to show the audience. Also, be careful about asking audience members to help you with a demonstration; you can easily lose control of your audience if members are all working on something at their own pace. You may wish to only ask one or two audience members to participate while others watch.

If Appropriate, Allow Time for Feedback

In some how-to presentations, audiences are not expected to actually perform the task but rather simply to obtain an understanding about how the process or product works. Audience members in these cases will take the accompanying handouts and try the process at their individual work sites. In other situations, especially hands-on training sessions, audiences are expected to learn the skill as part of the presentation itself. Word processing training in a computer lab is one example of this sort of how-to presentation. If this is the case, you need to allow ample time for the audience to practice the skills learned and then demonstrate the skill if appropriate.

Preparing Your First How-To Presentation

Select a topic for a how-to presentation that is appropriate for your career or field of study. Using the techniques you learned in previous chapters, perform an audience and purpose analysis. Then, outline your presentation. Use the outlining skills you are familiar with from basic public speaking or writing classes but concentrate on the specific tasks you want the audience to perform and the specific steps they'll need to learn in order to perform these tasks.

The following are some specifics for one possible how-to presentation. You may add or modify these specifics as needed for the assignment. Use the audience/purpose worksheets from Chapters 5 and 6. Possible topics might include:

- how to rewire a circuit
- how to install software on a laptop computer
- how to read an insurance policy
- how to use a voice messaging system
- how to see Jupiter at night through a simple telescope

Audience. You will present to a college-educated audience of mixed background—your classmates! You'll need to do a thorough audience analysis to determine the scope and detail of your presentation. Outline your presentation to include the steps you will explain to the audience.

Purpose. To instruct your audience about the use of a product or concept. The topic may require steps or a product demonstration.

Research. Your primary research will consist of being sure that your demonstration is adequate and allows your audience to understand your idea and perform the task(s) you describe.

Time. You may present your topic for ten to twelve minutes.

Visuals. Work with your instructor to determine what sort of visuals will be appropriate for your presentation. You may wish to list the steps of your procedure on an overhead projection transparency, and you should consider providing handouts. Your use of visuals should conform with the audience and purpose of the presentation. Make sure your text is large enough to read in the back of the room (14 point or larger works well). If your instructor wishes you to use more comprehensive visuals, then you may want to skip ahead to Chapters 16–18 for more information.

In Summary: Explaining How to Perform a Task

How-to presentations are one of the most frequently given in technical communication. Sometimes, along with a written document, users also require face-to-face instructions about how to operate a technology or complete a procedure. Types of how-to presentations include training presentations, product demonstrations, and procedural demonstrations. Remember to maintain a focus on your audience and the tasks they need to perform. Keep these tasks at an appropriate level, make sure your audience can follow the tasks, and don't overload them with too many steps.

QUESTIONS / EXERCISES / ASSIGNMENTS

Select an everyday task, such as starting your car. Now, define several different audiences for this task: young children, technical experts, people with no experience. For each audience, outline the steps and levels of steps you'd need in order to give a thorough how-to training presentation. Because you won't be able to perform a real audience analysis for this presentation, you can invent certain features about your audience as needed, including a pretend audience and task analysis. Notice how very different one task becomes depending on the audience and their differing backgrounds.

Presentations and Cyberspace. Learn more about training and instruction at the Website for the American Society for Training and Development (www.astd.org) or the International Society for Performance Improvement (www.ispi.org). Present your findings to the class.

Presentations and Teamwork. How-to presentations can be given individually or as part of a team. Often, these presentations will be designed collaboratively and then presented by one or two people. Form a team of three or four people from your class, and select a how-to topic that interests all of you. Assign each member a specific set of research tasks. Work as a group to design the presentation, and select two team members who will deliver the presentation. Work carefully on your audience analysis, paying special attention to the task analysis if you are going to be presenting a series of tasks. Then, decide how you will divide the presentation itself. Should one presenter do the first half and the other presenter the second half? Or should one presenter introduce and conclude the topic and circulate around the room, helping audience members (if it's a training presentation) while the other presenter continues to speak? As you work on your group presentation, keep track of group interaction, as you have done for other presentations in this section.

Presentations and International Communication. Locate a set of multilingual instructions (look at the instructions that came with your VCR, TV, computer, coffee pot, or other appliance, for example). Compare the various languages to the English-language instructions in terms of the number of steps given, the amount of space taken to give each step, the punctuation used by various cultures (does each language appear to use the same punctuation markings and are they used in the same places), and the use of images. How will these factors affect the way you plan a speech that will involve the use of a translator (consider the length of the presentation and the kinds of phrasing you will use)?

Presentations and Your Profession. Because so many professions offer such a variety of how-to presentations, you'll learn a great deal if you interview a professional in your field and ask about training and how-to presentations. Does the company have a special training department? Do scientists and engineers also give how-to presentations, or are all presentations given by professional communicators? Do presenters travel to customer sites or present at the company location? Present your findings in a two- to five-minute informative presentation in class.

REFERENCES

Barker, T. T. (1998). *Writing software documentation: A task-oriented approach.* Boston: Allyn & Bacon.

Gagné, R. (1985). *The conditions of learning.* New York: Holt, Rinehart, and Winston.

Hager, P. J., & Scheiber, H. J. (1997). *Designing and delivering scientific, technical, and managerial presentations.* New York: Wiley.

Horton, W. (1991). *Illustrating computer documentation: The art of presenting information graphically on paper and online.* New York: Wiley.

Houp, K. W., Pearsall, T. E., & Tebeaux, E. (1998). *Reporting technical information* (9th ed.). Boston: Allyn & Bacon.

Mirel, B. (1994). Analyzing electronic help exchanges. *Technical Communication, 41*(2), 210–223.

PRESENTING . . .

Kevin Kinneavy

Photo Credit: Josephine Lee

Kevin Kinneavy is a technology trainer and manager for Minnesota Education Technology Alliance in the Twin Cities, which provides technology leadership, training, and support services to schools and businesses throughout Minnesota. Here are his thoughts on Part Three, Types of Technical Presentations.

As a technology trainer, most of the formal presentations I give tend to be the "how-to" type either as training classes or conference sessions. As a manager, I find myself making presentations at meetings to persuade, inform, offer a plan, teach, or any combination of these types. These sorts of presentations can be formal or informal depending on the circumstance, but in all cases, I find that it's important to think about the purpose of the presentation and be well prepared. For me there's a fine line between being overprepared and underprepared. I like to give presentations that are informal in tone and invite participation from the audience, so it's important not to have a rigid format to follow. On the other hand, if I haven't thoroughly thought through what I'm presenting, I may get caught in some trap or led off on a tangent. To help guide me in my presentations, I create a detailed outline of what I intend to talk about without planning every word.

No matter what the main purpose, my presentations almost always cross the lines between types. Even a software training class, primarily a how-to presentation, has elements of other types embedded. During a training class I usually need to persuade the participants of the importance of using the software, inform the group of specific uses for it, and I try to give a plan for implementing regular use of the software. Because of this overlap, I find it's helpful to think of the overall purpose of the presentation as being of a particular type with interludes of other types sprinkled throughout. It's important that I think about and plan the purpose of each section so that I prepare appropriately and communicate clearly. If I'm not sure what my purpose is, I'll send mixed messages, and the audience won't understand what I'm trying to convey.

For almost any type of presentation these days, most people have the opportunity to use presentation software such as PowerPoint [something you'll learn more about in Part Five]. People have differing opinions on the use of such presentation software, but as a visual learner, I think it's important to include a variety of media in my presentations, and generally I like using presentation software. In any case, I try to be sure that whatever visual aids or other media I use in my presentation add to it rather than just distract the audience. I find it's helpful to use the software to present a broad outline of my presentation with supporting audio or visual aids, but I'm careful not to just read the outline during my presentation. There's nothing worse than a presenter who simply reads a handout or slides! Most

(continued)

PRESENTING... Continued

presentation software includes templates to help prepare presentations of various types. Usually one of those will provide the basic structure for a certain type of presentation, but I always make modifications so that the presentation fits my specific needs for each situation. I always try to get set up in the presentation space well ahead of time, especially when I plan to use some form of technology for the presentation. It's amazing how often there are technical difficulties, so I'm always prepared to present without the visual aids in that event.

Regardless of the topic or audience, whether the setting is formal or informal, or the tools used, I think it's important to keep the purpose in mind during the planning and preparation. In spite of the fact that a particular presentation may not fall neatly into one of the categories, thinking about those types helps me make a clear and concise presentation that accomplishes my goals. Ultimately, the audience and purpose shape the content and type of every presentation.

PART FOUR

Science, Technology, and Non-Expert Audiences

Now that you are familiar with the principles of technical presentations and have given some basic presentations, it's time to consider some advanced concepts and techniques. Part Four will introduce you to some advanced concepts for technical presentations: examining your role in communicating technical information to the public; using a technique from classical rhetoric, called stasis theory, to make information accessible; using analogy and metaphor in your presentations; and information about using visual information wisely. This section does not offer specific types of presentations but rather gives you more tools and concepts that you can use to tailor a presentation for a specific audience and purpose.

You will notice that most of the examples in this section are from printed sources, not oral presentations. There are many reasons for this. First, oral presentations are not always recorded and transcribed into text. Like most oral communication, speeches and presentations tend to disappear once they are given. Therefore, material from oral presentations is difficult to use in a textbook, where you need to be able to see and study examples and analyze how they are constructed. Printed sources provide you with those opportunities, and you will be able to apply what you learn from these sources to your work on oral presentations. In addition, students of oral presentations in technical communication have much to learn from what is being done in science and technology journalism. Science and technology articles aimed at public audiences offer us valuable tools and techniques that can be easily applied to oral presentations.

CHAPTER 13 Technical Presentations: Beyond Efficiency

CHAPTER OVERVIEW

So far, you have learned a bit about the role of a technical communicator in relation to science and technology. But until now, this book has focused primarily on techniques for giving effective presentations. This chapter continues a discussion about the unique role of communicators in a world of highly complex information—information that is often important for the public but, unfortunately, only understood by experts. Technical communicators play an important role in making this information understandable for all. This chapter covers the following topics:

- Making a Difference in Science/Technology Culture
- Beyond Efficiency: Technical Communicators and the Public
- The Introduction: A Good Place to Start
- Using These Techniques for Oral Presentations

Making a Difference in Science/Technology Culture

As noted throughout this book, technical communication is on the rise, due in large part to the highly specialized, information-saturated world. This trend toward more and more information will only increase as people continue to invent, research, and discover new scientific ideas and turn these ideas into technologies for medicine, the workplace, the home, and other uses. Yet all of this information is of no use to anyone unless it is communicated in a format that is understandable to audiences.

In this and the next three chapters, you will concentrate on an imagined audience called the public. At first, this concept may seem at odds with what we've discussed in previous chapters, where you learned that the best oral presentations are those given by presenters who understand the specific audience and their knowledge levels, backgrounds, and needs. Yet there are many times when the technical communicator's role involves communicating to a large audience of people with mixed backgrounds who are not experts in the specific field. For example, if you are a communicator with a large government research laboratory, you may be asked to give a presentation to the local community about a scientific project taking place at the lab. Or if you are a scientist working on that project, you may need to give a talk to a local high school or college. In these and similar instances, the communicator's role involves making the complex scientific material interesting and accessible to a mixed audience. More importantly for this chapter, the role also involves a special relationship between the communicator and the public—citizens from a variety of backgrounds who may know very little about the subject matter at hand.

A word of reminder from Chapter 1—technical communicators can be full-time professional communicators, or they can be scientists or engineers who are communicating their ideas to the public. In either case, communicating technical information so it can be understood by the public makes a major difference in how people learn about important new topics.

Beyond Efficiency: Technical Communicators and the Public

In Chapter 10, you learned about the syllogism: a form of argument where the presenter and the listener share a common premise. In a sense, this book so far has been something of a large syllogism. If you've noticed, the underlying premise to this book has been that effective oral presentations are presentations that most *efficiently* explain information in a way that the audience can use. This premise—efficiency—underlies many technical communication books and classes. Good technical communication, as the books often say, is efficient, clear, and accessible to its audience members.

These premises of efficiency, clarity, and accessibility are important. But there is another very important reason for working in technical communication, and that reason is *responsibility.* Good technical communication, while it must be usable, should also be responsible. Technical communicators should take seriously their relationship with the public. This relationship reflects a special responsibility on the part of the communicator to help audiences understand the importance and relevance of a scientific or technical topic. As one expert in science communication put it, "[s]cience could not survive as anything but an interested attitude toward the universe if nobody wrote about their discoveries" (Porush, 1995, p. 2). Change "wrote" to "communicate" in this sentence, and you have it in a nutshell. If no one communicated about science and technology, there would be very little of it available to use and understand. Communicators are a critical link in this process—they help entice audiences to listen to new information presented in a format that is interesting, fun, exciting, and useful. In short, technical communicators have a major responsibility for mediating between science and technology and the public.

The Introduction: A Good Place to Start

A good place to learn lessons about communicating science and technology to the public is on the pages of science journalism. Science and technology writers for major newspapers and magazines often compose their material for the most broad of audiences: the reading public. These writers have learned the art of making complex information interesting, and they understand that their words are shaping the public's understanding of a topic that otherwise might never be understood. Science and technology writers are in fact acting as technical communicators when they take complex topics like the human genome project (a project to map the entire human DNA structure), encryption (a mathematical algorithm used to keep cellular phone conversations private), or cancer prevention and make this information interesting and understandable for the public. Most science and technology writers recognize their special role in dealing with the public, and they are aware of their responsibility.

You can learn a great deal about communicating technical information to the public by looking at the introductory paragraphs used in high quality science and technology publications. These paragraphs exhibit a series of techniques that can be used not only in writing but also in oral presentations. Some of these techniques will be similar to those discussed in Chapter 7, but what you will see in the sections that follow are specialized ways of making complex material compelling and interesting. Remember that the introduction is the place where you arouse audience interest and create the ethos for the entire presentation. The techniques used by these journalists in their writing are easily translated into techniques that you can use for presentations. However, note that journalists often take more liberty and employ more creativity with their writing than do technical communicators—part of a technical communicator's responsibility, in writing and in presentations, is to aim for accuracy of information. So, although the following techniques are useful and effective ways to capture an audience's attention, you should also attempt to strike a balance between creativity on the one hand and accuracy on the other.

Science Fiction and the Imagination

One way science and technology journalists often grab audience attention is to invoke images from science fiction—images that stir the imagination and create a sense of wonder and awe. For example, in an article about an ancient dinosaur called *megaraptor namunhuaiquii*, an ancient dinosaur whose fossilized remains were recently discovered, the author uses this introductory paragraph:

> It was the last day of his expedition, and Fernando Novas was pleased. The Argentine paleontologist, who works at the Museum of Natural Sciences in Buenos Aires, had been looking for carnivorous dinosaurs in northwestern Patagonia, a dinosaur-fossil hot spot. The region had already yielded the 42-foot-long terror *Giganotosaurus*, possibly the largest carnivore of all time, and the 100-ton *Argentinosaurus*,

> the heaviest beast to walk on land. Novas himself had found a curiously birdlike nonflying dinosaur, which he called *Unenlagia,* and several other predatory species. On the last day of his successful expedition, in January 1996, he decided to check out some bedrock at the top of a hill. Not surprisingly, given the arid, fossil-friendly landscape of northwestern Patagonia, Novas found some bones (Menon, 1998, p. 30).

Notice how this introduction uses elements from science fiction to entice you to read on: Readers are told of strange and unusual beasts like the "carnivorous dinosaurs," a "42-foot-long terror," and "a curiously birdlike nonflying dinosaur." Even the "arid, fossil-friendly landscape of northwestern Patagonia" invokes an other-worldliness and invites audiences to read further. Instead of starting the story with the long and cumbersome Latin names of these creatures, which would probably be too technical for a mixed audience, this introduction appeals to the science fiction-like quality of this true story.

Linking to a Timely Event *(Kairos)*

A concept from classical rhetoric known as *kairos* is very useful for communicating science and technology to the public. Simply stated, *kairos* means "opportune or timely moment." Mixed (public) audiences are most interested in topics that relate to an event connected with something in their immediate surroundings or environment. Notice, for example, how television networks run specials related to hot topics in the news that week; during the O. J. Simpson trial, for example, the airwaves were full of shows about court systems, domestic violence, and other related topics. This same technique is used by science and technology journalists, who often try to connect their story to an item that is timely. For example, the August 1996 issue of *Scientific American* ran a story about sand, beginning with the following paragraph:

> When we pick up a handful of sand from the beach and watch it sift through our fingers, we are seeing the product of millions of years of geologic history. Much of this history can be uncovered by examining the particles under magnification, where they give up the secrets of their origin and subsequent travels. (Mack & Leistikow, 1996, p. 63.)

This article is ultimately about geology and the way sand forms. It could have been a rather technical article about the earth's geological cycles. Instead, the authors linked the topic to a timely event. How is sand timely, you ask? Well, the magazine article ran in the August issue, a month when many North Americans head to the beach for vacation. By starting with the sentence about watching sand sift through one's fingers, the authors used the rhetorical notion of *kairos* to link a scientific topic to an event of immediacy in the mind of the audience.

Narratives and Good Stories

Another technique used by science and technology writers involves telling a compelling story as part of the introduction. As noted in Chapter 7, a story draws the reader into the material using a narrative format: It puts the audience members into a listening mode and makes them curious to know more. In an article about how flu epidemics arise, author begins with such a story:

> On September 24, 1918, three days after setting sail from Norway's northern coast, the *Forsete* arrived in Longyearbyen, a tiny mining town on one of the Norwegian islands north of the Arctic Circle. It was the last ship of the year, before ice made the Arctic fjords impassable, and it carried among its passengers a number of fishermen and farmers going north for the winter to earn extra money in Longyearbyen's coal mines. During the voyage, however, the ship had been hit with an outbreak of the flu. Upon landing, many of the passengers had to be taken to the local hospital, and over the next two weeks seven of them died. They were buried side by side in the local cemetery, their graves marked by six white crosses and one headstone. (Gladwell, 1997, p. 52)

This paragraph is followed by a list of the seven names and their birth and death dates. The story is compelling: One can feel the icy waters in the fjords and can imagine the fishermen and farmers traveling to earn some extra money. The list of names adds a personal touch, giving a human face to the story. The subject of influenza outbreaks could be communicated in a highly technical fashion, but instead, the writer puts a human face to his introduction, which makes audiences want to find out exactly what happened. It also links the dangers of flu directly to humans, who could also be at risk.

The Personal Scientist

Many times, if a scientific or technical topic involves certain individuals, a journalist will begin a story with a personal snapshot of the researcher as a way of adding a human touch to what might otherwise be a highly technical article. The earlier example about dinosaurs, for instance, features paleontologist Fernando Novas; a similar approach is taken in the introduction to the following article about the physics of magnets:

> David Durlach was a child when he discovered electromagnets. But not until he was in high school did it strike him like a poem that each winding of a wire coil increases the strength of its magnetic field. At that point, he remembers, he started winding electromagnets until his wrists got tired. Once, when a coil grew to the size of an acorn squash and the weight of a bowling ball, he lugged it over to a wall socket and plugged it in. By some miracle the fuses held, but lights throughout the house grew dim. "My parents asked me not to plug it in in the evenings when they were trying to read," he recalls. (Guterl, 1997, p. 38)

Not only does this introduction personalize the scientist, but it does so by telling audiences about him as a young child. Children are what Aristotle would call a common topic—a theme that almost anyone can relate to. Whether you have children or just spend time around them, the idea of a curious child is appealing to almost anyone. Again, a topic like physics and magnetism might be hard to connect to a mixed audience unless the writer used this technique in his introduction.

Irony and a Sense of Humor

As noted before, humor must be used carefully. But humor or irony can often be a good way to start off any communication about a technical topic. One science writer seems to have understood that the topic of interplanetary travel might intimidate readers unless it began with a bit of light-heartedness, so he began his article, titled "It's Only Rocket Science," this way:

> You don't happen to have a spare half-trillion dollars? Cheer up. There's more than one way to fly to Mars. (Krauss, 1997, p. 59)

Of course, few if any of the magazine's readers have that much money. This line, and the slightly ironic "Cheer up," are intended to create a sense of comfortableness in the audience and tone down what might otherwise be an intimidating technical topic.

Suspense and Mystery

One common feature you might have noticed in all of the previous examples is that, to differing extents, each invokes a sense of suspense and mystery. Sometimes this suspense is created by a science fiction-like story, such as the introduction to the article about dinosaurs, which invites audience members to join the tale and learn more. Other times, as in the influenza outbreak story, this suspense comes in the form of a mystery: Why did those seven people die, and what do scientists know today about such outbreaks? Another way to create this suspense is to do something mentioned in Chapter 7, and that is to leave your audience with a sense of dissonance. (Dissonance is a feeling where things are just a bit unsettled.) In an article about melatonin, a purported sleep aid sold in health food stores, one author starts her article this way:

> As we drift into sleep, our temperatures drop, our metabolisms slow, and a chemical called melatonin begins to circulate in the blood. Melatonin is made in tiny amounts by the pineal gland, a quarter-inch-long gland at the base of the brain, and little is known about the hormone's effects on the body. Nonetheless, health food stores around the country sell bottles of melatonin, billing it as soporific, and thousands of users tout its powers. Yet there is now evidence that melatonin not only sometimes fails to promote sleep but in fact disrupts it. (Preiser, 1997, p. 28)

Notice how this introduction begins with some basic information but then quickly shifts into a mode whereby audience members feel concerned about the effects of taking melatonin. By using the transitions "nonetheless" and "yet," the author signals a contrast between what the audience might have heard about how good melatonin is on the one hand and certain potential dangers associated with taking the supplement on the other hand. This contrast sets up a tension, or dissonance, and audience members want to learn more about the topic.

Using These Techniques for Oral Presentations

At this point, you may be wondering how you can use the techniques of these journalists for your own oral presentations. In general, you should be able to translate what these writers did into ideas you can use when introducing your own scientific or technical presentations. But there are a few things you'll need to watch out for when doing this.

Don't Overdo the Storytelling

In a written article, it's often acceptable to take a little while to tell an introductory story before beginning the main body of the piece, especially if the format of the article allows for a bit of length. In oral presentations, audiences do not have the advantage of looking down at a piece of paper to help them stay on track. They are listening intently to your introduction and hoping you will get to the point so that they can follow the rest of your talk. So, although some of these examples are excellent ways to start a written piece, they might be too long or too hard to follow for an oral presentation. Storytelling and suspense are great ways to introduce your technical presentation, but don't go into too much detail or people will lose track of what you are telling them. Also, remember that part of your responsibility is to balance the creative aspects of your presentation with the accurate reporting of the technical or scientific information.

Keep It Short

Along the same lines, you should keep the introductory material short, concise, and in proportion to the rest of your presentation. If you are giving a ten- to twelve-minute presentation, your entire introduction should probably be no longer than two or three minutes. Stories and suspenseful narratives sometimes have a way of taking on a life of their own. Time your introduction, including all the other important parts (overview of your presentation; credibility statement), and, when you get up to deliver your actual presentation, don't allow yourself to run any longer than the length of time you practiced.

Make It Appropriate for the Audience

The techniques used by the journalists in the previous examples are useful illustrations of how to connect scientific and technical topics to the public. Yet you cannot simply use one of these techniques at random. It's still important to do as much of an audience analysis as possible. In a way, imagine that there are many types of "public." A lecture at a university might yield an audience with a certain educational level; a presentation for local high school students would yield quite another. The techniques you choose in your introduction should be appropriate for the particular "public" you'll be addressing, and you can determine what might be appropriate by performing a careful audience and purpose analysis.

Remember Your Responsibility

As you've learned in other parts of this book, it's usually appropriate to be excited and enthusiastic about your role in bringing important, cutting-edge scientific and technical information to the public. A strong introduction, based on the techniques illustrated in this chapter, can add to this enthusiasm. But be sure that you are also responsible about making your information clear, accurate, and as precise as possible.

Make It Oral and Natural, Not Written and Scripted

The previous examples sound great in writing, but they may not all work very well in an oral presentation. As mentioned earlier, you shouldn't write down your introduction word for word: If you do, then forget your place while speaking, you'll become confused and falter. Instead, use the ancient art of human memory to remind yourself of what you will say. Telling a story is one of the most natural of human abilities. If you think one of the techniques used by the journalists will be appropriate for your presentation, make an outline of the story, then practice it in your own natural speaking style.

Return to the Story or Idea during the Body and Conclusion

Don't just use these techniques to start your presentation. A narrative or suspenseful story can give your presentation a theme that works its way through the presentation. Also, if you begin with a compelling story or personal note about the scientist or engineer, return to this idea during the conclusion of the presentation.

In Summary: Beyond Efficiency

Technical presentations should be designed to go beyond efficiency—to reach out to the audience's imagination and sense of interest and wonder in science and technology. By doing so, technical communicators help make a difference in science and technology culture. Journalists who specialize in science and technology writing offer some useful techniques for making scientific and technical topics compelling to an audience. These techniques include appealing to science fiction and the imagination, linking to a timely event, using narrative, connecting to the personal scientist, using irony, and creating suspense and mystery. These advanced techniques will make your presentation appealing and enjoyable for your audience.

QUESTIONS / EXERCISES / ASSIGNMENTS

1. Prepare a short informative presentation (five or six minutes) in which you describe your responsibilities as a technical communicator—either at your current job or internship or as you might see these responsibilities in your future career.

2. Find several articles in a science or technology magazine and look for both positive and negative features in how the writer used language to make the topic accessible to a lay audience. Prepare a short informative presentation (five or six minutes) outlining your findings and explaining which of these positive features you could use in an oral presentation.

Presentations and Cyberspace. A number of Web pages offer excellent examples of making science and technology accessible, exciting, and important for the public. Two good examples are the informational pages for the Lawrence Berkeley National Laboratory (www.lbl.gov/LBL-PID/LBL-Overview.html) or the Los Alamos National Laboratory (www.lanl.gov/external/welcome/). Look at these and other science or technology Web pages, and note what features are used. Consider how you might use similar features in a scientific or technical presentation.

Presentations and Teamwork. As a team, review the informative presentations you gave after studying Chapter 9. Select a few that deal with overtly scientific or technical topics. Using one of the techniques illustrated in this chapter, create a new introduction and conclusion. List the characteristics you are assuming about your public audience.

Presentations and International Communication. Remaining competitive in the new global marketplace means keeping up with new developments and advances in technology and processes. However, as other countries are often involved in the same industry, some information required to remain on the cutting edge is often published in another language. Identify the languages that might be important to your given field and determine what non-English publications might contain information essential to being competitive in your field.

Presentations and Your Profession. Talk to one or several professionals in your field, and ask them about instances when they must give presentations that make their technical knowledge useful and interesting to the public. Ask them about what responsibilities they feel in this role.

REFERENCES

Gladwell, M. (1997, September 29). The dead zone. *New Yorker,* pp. 52–65.
Guterl, F. (1997, March). Beauty and magnets. *Discover,* pp. 38–43.
Krauss, L. M. (1997, May). It's only rocket science. *Discover,* pp. 59–62.
Mack, W. N., & Leistikow, E. A. (1996, August). Sands of the world. *Scientific American,* pp. 62–67.
Menon, S. (1998, April). King claw. *Discover,* p. 30.
Porush, D. (1995). *A short guide to writing about science.* New York: HarperCollins.
Preiser, R. (1997, March). Sleep and snake oil. *Discover,* p. 28.

CHAPTER

14 Shifting Science and Technology to the Public

CHAPTER OVERVIEW

The previous chapter discussed advanced techniques for creating introductions that draw audiences into highly technical or complex topics by way of stories, humor, and suspense. This chapter examines several additional advanced concepts—genre shifts and stasis theory—and illustrates how you can use these concepts to shift from an overly complex, scientific or technical content to content that is meaningful to mixed audiences. This chapter covers the following topics:

- More Lessons from Science and Technology Journalism
- Genre: Shifting Modes
- Stasis: Shifting Points of Interest

More Lessons from Science and Technology Journalism

As you learned in the previous chapter, science and technology journalists have developed many techniques for making complex subject matter interesting and relevant for the public. By creating introductions to their articles that are compelling, story-like, and personal, these writers help readers connect to the topic and thus entice them to read on. By using these same techniques, presenters can intrigue their audiences, enticing them to continue listening to a scientific or technical presentation. In Chapter 13, you learned several of these techniques and practiced using these to create introductions for your technical presentations.

In a similar fashion, many science and technology writers have a knack for making the body of their article, the subject matter itself, useful and interesting for a public audience. As with introductions, the techniques for dealing with highly complex technical content can be used not only for written material but also for oral presentations.

Classical rhetoric provides two concepts that help explain how these writers make technical content accessible for a mixed audience. These concepts are *genre* and *stasis theory.*

Genre: Shifting Modes

Genre is a French word generally defined as a particular category of creative or expressive work (such as painting, music, film, literature) that is categorized as such due to certain unique characteristics (such as content, style, or tone). For example, expressionism may be considered one genre of painting; blues may be considered a genre of music. When Aristotle studied the types of speeches given in ancient Greece, he determined that these speeches fell into three distinct genres: forensic, deliberative, and epideictic. Forensic rhetoric involved speeches that dealt with issues of the past: In a court of law, for example, lawyers often debate past actions, such as a crime that has been committed. Deliberative rhetoric dealt with issues of the future: Governing bodies, such as Congress, often deal in deliberative rhetoric as they debate new programs for education, health care, and so on. Epideictic rhetoric was based in the present and involved speeches that praised or blamed, such as acceptance speeches at an awards ceremony.

Jeanne Fahnestock, a professor of rhetoric who has studied how scientific information is written for public audiences, has successfully used Aristotle's three concepts to explain how communicators make the shift from science communicated to scientists to science communicated to a mixed audience. Her technique involves finding a scientific study that's become popularized: for example, a study about a new cancer medication that is being featured on the local news and in the papers. By looking at the original study, written by and for scientists, and then looking at the television or newspaper version, she noticed that writers of the popularized pieces had intentionally made a genre shift to help readers understand the complex material. Though these writers may not have known anything about Aristotle or his conceptions of genre, these categories provide a way to make technical content, whether in writing or in an oral presentation, more accessible and useful to a mixed audience. In doing so, you take seriously your responsibility as technical communicators to help people understand groundbreaking advances in science, medicine, and technology.

Following Fahnestock's suggestions, here is a pair of articles addressing the same topic. The first article is from a scientific journal called *Behavioral Ecology & Sociobiology* and is written for an audience of scientists (Figure 14.1). The title is "Male-male association patterns and female proximity in the guppy, *Poecilia reticulata.*" The second article, based on the same study but written for a mixed audience of *New York Times* readers, is titled "Males, Take Heed: Guppies Offer a Tip On Attracting a Mate" (Figure 14.2). Read these articles and pay careful attention to what the writers are doing with language.

Even without any detailed analysis, you can clearly tell that the scientific article ("Male-male association patterns") sounds typically scientific, understandable only to a select audience of people trained in this field—insiders who know and use the jargon and concepts of this area of biological study. The *New York Times* article, however, is snappy, easy to understand, and much more suited for a mixed audience. What you may also have noticed is that, unfortunately, the scientific article sounds a lot like the kind of difficult-to-understand information usually associated with science and technology. Often, when writers or presenters are asked to

Lee Alan Dugatkin • Robert Craig Sargent

Male-male association patterns and female proximity in the guppy, *Poecilia reticulata*

Received: 24 October 1993, Accepted after revision: 30 May 1994

Abstract If males differ in their ability to attract potential mates, and are able to perceive such differences, theory predicts they should distribute themselves in a manner that increases their probability of obtaining potential matings. The relationship between male-male association patterns and the proximity of females in social groups, however, remains virtually unexplored. Experimental analysis of this relationship in the guppy, *Poecilia reticulata*, demonstrates that in preference tests males showed a strong tendency to associate with other males that were further away from potential mates than they were themselves. Male guppies pursue a behavioral strategy that involves categorizing other males based on their proximity (and possibly relative attractiveness) to females, remembering the identity of such individuals, and using this information when choosing between other males as associates. Such a strategy may increase a male's chances of being the individual chosen by a female assessing nearby males.

Key words Association pattern • Mate choice • Guppy

Introduction

If males are able to assess their relative attractiveness to females, then females may play a role in the structuring of (behavioral) association patterns within group-living species, by providing information that males may use when choosing conspecifics with whom to associate. If this proves to be the case, the logic of ideal free distribution models (Brown 1969; Fretwell 1972; Sutherland and Parker 1985; Parker and Sutherland 1986), wherein potential matings are a resource that either directly or indirectly affects the distribution of male behavioral association patterns, may be heuristic. At least three very different outcomes are possible: males may ignore, or be unable to assess, information on their relative attractiveness to females when choosing between other males with whom to associate; they may choose to associate with males whom they view as more attractive than themselves; or they may prefer to associate with other males that are viewed as less attractive. Dependent on the type of mating system, any of these possibilities may increase a male's subsequent probability of mating, either by being chosen by a female, or by engaging in a 'sneak' copulation. For example, in lek breeding species, evidence suggests that satellite males station themselves near territorial males and 'intercept' females on their way to such territories (Wells 1977; Fellers 1979; Gatz 1981; Bradbury and Gibson 1983; Höglund and Robertson 1990). Under such conditions, one might predict that satellites would associate with other males who are viewed as more attractive. Such studies, however, normally lack the controls necessary to rule out alternative hypotheses. For example, it is often very difficult to separate 'hot shots' (males that attract many females) from 'hot spots' (areas that females prefer) (Wiley 1991; but see Höglund and Robertson 1990 and Clutton-Brock et al. 1989 for exceptions).

No study to date has examined whether males tend to avoid, rather than associate with, more attractive conspecifics. Such a preference on the part of males might evolve in non-territorial systems, in which females assess male quality and attempt to mate with the most attractive of the males they have sampled (Real 1991). Here, we investigated whether proximity to females might influence male association patterns in the guppy, *Poecilia reticulata.* Although the cohesion of groups depends on the level of predation pressure (Seghers 1973), the guppy is typically classified as a schooling fish with a mating system that is non-resource based and non-territorial (Liley and Seghers 1975). Female guppies assess males as potential mates on various

L.A. Dugatkin (✉)
Division of Biological Sciences, University of Missouri, Columbia, Missouri, USA

R.C. Sargent
Center for Evolutionary Ecology,
T.H. Morgan School of Biological Sciences,
University of Kentucky, Lexington, KY 40506–0225, USA

FIGURE 14.1 From *Behavioral Ecology & Sociobiology*, for an audience of scientists.

Source: Dugatkin, L. A., & Sargent, R. C. (1994). Male-male association patterns and female proximity in the guppy, *Poecilia reticulata*. *Behavioral Ecology & Sociobiology, 35*, 141. Reprinted with permission.

Males, Take Heed: Guppies Offer a Tip on Attracting a Mate

By NATALIE ANGIER

Gentlemen! Ask yourselves the following question. If you were hoping to attract the woman of your fantasies over to your table in a bar, would you rather be sitting next to a guy who looks like Mel Gibson, or like Jerry Lewis in "The Nutty Professor"? Against which backdrop are you likelier to shine, or even appear visible at all? Think carefully and realistically—the future of your chromosomes may depend upon it.

Scientists have devoted thousands of hours studying the details of how female animals choose their mates and how that pickiness drives the evolution of male finery and flamboyance. They have also looked at how males fight one another for access to those females, engaging in ritualistic displays of sound and fury known among biologists as male-male competition.

Now researchers have discovered a new twist to the struts and frets of animal courtship. They have found that a male will preferentially congregate with other males who have proved to be lousy Lotharios, the better to appear himself as a comely alternative—or at least the lesser of two evils.

Studying the behavior of guppies, colorful little fish that have made sizable contributions to evolutionary science, Dr. Lee Alan Dugatkin of the University of Missouri in Columbia and Dr. Robert Craig Sargent of the University of Kentucky in Lexington have determined that males will observe the performance of their competitors, to see which the females prefer and which they avoid. When given a choice to swim beside a loser at love or a winner, the observing males overwhelmingly opt to situate themselves cheek by gill with the chump.

The latest results, which appear in the current issue of the journal Behavioral Ecology and Sociobiology, not only demonstrate that males will go to any length to appear good to females, but that even fish with brains as small as pinheads are capable of surprisingly sophisticated social behavior.

"This kind of behavior requires an if-then sequence of thought," said Dr. Dugatkin. "If I see a particular outcome with another male, then I behave accordingly. It's not the sort of ability you normally expect from a guppy."

Dr. David Sloan Wilson, a professor of biology at the State University of New York at Binghamton, said of the research, "The message that comes out of all these stories is that we have to revise upwards our estimates of the cognitive abilities of nonhuman animals."

Dr. Dugatkin had earlier shown that female fish often make their choice of a mate through imitation, observing which male their peers prefer and then picking the same male. The latest research suggests that males, too, act on their assessments of their peers, though to very different ends.

In the experiments, the scientists rigged up a tank with various partitions to place fish closer together or farther apart. They allowed a male to observe a female swimming in a tank with another male that either was permitted to be close to her or was kept away from her by an invisible partition. The distance between the female and the male under observation served as a controllable proxy for her preference. In general, the closer a female guppy stays to a male, the more she fancies him.

The observing male was then put in a tank with both the faux winner and faux loser in the battle for the female's affections. In 24 out of 30 independent trials with 30 different sets of guppies, the observing male swam right over to the part of the tank where the loser was kept, and lingered there as though he just happened to like his company.

To assure that the observing male was not merely responding to indirect cues from the victorious male, whose recent proximity to a female could in theory have aroused him and made him

Continued on Page B11

FIGURE 14.2 From *The New York Times*, for a mixed audience.

Guppies and a Tip on Attracting a Mate

Continued From Page B5

more aggressive and unapproachable, the scientists also did the same experiments without letting male No. 1 observe the interactions between the two males and the female. When the male had no clue who had been beside the female and who had been kept away, he chose to swim beside one or another with equal frequency.

Dr. Dugatkin admits that the experiment was performed under artificial laboratory conditions. He hopes soon to observe the guppies in their native Trinidad to see if they perform similarly in the wild. Nevertheless, he proposes the results are meaningful in their surprising consistency. Among guppies, which aggregate in loose schools of 15 to 100 fish, males cannot monopolize territories or harems and therefore have trouble making themselves stand out to potential mates. Finding a less attractive foil to underscore one's graces may be a male's easiest route to reproductive success. Dr. Dugatkin also suggests that such a strategy of conquest by contrast is not likely to be limited to guppies, but may apply to other social animals like birds, dolphins or primates, in which individuals are perpetually assessing the strengths and weaknesses of their neighbors.

Even a fish with a tiny brain uses a social stratagem.

"I wouldn't hesitate to say the same things may be going on with humans," Dr. Dugatkin said. He is hoping to do experiments shortly to see if people, like guppies, choose their cruising companions in part to make themselves appear the choicest catch of the sea.

FIGURE 14.2 *(continued)*

write or give a talk about a subject they know well, what they come up with sounds just like the "Male-male association patterns" article. That's because most technical experts have difficulty speaking to public audiences, and that's where your role as a communicator comes in. How can you use the concept of genre to explain what the "Males, Take Heed" author did, and how can you use this concept in your own oral presentations?

To answer these questions, return to the work of Aristotle and Fahnestock. In her own analyses, Fahnestock illustrates how you can use genre theory to explain what is happening in each of these articles. The scientific article ("Male-male association") would, in her analysis, be considered a forensic piece—forensic because it primarily analyzes something that happened in the past (a study performed by these scientists) and debates these actions (how the study was conducted, what it meant in the context of other scientific data, and so on). The popularized article ("Males, Take Heed"), she would say, is an epideictic piece—though it does discuss the study, it does not dwell on the fine points of what happened as much as it explains the study in the context of the present, beginning with an introduction that connects the study to a scenario that could be happening to anyone at any time. Instead of debating the actions of the study itself, the second piece celebrates the study, using glowing language and an air of excitement.

According to Fahnestock, the shift from the forensic genre to the epideictic genre is one technique used by science and technology journalists to move information from the scientific sphere into the realm of the public. By shifting the analytical, forensic style of scientific communication into the more invigorating, celebratory, epideictic mode, communicators take specialized information and make it useful and interesting to a non-expert audience. By looking more closely at each article and noticing the features of language that change with this genre shift, you should be able to use these features to create the body of your oral presentation on a scientific or technical topic.

Create Excitement and Enthusiasm

Perhaps the first difference of interest between the two articles is the shift in tone from an objective, nonemotional, scientific tone to one of excitement and enthusiasm. This shift is immediately apparent in the titles. The scientific paper's title, "Male-male association patterns and female proximity in the guppy, *Poecilia reticulata*," may appeal to other biologists who are studying this subject. But such a title does little to excite a mixed audience. The concept of "male-male association patterns" is probably not familiar to those outside this field of science. And the Latin name for guppy, *Poecilia reticulata,* would do little to capture the interest of a non-expert audience. In the *New York Times* article, "Males, Take Heed," a short title written in the imperative voice, catches an audience's attention immediately. It's intriguing, and audiences would wonder about its meaning.

Within the article itself, this same sense of enthusiasm is evident. Futuristic lines such as "the future of your chromosomes may depend on it" convey a sense of the unknown, using the sort of science fiction-like appeal mentioned in the previous chapter; descriptive phrases like "the evolution of male finery and flamboyance" add excitement and a sense of color and texture to the article. And, whereas the scientific paper makes no mention of how many hours were spent performing the study, the popularized version explains that "[s]cientists have devoted thousands of hours" studying this subject. "Thousands of hours" also conveys a sense of excitement and interest and suggests that this is an important topic. Remember to strike a balance when using these techniques—don't overuse dramatic lines at the expense of providing your audience with accurate information. It only takes a little bit of enthusiasm to help retain audience interest.

For oral presentations to mixed audiences that involve complex technical information, make sure that the body of your presentation doesn't digress into a specialized discussion, interesting only to others in the field and devoid of any excitement or enthusiasm. Use language that is rich with the importance of the material you are discussing.

Use an Effective Introduction

Following the standard practice of most scientific papers, the "Male-male association" article doesn't really have an introduction of the sort you have learned about in this book. There is no attempt to grab the audience's attention with a story or anecdote; no science fiction-like overtones; no appeals based on the personal nature of the scientists. Instead, it begins by jumping directly into the main subject: "If males are able to assess their relative attractiveness to females, then females may play a role in the structuring of (behavioral) association patterns. . . ." In "Males, Take Heed," however, the author knows that mixed audiences would not have any idea what this first sentence means. So the author uses several techniques described in Chapter 13 to create an introduction that catches the audience's attention and makes them want to read further. The subtitle "Guppies Offer a Tip On Attracting a Mate" is obviously of a broader appeal than the title of the scientific paper. Even if a reader were happily in a relationship, she or he still might be curious to see what guppies could possibly have to do with the idea of dating.

This aspect of the genre shift from a forensic paper to an epideictic one reinforces something we've discussed throughout this book—make sure you have a very interesting, well-crafted introduction that is best suited for your specific audience.

Speak in First Person

In science and technology writing and speaking, the passive voice is often used. If you've taken a technical writing course lately, you probably know that passive voice is the combination of the verb "to be" and another verb. Passive constructions usually do not have any identifiable sense of who is doing the action. In the first sentence of this paragraph, for example, you read the phrase "the passive voice is often used." This phrase is passive. You have the verb "to be" ("is") along with the other verb ("used"). The active construction would be "Scientists use the passive voice": "scientists" is the subject, "use" is the verb, and you can tell who is doing the action.

Scientists and engineers often write in passive voice for many reasons. Probably the biggest reason is that in these fields, it often is not important to know who performed the action. The data, not the scientists, take the lead role. For example, in "Male-male association patterns," under the section "Materials and methods," the authors note that "[p]reference was determined by examining whether the focal spent more time in the third of the tank near the winner or loser." This passive construction ("[p]reference was determined") would be active if stated as "We determined the preference." But in this case, the scientists probably felt that the method of determining the preference was more important than who did it.

For scientists and engineers, passive voice is often a way of life, and although many in these fields are learning to speak and write in active voice, within their specialized communities of other scientists and engineers, passive voice is often acceptable. Passive voice is also used to avoid blame; the famous saying "A mistake was made" is a classic example of how passive voice can be used so that no person or organization would need to be blamed. When presenting to mixed audiences, active voice is easier to understand and generally a better choice. In the third paragraph of "Males, Take Heed," the author chooses an active construction to explain the work to a mixed audience: "Now researchers have discovered a new twist."

In oral presentations that involve complex technical information for mixed audiences, try to use active voice. If you are used to speaking in passive voice, you will probably need to practice using active voice in order to change your habits.

Use Shorter Sentences

Notice the first sentence of the "Male-male association" article:

> If males are able to assess their relative attractiveness to females, then females may play a role in the structuring of (behavioral) association patterns within group-living species, by providing information that males may use when choosing conspecifics with whom to associate.

This is simply too long a sentence for a mixed audience to understand. Along with containing a good deal of jargon, it is difficult to follow because of the amount of information contained in this one unit of thought. The popularized article, in contrast, begins with very short statements:

> Gentlemen! Ask yourselves the following question.

Generally, when shifting from a scientific, technical, or other specialized audience, you should use shorter sentences. Unlike writing, where authors do not need to stop and take a breath, oral presentations tend to force people to use shorter sentences anyway. Still, be careful not to conflate too many ideas into one sentence, or your audience will not be able to follow you.

Use Simpler Language

Another obvious difference between the scientific paper and the *New York Times* article is in the uses of language. The scientific paper is written for an audience of biologists. It can, therefore, make use of all the specialized language of that field: "(behavioral) association patterns," "group-living species," "conspecifics." The *New York Times* article, on the other hand, must make this information accessible to a far wider audience of mixed backgrounds; thus, it uses far less specialized language: "the details of how female animals choose their mates," "make their choice through imitation." As discussed elsewhere in this book, effective and interesting oral presentations use language that is at the appropriate level for a given audience.

Remember Your Responsibilities

As you "translate" from science and technology to the public, you are taking on an important job. Your presentation should be suited for its audience, but at the same time, you should not shortchange your audience of valuable information. Sometimes, people use the phrase "to dumb down" when they talk about how to make information accessible to wider audiences. Yet this phrase is insulting and doesn't reflect the truth. A good piece of technical communication, written or oral, does not make anything "dumb," and it does not cut corners. It selects the most useful information for a given audience and makes that information exciting, interesting, and useful while at the same time keeps the information accurate. It also tries hard to keep the sometimes subtle distinctions clear to its new audience. For example,

Fahnestock noticed that in most scientific papers, scientists were careful to "hedge" their conclusions, noting that their findings may need further research or are still questionable, but in most popularized accounts of the same studies, these findings were stated as if they were final or conclusive (1986, p. 287). By overstating the original scientific claims, the communicator robs the audience of a chance to actually see how science is done—cautiously, and through repeated experiments. Therefore, when you are preparing oral presentations for mixed audiences, don't be overly dramatic, and try keeping the scientific or technical information as accurate as possible.

Watch for Offensive or Stereotypical Language

In an attempt to shift information from the highly scientific or technical to the public sphere, communicators sometimes make the mistake of using a story line that, although it may appeal to many, is offensive and therefore not useful to others. The "Males, Take Heed" article, for example, might be amusing to some, but others might find it offensive to read the initial story about how men can pick up women in a bar. Still others, who might look a little bit like Jerry Lewis, might not enjoy the connotation that they will be unable to meet a partner due entirely to their looks. The introduction to "Males, Take Heed" may actually deter some people from reading the article. So, for your oral presentations, be sure to watch for offensive language or stories that, although they may appeal to some audience members, will offend others. Some of this choice comes in the form of good taste; other times, you will need to rely on your audience analysis to know what your audience will listen to.

Stasis: Shifting Points of Interest

Another technique from classical rhetoric that is useful in making complex information accessible for mixed audiences is an ancient idea called *stasis theory.* Several rhetoric scholars who study scientific and technical communication, such as Jeanne Fahnestock and Lawrence Prelli, have used stasis theory to examine what happens when scientific and technical information is conveyed to non-expert audiences. Stasis theory provides a useful framework for understanding how complex topics can be made interesting to mixed audiences.

Stasis theory is based on work by the Roman teacher of rhetoric, Cicero. His work in rhetoric was designed primarily to teach lawyers about the most effective ways of making arguments in the courts. Yet his stasis theory has withheld the test of time and is useful for technical communication as well.

Basically, stasis theory suggests that most communication involves four stasis points, or points where the discussion is focused. These questions are

1st stasis	Conjectural	Is it?
2nd stasis	Definitional	What is it?
3rd stasis	Qualitative	Of what nature?
4th stasis	Translative	What procedures should be followed?

Arguments or communication that are focused in the first and second stasis deal primarily with defining the issue at hand. The conjectural, or first stasis, asks "is it?"—in other words, it asks if a phenomonon actually exists. The definitional, or second stasis, asks for a definition of the phenomenon: If in fact this thing exists, what is it? How do we define it? Arguments in the third and fourth stasis focus more on the policy and procedural nature of the issue at hand: What is the nature of this thing (third stasis), and how should we deal with it (fourth stasis)?

Fahnestock shows that most scientific papers are involved in questions of the first and second stasis. Scientists and engineers who report their experiments are usually writing or presenting for others in their field, and the main goal of the communication is to prove conjectural and definitional items. Scientific papers often ask and answer questions in these two stasis points, questions such as "does this phenomenon exist?" (first stasis: conjectural) and "what shall we call it?" (second stasis: definitional).

In communication designed for a mixed audience, however, the focus shifts. Public audiences generally are less concerned with questions about the phenomenon itself than they are with issues in the third and fourth stasis: What is the nature of this event, and how will it affect me? In the two articles about guppy mating habits, it is clear that the scientific article focuses on reporting the experiment and establishing that 1) a phenomenon did occur (first stasis: conjectural), and 2) the phenomenon is as they described it (second stasis: definitional). The popularized article, on the other hand, focuses on the broader nature of the study and on how this study might affect humans; instead of reporting the specifics of how the study was conducted, the *Times* article reveals how this study might affect people's lives (perhaps help people to meet a mate, for example).

In two articles, one from a scientific journal and the other from the *New York Times*, you can see the same shift in stasis point. The scientific paper, published in *Nature* (Figure 14.3), reports the results of the study and stays focused on the first two stasis points. It establishes that a particular study took place and that a particular set of results were obtained by the researchers. The popularized piece (Figure 14.4) illustrates a shift away from the data and experiment and toward questions related to human use, even beginning with an introductory paragraph that asks direct questions of its audience ("Do you remember where you went on your first date? Or the most terrifying scene of the last movie that really frightened you?"). These questions focus not on the data or results of the study, but on the human impact this study might have. Research that might help people with their memory could be of benefit to many. The *New York Times* writer designed communication that focused on the nature of the study and the possible procedures that might arise from this study. Again, as with the guppy article, you can see a shift from the first and second stasis questions to the third and fourth.

So, how can stasis theory help you with oral presentations for technical communication? In short, what a stasis-based analysis suggests is that when communicating science and technology to mixed, public audiences, the focus should be on how this information might affect or connect to your audience members. Will the results of a new study lead to new medications, advances in information technology, or less expensive ways to feed the growing world population? The lesson to be

β-Adrenergic activation and memory for emotional events

Larry Cahill*, Bruce Prins†, Michael Weber†‡ & James L. McGaugh*

* Center for the Neurobiology of Learning and Memory, and Department of Psychobiology, University of California, Irvine, California 92717-3800, USA
†Hypertension Center, Long Beach Veteran's Affairs Medical Center, Long Beach, California 90822, USA
‡Department of Medicine, University of California, Irvine, California 92717-4075, USA

SUBSTANTIAL evidence from animal studies suggests that enhanced memory associated with emotional arousal results from an activation of β-adrenergic stress hormone systems during and after an emotional experience[1-3]. To examine this implication in human subjects, we investigated the effect of the β-adrenergic receptor antagonist propranolol hydrochloride on long-term memory for an emotionally arousing short story, or a closely matched but more emotionally neutral story. We report here that propranolol significantly impaired memory of the emotionally arousing story but did not affect memory of the emotionally neutral story. The impairing effect of propranolol on memory of the emotional story was not due either to reduced emotional responsiveness or to nonspecific sedative or attentional effects. The results support the hypothesis that enhanced memory associated with emotional experiences involves activation of the β-adrenergic system.

Subjects received either propranolol or a placebo 1 h before viewing a series of slides accompanied by an emotional or neutral narrative, and were tested for memory of the story one week later (see Fig. 1 for methods). The stories were those used in an earlier study demonstrating an enhancing effect of emotional arousal on memory (L.C. and J.L. McG., manuscript in preparation), and were developed from earlier work by other investigators demonstrating enhancing effects of emotional arousal on memory[4] (Box 1). If the enhanced memory for the emotional story involved activation of β-adrenergic receptors (either centrally or peripherally), then blockade of those receptors should impair memory for the emotional story, while leaving memory for the neutral story relatively unaffected. Our results confirm this prediction.

The memory test results revealed significant and selective effects of propranolol on memory of the emotional story. Focusing first on the free recall results, we examined the mean number of slides recalled (out of 12 possible). The placebo subjects who viewed the emotional story recalled significantly more slides (6.0±0.6) than did propranolol subjects (4.09 ± 0.55) (t (17) = 2.33, P< 0.05). In contrast, the placebo and propranolol groups who viewed the neutral story did not differ in the number of slides recalled. Similar results were obtained in an 80-item multiple-choice recognition memory test (which assessed memory for both visual and narrative story elements). Placebo subjects who viewed the emotional story answered signficantly more questions correctly (48.9 ± 1.47) than did the propranolol subjects (42.4 ± 1.72) (t(17) = 2.73, P<0.02). The placebo and propranolol groups who viewed the neutral story did not differ in number of questions correctly answered.

The enhancing effects of emotional activation on recognition memory and the impairing effects of propranolol on emotionally enhanced memory were obtained primarily in story phase 2, the phase in which the emotional elements were introduced (Fig. 1). The placebo subjects displayed superior memory for those story elements associated with emotional arousal, whereas the propranolol subjects did not. A 2-factor ANOVA for the arousal story results with repeated measures on the story phase revealed significant effects of the drug treatment (P<0.05) and story phase (P<0.01). Subjects in the placebo/arousal story condition answered significantly more phase 2 questions correctly than either phase 1 (P<0.01) or phase 3 (P<0.05) questions. Furthermore, and most importantly, the retention performance of the placebo group was significantly better than that of the propranolol group for questions pertaining to phase 2 of the arousal story (P0.02). In contrast, for subjects

BOX 1 Narratives accompanying slide presentation

Slide	Neutral version	Arousal version
1.	A mother and her son are leaving home in the morning.	A mother and her son are leaving home in the morning.
2.	She is taking him to visit his father's workplace.	She is taking him to visit his father's workplace.
3.	The father is a laboratory technician at Victory Memorial Hospital.	The father is a laboratory technician at Victory Memorial Hospital.
4.	They check before crossing a busy road.	They check before crossing a busy road.
5.	While walking along, the boy sees some wrecked cars in a junk yard, which he finds interesting.	While crossing the road, the boy is caught in a terrible accident, which critically injures him.
6.	At the hospital, the staff are preparing for a practice disaster drill, which the boy will watch.	At the hospital, the staff prepare the emergency room, to which the boy is rushed.
7.	An image from a brain scan machine used in the drill attracts the boy's interest.	An image from a brain scan machine used in a trauma situation shows severe bleeding in the boy's brain.
8.	All morning long, a surgical team practised the disaster drill procedures.	All morning long, a surgical team struggled to save the boy's life.
9.	Make-up artists were able to create realistic-looking injuries on actors for the drill.	Specialized surgeons were able to re-attach the boy's severed feet.
10.	After the drill, while the father watched the boy, the mother left to phone her other child's pre-school.	After the surgery, while the father stayed with the boy, the mother left to phone her other child's pre-school.
11.	Running a little late, she phones the pre-school to tell them she will soon pick up her child.	Feeling distraught, she phones the pre-school to tell them she will soon pick up her child.
12.	Heading to pick up her child, she hails a taxi at the number nine bus stop.	Heading to pick up her child, she hails a taxi at the number nine bus stop.

FIGURE 14.3 Scientific journal article uses conjectural and definitional stasis points.

Source: Reprinted by permission from Nature, 371, 702.

New Kind of Memory Found to Preserve Moments of Emotion

By DANIEL GOLEMAN

Do you remember where you went on your first date? Or the most terrifying scene of the last movie that really frightened you? Or what you were doing when you heard the news that the space shuttle Challenger had blown up?

The fact that most people have detailed answers for such questions testifies to the power of emotion-arousing events to sear a lasting impression in memory.

Scientists believe they have now identified the simple but cunning method that makes emotional moments register with such potency: it is the very same alerting system that primes the body to react to life-threatening emergencies by fighting or fleeing.

The "fight or flight" reaction has long been known to physiologists: the heart beats faster, the muscles are readied and the body is primed in the most primitive of survival instincts. These and other distinctive reactions are triggered by the release into the bloodstream of the hormones adrenaline and noradrenaline.

The same two hormones, it now appears, also prime the brain to take very special note in its memory banks of the circumstance that set off the flight-or-fight reaction.

The discovery "suggests that the brain has two memory systems, one for ordinary information and one for emotionally charged information," said Dr. Larry Cahill, a researcher at the Center for the Neurobiology of Learning and Memory at the University of California at Irvine. Dr. Cahill and colleagues published the findings in the current issue of the journal Nature.

The emotional memory system may have evolved because it had great survival value, researchers say, insuring that animals would vividly remember the events and circumstances most threatening to them. The findings confirm in humans the relevance of 15 years of research on the neurochemistry of memory with laboratory rats by Dr. James L. McGaugh, director of

Adrenaline makes mind take snapshot of fraught events.

the Irvine center and a co-author of the paper. His work with animals had implicated adrenaline and noradrenaline in emotional arousal and memory.

"I think it's very exciting," said Dr. McGau-

Continued on Page B10

FIGURE 14.4 Newspaper article uses qualitative and translative stasis points.

learned from the ancient concept of stasis theory is this: When designing oral presentations for mixed audiences, keep in mind that these audiences will be primarily interested in how they can interpret the information in ways that are meaningful to them and their daily lives.

In Summary: Shifting Information to the Public

In this chapter, you have learned two advanced theories from rhetoric to help you create presentations that make scientific and technical information accessible, exciting, and useful to mixed audiences. These techniques, genre and stasis theory, require you to shift information from a scientific or technical stance to a public one. Such a shift involves a more excited and enthusiastic tone, effective introductions, language and word choice, and a focus on the stasis points of how such information will apply to your audience's everyday lives.

QUESTIONS / EXERCISES / ASSIGNMENTS

1. Begin to notice how scientific and technical information is presented in the media, and look for examples of the genre shifts and stasis shifts described in this chapter. Look in the newspaper, in popular science magazines, on the radio, and on television. Keep a list of both positive and negative features used by the writer or speaker when shifting science and technology into the public. Discuss these in class.

2. Go back to your first informative presentation, and redesign the body of this presentation using some of the concepts and techniques described in this chapter.

Presentations and Cyberspace. The Web could easily be considered the largest public forum in the world. Anyone with the right computer connections can begin surfing through vast amounts of information. Some of this information is designed to present science and technology to the public, whereas other sites are clearly designed only for specialists in those fields. Do a Web search on a topic that is related to your career or of interest to you. Locate ten to twelve Websites. Note which of these are designed for the public, and analyze these for the features described in this chapter (genre, stasis). Does the Web make it easier or more difficult to present complex information to mixed audiences? What special challenges are faced by Web designers who choose to create these sorts of pages?

Presentations and Teamwork. With your study group, identify and videotape a television program focusing on a scientific or technical topic in your field, and suitable for a mixed audience (alternatively, locate an article in the general press focusing on a scientific or technical topic in your field). Identify the techniques used to make the technical content accessible to the mixed audience and discuss the effectiveness of these techniques.

Presentations and International Communication. Talk with someone who presents scientific and technical information to international audiences. Discuss the use of genre and stasis theory in such presentations, and ask how he or she uses those and any other concepts to deliver effective presentations.

Presentations and Your Profession. Talk with a professional in your field and ask what techniques and strategies he or she uses to explain technical information when speaking to a mixed audience.

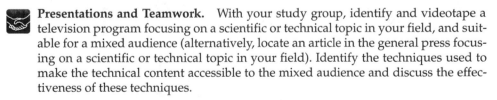

REFERENCES

Angier, N. (1994, November 8). Males, take heed: Guppies offer a tip on attracting a mate. *New York Times*, pp. B-5, B-11.

Cahill, L., Prins, B., Weber, M., & McGaugh, J. L. (1994). ß-Adrenergic activation and memory for emotional events. *Nature, 371,* 702.

Dugatkin, L. A., & Sargent, R. C. (1994). Male-male association patterns and female proximity in the guppy, *Poecilia reticulata. Behavioral Ecology & Sociobiology, 35,* 141–145.

Fahnestock, J. (1986). Accommodating science: The rhetorical life of scientific facts. *Written Communication, 3*(3), 275–296.

Goleman, D. (1994, October 25). New kind of memory found to preserve moments of emotion. *New York Times*, pp. B-5, B-10.

Prelli, L. J. (1989). *A rhetoric of science: Inventing scientific discourse.* Columbia: University of South Carolina Press.

Rude, C. D. (1998). *Technical Editing*. 2nd ed. Boston: Allyn & Bacon.

Williams, J. M. (1997). *Style: Ten lessons in clarity and grace.* 5th ed. New York: Longman.

CHAPTER

15 Using Analogy to Explain Technical Ideas

CHAPTER OVERVIEW

This chapter continues the discussion of advanced concepts and techniques for making complex technical information accessible to your audience. Chapter 13 discussed introductions; Chapter 14 discussed theories you can use to make the body of your presentation more directed to a mixed audience. Chapter 15 offers another technique, using analogies, that will make your technical information appealing and understandable. This chapter covers the following topics:

- What Are Analogies?
- The Power of the Familiar
- Analogies in Scientific and Technical Communication
- Using Analogies Wisely

What Are Analogies?

An analogy is a comparison of two ideas that are similar or that somehow explain each other. Even without thinking about it, you use analogies every day—either to explain new ideas and concepts or to understand them. As you'll discover in this chapter, analogies are powerful rhetorical devices that work because humans learn well when they can connect new, abstract ideas to familiar, tangible ones.

There are many ways in which analogy can be used. Probably the two with which you are most familiar are the *simile* and the *metaphor.* Both of these figures of speech work by comparing two ideas: an idea the audience is often familiar with, and a new idea. Similes usually are constructed with the words "as" or "like;" for example:

> Your computer filing system is like a large file cabinet.

Metaphors, on the other hand, make a direct mapping of one concept to another, leaving out the "like" or "as":

> Your computer filing system is essentially a large file cabinet.

Notice that in both examples, the rather basic concept of a file cabinet is used to help the audience understand the more complex idea of a set of computer files. Most people know that computer files are actually made up of digital data, where information is represented in the computer by the numbers 1 and 0. But that concept is a bit abstract, so connecting it by analogy to something more tangible and familiar (a file cabinet) helps the audience link this abstract idea to something they understand and are familiar with.

Throughout the rest of this chapter, the term "analogy" will be used to mean both similes and metaphors as well as other forms of analogy (other types of comparisons that don't necessarily use the constructions of the metaphor or simile).

The Power of the Familiar

When you use analogies to explain a complex idea, you are drawing upon one of the very fundamental ways in which humans learn. According to Lakoff and Johnson, two researchers whose book on metaphor is widely cited, people tend to think of metaphor only as window-dressing: pretty words and ideas that can be used to dress up ideas. But, they argue, metaphor (they use "metaphor" in a broad sense, to mean all kinds of analogizing) is more than a "rhetorical flourish." Indeed, they say, metaphors are "pervasive in everyday life, not just in language but in thought and action. Our ordinary conceptual system, in terms of which we both think and act, is fundamentally metaphorical in nature" (1980, p. 3). In other words, at a very basic level, humans learn by analogy—by comparing new, unfamiliar ideas with concepts and ideas that they already understand.

For Lakoff and Johnson, "the essence of metaphor is understanding and experiencing one thing in terms of another" (1980. p. 5), and "its primary function is understanding" (1980, p. 36). So, when a computer filing system is described in terms of a filing cabinet, audiences are able to understand one thing (computers) in terms of another (filing cabinets). Though these researchers were not describing the job of a technical communicator, they very well might have been when they noted that "[b]ecause so many of the concepts that are important to us are either abstract or not clearly delineated in our experience . . . we need to get a grasp on them by means of other concepts that we understand in clearer terms" (1980, p. 115). As you have learned throughout this book, the world of science and technology is becoming more and more complex. New ideas that are important to the public are often abstract, technical, and difficult (if not impossible) to understand unless these ideas can be linked to concepts that these audiences are familiar with.

The idea of using metaphors, similes, and other analogies to help audiences learn is certainly not new. Aristotle, more than 2,000 years ago, recognized the power of a good metaphor. Today, psychologists and education specialists rely on the concept of *schema theory* to explain how audiences learn. This theory provides solid evidence for what Aristotle observed in the power of analogy, for it states that people learn best if a new idea is linked to a schema, that is, a "collection of ideas and the relationships among them that form a category that the learner 'understands' " (Gagné, 1985, p. 168). In other words, when people can connect new concepts to things they already understand and for which they already have existing mental categories, they will learn far more quickly and accurately.

In previous chapters, this point has already been made by suggesting that you use introductions that connect with your audience or that you change the focus to the third and fourth stasis, which involve questions that matter to the audience. This chapter examines the use of analogic language (metaphors and similes) to see how these features can work in oral presentations.

Analogies in Scientific and Technical Communication

Analogies abound in scientific and technical communication; in fact, one author goes so far as to say that "[i]n a way, the very essence of [scientific communication] is oftentimes an analogic construction" (Harmon, 1994, p. 182). If you think about it, this makes a good deal of sense. Many scientific and technical concepts are abstract and often cannot be seen by human eyes, and in these cases, a good analogy is sometimes the only way to make new ideas take on any sort of understandable form or shape.

Analogies have played a large role in the history of scientific and technical communication. An early example is seen in the writings of Charles Darwin, the nineteenth-century scientist generally credited with advancing the theory of natural selection (evolution). As Darwin attempted to explain his theory of natural selection to a mixed audience of other scientists, church officials (the Catholic church was very involved in science at that time), and the public, he compared his theory with animal breeding, something that was familiar and understandable to his audience (Campbell, 1986; Gross, 1996).

Other uses of analogy have been even more overt. Notice this line from T. H. Huxley, a scientist who also studied evolution and natural selection. It is from a public lecture he gave in 1863:

> A horse is not a mere dead structure: it is an active, living machine.

And, in 1950, almost 100 years later, anatomy professor J. Z. Young included this line in a lecture:

> The model of the body as a machine has been the basis of much of the most useful part of our biology.

These sentences use the metaphors of the horse and the human body as a machine. In doing so, the speaker will now be able to explain the complexities of biology, something unfamiliar to their audiences, using the familiar machine metaphor as a basis. Huxley goes on to explain how a horse's digestive system is like a large factory:

> [The horse's] jaws are working as a mill—and a very complex mill, too—grinding the corn, or crushing the grass to a pulp.

For audiences of Huxley's time, the metaphor of horse as machine, particularly his comparison of the horse's digestive system to a mill, was very understandable—most citizens of this agrarian period in England were familiar with the mills that ground the corn, wheat, and other grains that came from local farms.

In 1953, when James Watson and Francis Crick described their discovery of the shape of the human DNA molecule, they, too, relied on metaphor to explain their findings. Two rhetoric scholars who have studied the writings of these famous geneticists note that when describing how DNA passes its genetic information along, Watson and Crick used the metaphor of a human messenger. This metaphor "adds presence and life to an idea that is otherwise remote and lifeless," say these rhetoric scholars (Halloran & Bradford, 1984, p. 184). Thus, metaphor and analogy not only help connect new ideas to familiar ones, they can also lend excitement and life to a concept that might seem flat, too technical, or too difficult to conceptualize.

These examples show how analogy has been used historically in scientific and technical communication. In today's digital, information-saturated society, analogies continue as useful tools for making technical information understandable to mixed audiences. In science and technology communication, powerful uses of analogy often help audiences understand complex topics. For example, in an article about computer hackers, one author uses the following analogy to describe the online chat program known as "Internet Relay Chat":

> Sitting at his home computer one night, Abednego logs on to the Internet Relay Chat, the cyberspace equivalent of CB radio. (Meinel, 1998, p. 98)

By comparing Internet Relay Chat, something her audience may not know about, with the more familiar CB radio, something she assumes (and hopefully has researched, via audience analysis) her audience understands, this author helps people learn about a new idea via the familiar concept of something they already know.

The more closely you look and listen, the more you will see how analogies play a major role in how people communicate. Everywhere, you will hear similes such as "the human brain is one big computer" or "our ecosystem is a living entity." Particularly when communicating new, difficult-to-understand topics, analogies are the primary way in which audiences learn this new knowledge. Analogies also can bring excitement and dimension to an otherwise abstract topic.

Using Analogies Wisely

The previous examples illustrate the power of using analogy to explain scientific and technical concepts. You will want to experiment with using analogy in your own oral presentations so you can use this technique to make your topic understandable for your audience. There are some tips for using analogies wisely, however, and you can review these here.

Determine Your Use

Harmon (1998, p. 180) lists four basic uses of metaphor and analogy in scientific communication.

1. *To introduce colorful imagery.* In these cases, a presenter uses analogies to give energy and excitement to something that might otherwise seem boring or flat. The idea of DNA as a messenger, described earlier, is one example. Because audiences listen more closely when technical topics are expressed with excitement, using analogy to add energy to your topic may be effective.

2. *To convey information that would be difficult to express with ordinary language.* Sometimes, a topic is too abstract to be understandable with ordinary, nonanalogic language. For example, when Watson and Crick described how the two strands of DNA connect together, they used the analogy of a zipper (Halloran & Bradford, 1984, p. 188). A zipper is something people can understand and visualize far more easily than a tiny, abstract DNA molecule.

3. *To express something in a more concise fashion than with ordinary language.* A good analogy often sums up an idea that would take a lot of words to explain. Again, drawing on the Watson and Crick analogy of a zipper to explain the structure of DNA, it's easy to see how the idea of a zipper conveys so much with so few words. Zippers connect two sides of a pair together; they interlock each side, and so on.

4. *To aid in problem solving.* Many times, a good metaphor or simile provides such a stable and understandable framework for an abstract idea that the metaphor itself helps people solve scientific or technical problems. When students learn basic chemistry in high school, for example, they often are told to think of molecules as structures that look like Tinkertoy combinations of balls and sticks. From this analogy, students are then able to visualize how a hydrogen atom connects to a carbon one and how larger molecules are made up of smaller ones. So, an analogy of this sort will be useful if you are trying to help your audience understand how something works or how to solve a particular problem.

Align Analogies with Your Audience

An analogy is only effective if it connects to your audience's frame of reference. Unless you align your analogies with your audience's understandings, the analogy will not make sense and, in fact, could cause confusion. This confusion can be especially problematic if you are speaking to an international audience. What makes sense to one culture might have no meaning to another; as one author of a book on international technical communication puts it, "metaphors and similes can introduce culture-specific, industry-specific, or company-specific references that may make no sense to your target audience" (Hoft, 1995, p. 225). So, make sure you consider the backgrounds of your audience as you look for analogies to explain your topics.

Adapt If Your Audience Doesn't Understand the Analogy

If you begin your presentation with a series of analogies but notice that your audience is not following the connections you are trying to make, you should be prepared to scrap the metaphor and use another technique to make your point. Don't base your entire presentation around a single analogy unless you know this analogy will work. For instance, if Huxley were to return and use his analogy of a grinding mill to explain the biological structures of a horse, he would soon discover that most twenty-first-century United States citizens don't know anything about grinding mills! Be prepared to explain your idea in several different ways.

Avoid Mixed Metaphors

Metaphors and similes work well as long as you do not stray and begin to mix several different concepts at the same time. For example, if you begin by comparing the workings of a computer to those of the human brain, you will get your audience thinking in one direction. If later you begin comparing the computer to cable television, you might confuse your audience.

Use Analogies Responsibly

As Lakoff and Johnson clearly illustrate, analogies are not just neutral ideas to convey information. They carry cultural and political overtones, and, especially if the subject of your presentation is new for your audience, the analogies you choose will affect how they view this topic. If you choose to describe a computer as something like a human brain, for example, you are making a statement about how computers may someday be able to think and make decisions like humans. You are also suggesting that humans operate in purely logical states, like computers, where decisions are based not on emotions but on ones and zeros. Earlier in this chapter, you learned about Huxley's description of a horse as a machine. This analogy suggests that horses are more mechanical than flesh-and-bone; more of a commodity and a money-making apparatus than a living thing. As a technical communicator, responsible for helping the public understand science and technology, you must choose your metaphors wisely, because the ways you present information will form the public's perception of many important new ideas.

Use Analogies Sparingly

Too many analogies can be confusing for an audience. Try only using analogies in certain key moments, where the analogy is truly needed to explain or illuminate your topic. Analogies work well when they are used sparingly and in the appropriate moments. If you make too many comparisons, your audience will not be able to learn what you are trying to convey.

In Summary: Using Analogy

Technical presentations can be enhanced if the presenter learns how to properly harness the power of analogy. Analogies, in the form of similes and metaphors, have been used throughout history to help explain scientific and technical concepts. These techniques work because they connect new, complex ideas that are unfamiliar for an audience to older, more familiar concepts. By relying on this process and using analogy, you will help your audience understand, enjoy, and be able to visualize your topic. Analogies should be aligned with your audience's frame of reference, and you should be ready to adapt if your analogy is not working. You should also use analogies consistently (avoiding mixed metaphors), responsibly, and sparingly.

QUESTIONS / EXERCISES / ASSIGNMENTS

1. One of the easiest ways to practice using analogies is the following: Select a topic that you know well but that would be new, slightly difficult knowledge for a class of sixth graders. Make a list of possible analogies you could use to explain your topic to this audience. Your analogies should be suited for a sixth-grade audience, so if you are not familiar with children of that age group, you'll need to do some audience analysis to determine what these children know and understand. But because most people have some exposure to children, it is very natural to explain new concepts to them and to do so via analogy.

2. Take the same topic in question #1, but choose a new audience: adults, not children. Select an audience you are familiar with (classmates, neighbors, coworkers). Make a list of the analogies you might use to teach them about this new topic. Note how these analogies differ from the ones you selected to present to children.

Presentations and Cyberspace. Perform a search on the Web for a scientific or technical topic that interests you. Locate ten to twelve sites related to the topic and look at these for uses of analogy. Examine these analogies with a group of your classmates: For what sort of audience were each of these analogies created? Are there some analogies that work well but others that do not? Why? Are there some Websites that encourage better presentations of technical material? Why or why not?

Presentations and Teamwork. With other classmates, attend a lecture or presentation on a scientific or technical topic. (At most universities, it's easy to find such presentations on campus.) Take notes about how the presenter uses analogies to explain the topic. As a team, present your findings to your class.

Presentations and International Communication. Analogies, especially metaphors and similes, are very culturally dependent, because they rely on common understandings about what things mean. A metaphor that might make sense to someone from the United States, for example, might not mean anything to a person from France, Japan, or India, even if that person speaks fluent English. And, if the metaphor is translated into the person's native language, it may make even less sense. Select several metaphors you might use while giving a presentation, and discuss these with a non-native speaker of English in your field. Get feedback on the effectiveness of using the metaphor in a technical presentation, and share this feedback with your class.

Presentations and Your Profession. Interview a professional in your field, and ask how he or she explains certain technical topics using analogies. Read magazine or journal articles in your field, or attend presentations, and listen for uses of analogic language. Note how you might use similar analogies in your own presentations.

REFERENCES

Campbell, J. A. (1986). Scientific revolution and the grammar of culture: The case of Darwin's "Origin." *Quarterly Journal of Speech, 72*(4), 351–376.

Gagné, R. M. (1985). *The conditions of learning.* New York: Holt, Rinehart, and Winston.

Gross, A. G. (1996). *The rhetoric of science.* Cambridge: Harvard University Press.

Halloran, S. M., & Bradford, A. N. (1984). Figures of speech in the rhetoric of science and technology. In R. J. Connors, L. S. Ede, & A. A. Lunsford (Eds.), *Essays on classical rhetoric and modern discourse* (pp. 179–192). Carbondale: Southern Illinois University Press.

Harmon, J. E. (1994). The uses of metaphor in citation classics from the scientific literature. *Technical Communication Quarterly, 3*(2), 179–194.

Hoft, N. L. (1995). *International technical communication: How to export information about high technology.* New York: Wiley.

Huxley, T. H. (orig. 1863; reprinted 1965). Six lectures to working men on the phenomena of organic nature. In J. Harrison (Ed.), *Scientists as writers* (pp. 47–48). Cambridge: MIT Press.

Lakoff, G., & Johnson, M. (1980). *Metaphors we live by.* Chicago: University of Chicago Press.

Meinel, C. P. (1998). How hackers break in . . . and how they are caught. *Scientific American, 279*(4), pp. 98–105.

Young, J. Z. (orig. 1951; reprinted 1965). Doubt and certainty in science. In J. Harrison (Ed.), *Scientists as writers* (pp. 49–51). Cambridge: MIT Press.

CHAPTER

16 Visual versus Verbal Communication

CHAPTER OVERVIEW

So far, this book has concentrated on physical techniques (memory, delivery), research techniques (performing an audience analysis, researching your topic), and verbal techniques (all aspects of language) for oral presentations. In Chapter 16, you will learn how visual communication is an important and necessary component of technical presentations. This chapter covers the following topics:

- Visual versus Verbal Communication
- Typefaces and Fonts
- Charts and Graphs
- Icons and Graphics
- Using Color

Visual versus Verbal Communication

Visual communication means communicating with more than just words. It means using drawings, diagrams, photos, charts, and other nonverbal forms to help explain new concepts and ideas to an audience. Until recently, technical communication was focused primarily on technical *writing*. Yet the use of visual information to communicate technical concepts has become increasingly important, for a variety of reasons.

International Communication. Increasingly, people speak about the world as a global marketplace. Technologies must be accessible to people who speak a variety of languages. Visual communication, including the use of symbols, can make these technologies understandable to audiences around the world.

Computers and Computer Graphics. Before the personal computer and laser printer became widely available, fancy graphics were the domain of graphic artists and other specialists. Accurate charts or color graphics were expensive to produce, so technical communication was mainly focused on words. Yet today, with desktop publishing software and laser printers, graphics are easy and inexpensive to produce. Thus, people tend to use them more.

Presentation Software and the Web. Presentation software, such as PowerPoint, makes it very simple to quickly create visuals that formerly took hours or days to make. Web software and the explosion of the Web for presenting all sorts of information also make visual communication a more dominant force in the world.

Underlying all of these global and technological changes is a basic fact about how humans learn. As one researcher put it, "[w]e all think visually" (Horton, 1991, p. 16). Visual communication is natural for humans, because people process this information with what psychologists call "preattentive vision" (Julesz, 1981), meaning that humans "process pattern information globally at a glance" (Legge, 1989). In simple terms, when people look at a visual pattern, like a chart or graph, they process it differently than text. Humans read each word of text and decipher it, but humans process visual communication as a large pattern. Because people see visual information as a whole unit, they perceive the unit quickly and efficiently.

Think of a time when you walked past a newsstand or glanced at the front page of a newspaper on your way out the door. You may have noticed a chart about the stock market, and the line on this chart was heading upward. Without even reading the text, you were able to perceive that some trend, perhaps stocks, bonds, or market prices, was on the rise. The power of the visual made this clear to you in a matter of seconds.

The natural human ability to learn from visuals, combined with the global workplace and new computer technologies, make visual communication a must for any effective oral presentation. When presenting information in front of a live audience, you have the advantage of being able to control how and when they look at your visuals. Also, unlike print, you have a variety of choices when presenting orally—PowerPoint and other technologies provide you with a multitude of backgrounds, fonts, colors, clip art, and other features that would usually be cost-prohibitive in a printed document. Some of these choices are examined in this chapter, but you will learn more about this topic in Chapter 17, which discusses presentation software.

Typefaces and Fonts

When you think of visual communication, you probably think of charts, graphs, drawings, and photos. These are visual, for certain, but before discussing these and other overtly visual forms of communication, it's important to consider the visual elements of text itself. Typefaces, fonts, and other text features are all part of communicating visually. When you create an overhead, slide, or presentation software screen, you need to choose the right combination of typefaces and fonts.

As with most visual communication, until recently typefaces and fonts were the domain of specialists: graphic artists, printers, and typographers. Before personal computers and laser printers, technical communicators relied on the equipment and

FYI

Visual Communication

Communicating visually is so important that it is really its own topic. This chapter will cover enough of the basics to get you started in your oral presentations. To learn more about visual communication in science and technology, see:

Horton, W. (1991). *Illustrating computer documentation: The art of presenting information graphically on paper and online.* New York: Wiley.

Kostelnick, C., & Roberts, D. D. 1998. *Designing visible language: Strategies for professional communicators.* Boston: Allyn & Bacon.

Tufte, E. R. (1990). *Envisioning information.* Cheshire, CT: Graphics Press.

Tufte, E. R. (1992). *The visual display of quantitative information.* Cheshire, CT: Graphics Press.

Your college or university may also offer courses in visual rhetoric or designing documents. If you are majoring in technical communication or are interested in effectively communicating technical topics, acquiring these skills is a must.

---

talent of this group of specialists to typeset plain text using appropriate typefaces and fonts. Today, even an eight-year-old child uses the word "font"; people use fonts and typesetting daily in word processing software or Web page designs.

Because typesetting is a regular part of today's communication technologies, it's important for you to understand how to use fonts and typefaces effectively. First, the terms themselves: Typeface refers to a family of type, such as Times Roman or Helvetica. Font refers to one specific item within that family, such as Times Roman 12 point bold, or Helvetica 14 point regular. In general, there are three categories of typefaces: serif, sans serif, and those that fall somewhere in between. Let's examine each of these in detail.

Serif

Serif typefaces are those whose letters have "feet," or small flourish strokes at the upper and lower end of the letter. For example, the following

ABCDEFGHIJKLMNOP
abcdefghijklmnop

is an example of Times Roman, which is probably the most familiar serif typeface. Notice the small feet that flow from the beginning and ending stroke of each letter.

Times Roman and other serif fonts are often considered the most readable, because the serifs help guide the eye from letter to letter. Also, serif typefaces are the oldest and thus, the most familiar. Serif fonts are also considered more formal.

Sans Serif

"Sans" is French for "without"; thus, sans serif typefaces do not have the feet of a serif typeface. For example, the following

ABCDEFGHIJKLMNOP
abcdefghijklmnop

represents Helvetica, a common sans serif typeface. Notice how, unlike Times Roman, Helvetica type is block type; the strokes forming its letters are straight up and down without any serifs. Helvetica and other sans serif typefaces are more modern than Times Roman and other serif fonts; thus, they convey a more modern and slightly less formal feeling.

Typefaces That Fall Somewhere in Between

In between pure serif typefaces like Times Roman and pure sans serif typefaces like Helvetica are other modern typefaces such as Optima:

ABCDEFGHIJKLMNOP
abcdefghijklmnop

In this typeface, there are no true serifs, but the letters are not purely block, either. The letters are slightly narrower in the middle and a bit wider at the edges.

Fonts

Within each typeface, you can choose a variety of different fonts. Two factors influence your choice: the font itself and its point size. Font refers to bold, italic, condensed, or other features. Here are four basic font choices in Times Roman:

ABCDEFGHIJKLMNOP
abcdefghijklmnop
(Regular)

ABCDEFGHIJKLMNOP
abcdefghijklmnop
(Bold)

ABCDEFGHIJKLMNOP
abcdefghijklmnop
(Italic)

ABCDEFGHIJKLMNOP
abcdefghijklmnop
(Bold Italic)

Within each of these fonts, you can also choose the size of the typeface. Type size is based on points, an old system of measuring type that has remained into the digital age. Type size affects legibility, as the following diagram indicates:

6	Typography is a form of visual language
7	Typography is a form of visual language
8	Typography is a form of visual language
9	Typography is a form of visual language
10	Typography is a form of visual language
11	Typography is a form of visual language
12	Typography is a form of visual language
13	Typography is a form of visual language
14	Typography is a form of visual language
15	Typography is a form of visual language
16	Typography is a form of visual language

Source: Kostelnick, C., & Roberts, D. D. (1998). *Designing visible language: Strategies for professional communicators.* Boston: Allyn & Bacon, p. 143. Reprinted by permission.

How to Choose Typefaces and Fonts for Oral Presentations

In times past, fonts were expensive. Each font was an actual physical device that the typographer purchased. For any given typeface, most typographers had four basic fonts (regular, bold, italic, bold italic). But an unusual font, such as a condensed, bold, scripted font, might not be available, because the typographer did not have any occasion to use it.

Today, however, you can change fonts and sizes with a simple click of your mouse or insertion of HTML code on a Web page. The choices are endless; there are even software packages that allow you to create a font, based on your handwriting or other features. With all of this choice, however, technical communicators must exercise discipline. Otherwise, if too many typefaces and fonts are mixed and matched, you end up with "visual noise" (Kostelnick & Roberts, 1998, p. 58); that is to say, your overuse of fonts will be so distracting that audiences will miss the message.

The following table gives basic advice on how to choose fonts for overheads (handouts would require you to use guidelines for printed material). Like all the information you design for your oral presentation, visual information, including typeface and font choice, must be based on the specific audience and purpose for that presentation.

Typefaces	Try not to mix typefaces. Stick with one family if you can. Or, use one family for the body copy and another for the headings. A good combination: Helvetica bold for headings, and Times Roman for body copy. Helvetica is best for captions and labels on charts and graphs. Sometimes, you'll need to follow your company's predetermined format for choosing typefaces and fonts for oral presentations.
Fonts	Use italic and bold sparingly. Do not overuse ALL CAPS, or people won't be able to read your overhead or other visual display.
Type size	The type size should be appropriate for the room layout and audience. Even in a small conference room, anything less than 14 point is usually hard to see when projected onto a screen (for large rooms, one expert suggests 30 point, boldface, san serif type) (Hay-Roe, 1999, p. 23). If your audience consists of older people, you may wish to increase the type size. Headings should be at least 2 points larger than body type.

Charts and Graphs

Typefaces and fonts are certainly one way of communicating visually. Charts and graphs can also be powerful tools. Especially in technical communication, where information is often numerical (statistics about a scientific study, for example), a good chart or graph can convey this data in a way that is easily understood by your audience. Like typefaces, charts and graphs used to be difficult and expensive to produce. Today, many software packages let you create complex graphs in no time at all. Charts and graphs come in a variety of styles. The following sections examine these visual aids.

Tables

A table is a good visual device to use when you are trying to show choices between different categories of information. Tables let you say a great deal with very few words. Consider the table in Figure 16.1, for example. Imagine how many words and sentences it would take to explain this information! And even then, your audience still would need to see the information in a visual format for it to be truly useful.

In print formats, tables such as Figure 16.1 can be referred to over and over if users need to reference information. But even for print, and especially for an oral presentation, this example is too complicated and contains too much information. One technical communicator noted that spreadsheets or tables containing too much information are "probably the worst type of visual aid," because the audience can never take in all of those columns and rows (Hay-Roe, 1999, p. 23). Tables displayed as part of your oral presentation should be very simple; too much information can be hard to read when projected onto a screen. If you need to present information that is too complex for an overhead or slide, try making a simpler version for your talk and bringing along handouts of more complex or detailed tables for your audience to review later.

No. 926. U.S. Postal Service Rates for Letters and Post Cards: 1958 to 1995

[Domestic airmail letters, as a separate class of service, discontinued in 1973 at 13 cents per ounce. See also *Historical Statistics, Colonial Times to 1970*, series R 188-191]

DATE OF RATE CHANGE	Letters			Postal and post cards	Express mail[1]	DATE OF RATE CHANGE	Letter			Postal and post cards	Express mail[1]
	Each oz.	First oz.	Each added oz.				Each oz.	First oz.	Each added oz.		
1958 (Aug. 1)	$0.04	(X)	(X)	$0.03	(X)	1978 (May 29)	(X)	$0.15	$0.13	$0.10	(X)
1963 (Jan. 7)	$0.05	(X)	(X)	$0.04	(X)	1981 (Mar. 22)	(X)	$0.18	$0.17	$0.12	(X)
1968 (Jan. 7)	$0.06	(X)	(X)	$0.05	(X)	1981 (Nov. 1)	(X)	$0.20	$0.17	$0.13	$9.35
1971 (May 16)	$0.08	(X)	(X)	$0.06	(X)	1985 (Feb. 17)	(X)	$0.22	$0.17	$0.14	$10.75
1974 (Mar. 2)	$0.10	(X)	(X)	$0.08	(X)	1988 (Apr. 3)	(X)	$0.25	$0.20	$0.15	[3]$12.00
1975 (Sept. 14)	(X)	$0.10	$0.09	$0.07	(X)	1991(Feb. 3)	(X)	$0.29	$0.23	$0.19	[3]$13.95
1975 (Dec. 31)[2]	(X)	$0.13	$0.11	$0.09	(X)	1995 (Jan. 1)	(X)	$0.32	$0.23	$0.20	[3]$15.00

X Not applicable. [1]Post Office to addressee rates. Rates shown are for weights up to 2 pounds, all zones. Beginning Feb. 17, 1985 for weights between 2 and 5 lbs, $12.85 is charged. Prior to Nov. 1, 1981, rate varied by weight and distances. Over 5 pounds still varies by distance. [2]As of October 11, 1975, surface mail service upgraded to level of air mail. [3]Over 8 ounces and up to 2 pounds.

FIGURE 16.1 Tables present categories of information.

Source: Houp, K., Pearsall, T. E., & Tebeaux, E. (1998). *Reporting technical information.* 9th ed. Boston: Allyn & Bacon. Reprinted by permission.

Bar Charts

A bar chart allows you to show trends and compare similar information spread over a period of time or a range of dates or costs. The bar chart in Figure 16.2 depicts various cost factors, spread over several years. Like any good piece of visual communication, this chart packs lots of information into a concise format. You can see the rising trend from 1992–1997, the breakdown of costs within each year, and the total cost per year.

As with tables, bar charts in oral presentations should be simple, clear, and easy to read. The number of bars and amount of detailed information should be visible from anywhere in the room. Axes should be labeled (the chart in Figure 16.2 could use some additional labeling on the y-axis), and further details should be saved for handouts.

Line Graphs

Line graphs illustrate trends. You are probably familiar with financial graphs; the graph in Figure 16.3 is from a newspaper business section.

Notice how this graph utilizes preattentive vision: Even without knowing what the different lines refer to, you can see that, although the top line has been higher all along, all three lines end up in roughly the same place.

Pie Charts

Pie charts illustrate the relationship of parts to a whole and to one another. The pie chart shown in Figure 16.4 portrays the relationship between different age groups (perhaps for an insurance company or a corporation) during 1988.

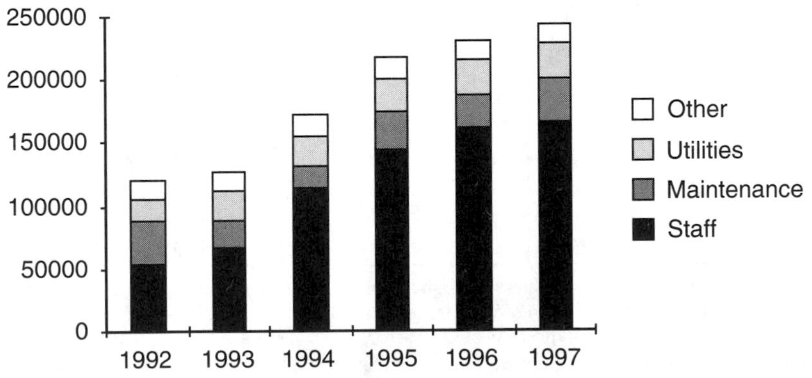

FIGURE 16.2 Bar chart shows trends and comparative information over time, dates, or costs.

Source: Kostelnick, C., & Roberts, D. D. (1998). *Designing visible language: Strategies for professional communicators.* Boston: Allyn & Bacon. Reprinted by permission.

Commodities

	$ Friday	Thursday
➤ Gold (Handy & Harman troy oz.)	$286.35	285.70
➤ Silver (Handy & Harman troy oz.)	$5.590	5.520
➤ Platinum	376.10	376.10
➤ Oil (W. Texas crude bbl.)	11.78	12.03
➤ Natural gas, gal.	1.78½	1.80
➤ Wheat (KBOT)	2.70½	2.69¼

Expanded listing, page Q5

Treasury yield curve/money rates

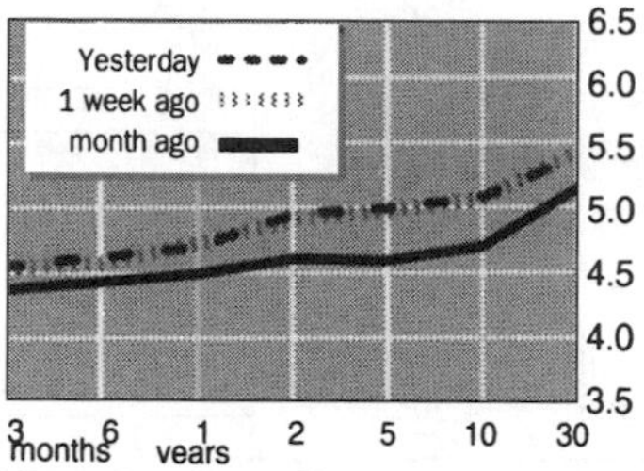

More Treasury listing, page Q5

	% Friday	%Wk. ago
➤ Bank prime rate	7.75	7.75
➤ Discount rate	4.50	4.50
➤ Fed. funds rate	4.625	4.625
➤ 3-mo. T-bill	4.54	4.52
➤ 3-mo. bank CD	4.45	4.45
➤ Money market funds avg.	4.50	
➤ Municipal bond index	5.15	5.14
➤ Fannie Mae 30-yr. mortgage	6.87	6.89
➤ 1-yr. T-bill (weekly avg.)	4.67	4.61

FIGURE 16.3 Line graph illustrates trends.

Source: Copyright © 1998, *Minneapolis Star Tribune.* Reprinted by permission.

Like most charts, pie charts are easily created with spreadsheet software. Be sure to label your pie's segments, and don't use too many different types of shading and screening to separate these segments. Like mixed typefaces, too much shading and screening can also cause visual noise.

Diagrams

We've all heard the phrase "a picture's worth a thousand words." In technical communication, especially documents and presentations that are designed to teach a user how to do something, a good diagram is invaluable. How many times have you tried to assemble something, and, after reading the instructions for only a moment or two, you find yourself turning to the diagram?

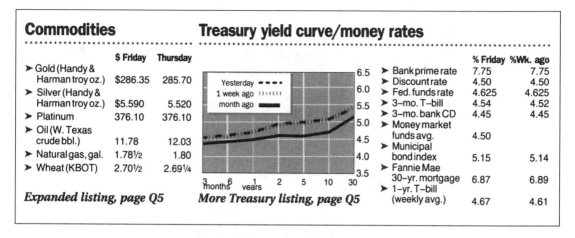

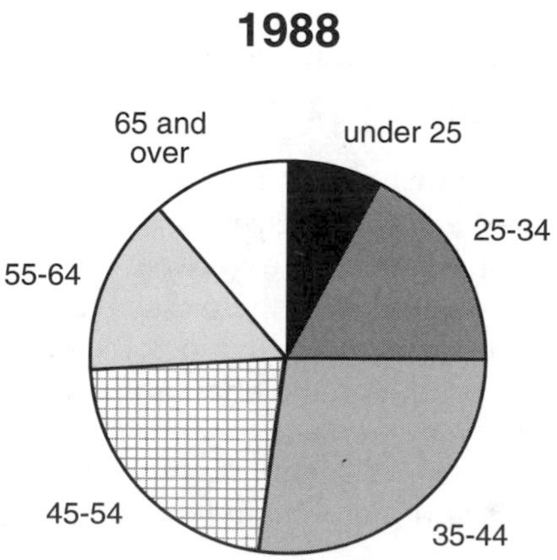

FIGURE 16.4 Pie chart illustrates relationships of parts to whole, and among parts.

Source: Kostelnick, C., & Roberts, D. D. (1998). *Designing visible language: Strategies for professional communicators.* Boston: Allyn & Bacon. Reprinted by permission.

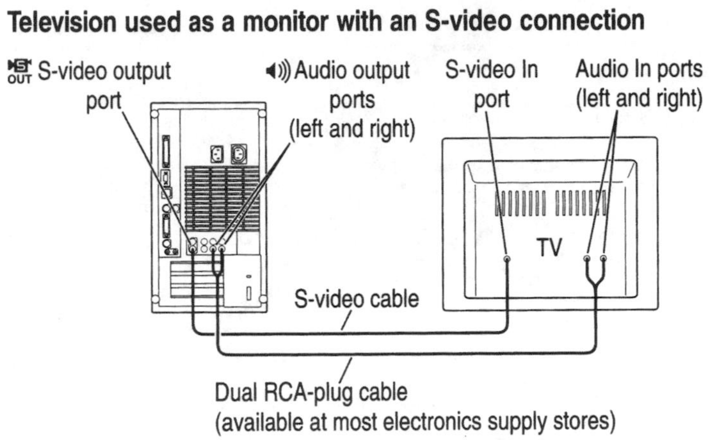

FIGURE 16.5 This diagram is too complex for an oral presentation.
Source: Diagram reprinted by permission from Apple Computers, Inc.

Diagrams should contain only as much detail as is helpful to your audience. Too much detail is usually difficult to see. The diagram in Figure 16.5 might be useful for the instruction manual, but it would be very difficult for an audience to follow at a presentation. For your presentation, you might isolate out one portion of this diagram, enlarge it, and use just that part.

How to Use Charts and Graphs in Your Oral Presentation

In the case of any of these visuals, you must choose a format that is appropriate for your presentation.

Select the Right Kind of Chart. If you want to show a trend, you would use a line graph, but if you want to show the relation of parts to a whole, you might use a pie chart.

Make Sure Your Chart Reproduces Well. Sometimes, charts that look great on your computer screen don't make very good overheads, because they contain too much detail that can't be copied when you put your chart onto a transparency. Or, you may create a wonderful chart in a spreadsheet program only to discover that when you copy that chart into your presentation software, it doesn't look the same! Test these items before spending too much time working on the final product.

Clearly Label the Chart. If you don't label things clearly, you might confuse or misguide your audience. Label all axes and parts and include a reference stating where you obtained this information.

Keep It Simple. Don't present too much information, or people won't be able to understand it. An overly complex table, for example, is very hard for people to read on an overhead.

Use an Appropriate Size. Be sure your chart is large enough for the size room in which you'll be presenting.

Test Your Visuals on a Sample Audience. Even though you may think your visual is easy to see, you should show it to a similar group of audience members and obtain their feedback before your actual presentation. What looks clear to you may be confusing to others.

Indicate Point of Visual. Explain to your audience what parts of the visual you want them to focus on. If you display a line graph with several lines, for example, you may want to direct your audience's attention to one trend in particular. The same is true for other visuals: Don't just put up the visual and expect your audience to know what to look for. Point out the important features.

Icons and Graphics

Icons and graphics are another form of visual communication that you can use effectively in your oral presentations. When you think of icons, you probably think of the symbols that are on your computer desktop—the trash can, the file folder, and more. The icons work like an analogy to represent abstract concepts by linking these concepts to things you already know; deleting a file is represented by putting something into the trash can, for example. Icons can be effective in your oral presentations, too. One nice way to use icons is to substitute them for bullets in listed items. For example, here is a standard bulleted list with plain, round bullets:

- Item A
- Item B
- Item C

Here is the same list with Apple icons:

 Item A
 Item B
 Item C

Be sure to choose icons that are somehow related to the topic of your presentation. For example, the Apple bullets might be appropriate for a presentation on Macintosh computers but would certainly not work for a presentation about PCs!

Much like icons, drawings and other graphics can also help to enliven your presentation and make information easier for your audience to understand. The drawing in Figure 16.6 adds action and adventure to a story on the possible evolutionary relationship between dinosaurs and birds. Imagine how this drawing would capture audience attention at the introduction of a presentation.

Graphics not only add life, they can help explain complex ideas. The graphic in Figure 16.7 illustrates the workings of a weather phenomenon called a bow echo, wind from a thunderstorm that can cause severe damage. This diagram is taken from a newspaper story. Would it work for an oral presentation? It may, if you were able to enlarge it and not lose too much information. Plan ahead if you wish to use something this complex.

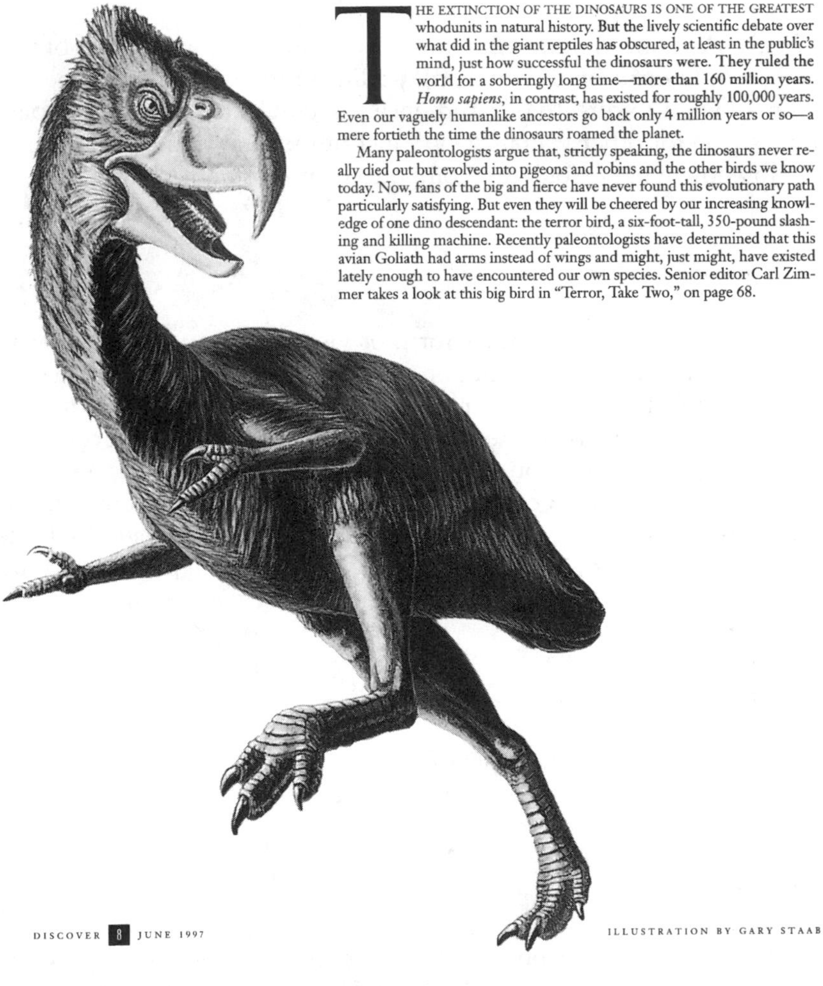

THE EXTINCTION OF THE DINOSAURS IS ONE OF THE GREATEST whodunits in natural history. But the lively scientific debate over what did in the giant reptiles has obscured, at least in the public's mind, just how successful the dinosaurs were. They ruled the world for a soberingly long time—more than 160 million years. *Homo sapiens*, in contrast, has existed for roughly 100,000 years. Even our vaguely humanlike ancestors go back only 4 million years or so—a mere fortieth the time the dinosaurs roamed the planet.

Many paleontologists argue that, strictly speaking, the dinosaurs never really died out but evolved into pigeons and robins and the other birds we know today. Now, fans of the big and fierce have never found this evolutionary path particularly satisfying. But even they will be cheered by our increasing knowledge of one dino descendant: the terror bird, a six-foot-tall, 350-pound slashing and killing machine. Recently paleontologists have determined that this avian Goliath had arms instead of wings and might, just might, have existed lately enough to have encountered our own species. Senior editor Carl Zimmer takes a look at this big bird in "Terror, Take Two," on page 68.

DISCOVER 8 JUNE 1997 ILLUSTRATION BY GARY STAAB

FIGURE 16.6 Drawings enliven a presentation and make information more understandable.

Source: Reprinted by permission of Discover Magazine.

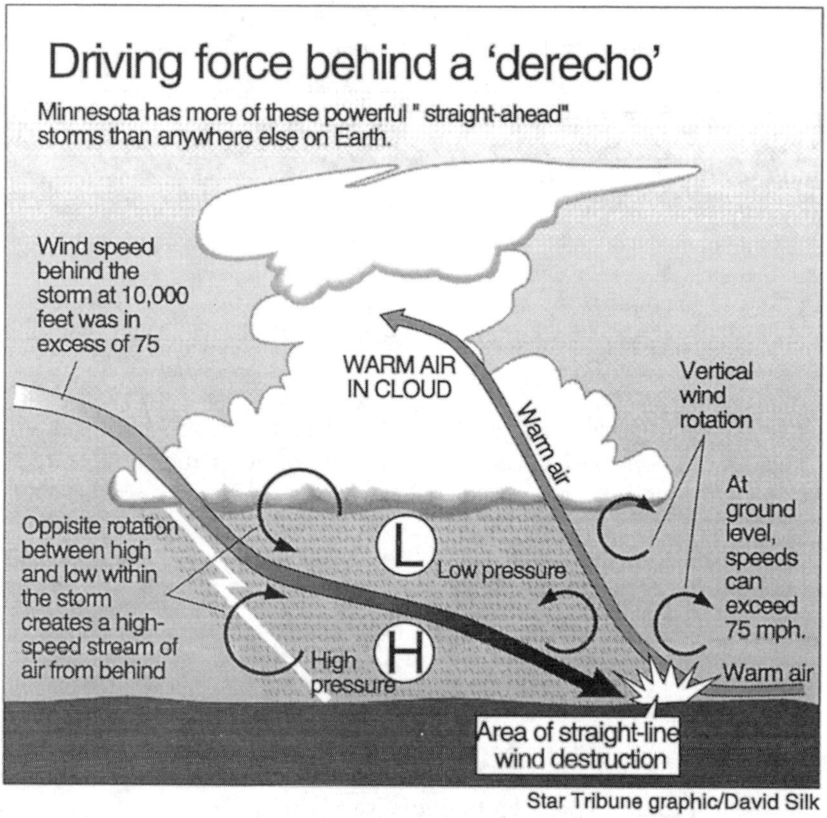

FIGURE 16.7 Graphics help explain complex ideas.

Source: Copyright © 1998, *Minneapolis Star Tribune.* Reprinted with permission.

Using Color

Color is another visual component of your oral presentations. Selective and appropriate uses of color can make your visuals truly effective. Like fonts, charts, and other visual communication, color used to be a scarce commodity. Color printing was expensive, and color overheads required hand applications of color overlay material. Today, you can use inexpensive color copiers for handouts, add color to computer projections with a few mouse clicks, or change colors on a Web page simply by modifying the HTML code. But although new technologies have simplified the technical aspects of using color, choosing the right color or color combinations is still complex.

Like most of the decisions you'll make about an oral presentation, questions about color also come down to audience and purpose. For example, if you were giving a presentation to a group affiliated with your college or university, you might choose the school colors to highlight your overhead transparencies or slides.

If you were speaking to a group of engineers or Internet designers, you might go with a wired, high tech look. Certain colors take on special meanings in different cultures around the world; red means prosperity in China but implies death in many African countries (Hoft, 1995, p. 267). Too much color, mixed together in too many combinations, may create the sort of visual noise discussed earlier and would tend to confuse your audience.

Just because you have the technology to use color doesn't mean you necessarily need to. According to one expert, there are several reasons for using color.

Audiences Enjoy Color. Color brings life and excitement to a presentation; it helps you catch people's attention. In this age of color television and Web surfing, people almost expect to see color in a presentation.

Color Helps Focus Audience Attention. Used selectively, color can help an audience focus on selected parts of your presentation. Thus, color can increase how much an audience learns.

Color Helps with Organization. Selective color use can help an audience see how your material is organized. If you use color for main headings or captions, audiences can quickly see how your visual was arranged.

Color Makes Material Resemble the Real Thing. For certain diagrams or illustrations, color can give audiences a better picture of what the actual item looks like (Horton, 1991, pp. 224–225).

However, even with color copiers, ink jet printers, and presentation software, color is still more expensive than black-and-white images. In addition, by using color, you've added a new dimension to your presentation: another aspect that will require your attention before you can give the presentation. In general, there are several guidelines to consider when determining whether to use color in your visuals.

Technology. Will you be using overhead transparencies? Slides? Presentation software? Flip charts? Each of these involves different considerations for using color. Color transparencies and slides mean that you'll need to pay a per-page or per-slide charge, and color is usually extra. Presentation software makes using color easy, but you need to be sure you've got the right computer and hookups at the presentation site (more on this in the next chapter). Flip charts or other large displays will require hand coloring or enlargements of color originals.

Cultural Considerations. As noted earlier, color and color combinations take on different meanings across different cultures. You should do a careful audience analysis to determine if certain color choices are appropriate.

Organizational Considerations. Does your company have guidelines for how you should use color in corporate communications? Many companies do, and you can often learn about these from a company style guide or someone in the marketing or communications department.

FYI

Using Color

Color, gesture, reading direction, and depictions of gender have all been identified as problematic areas in designing images for international audiences. For more on color in international communication, see:

Hoft, N. L. (1995). *International technical communication: How to export information about high technology.* New York: Wiley.

And, for more on color and visuals in communication, see:

Horton, W. (1991). *Illustrating computer documentation: The art of presenting information graphically on paper and online.* New York: Wiley.

Tufte, E. R. (1990). *Envisioning information.* Cheshire, CT: Graphics Press.

Room Lighting. What kind of lighting will be in the room where you are presenting? Colors that appear one way on your computer screen with an open window next to it will look very different in a room with fluorescent lighting or spotlighting. Check this in advance if you can.

Ergonomic Considerations. Ergonomics is the study of how certain features of technology, such as shape, size, and color, affect users' physical and psychological state. Certain colors are hard to read and can give audience members eyestrain as they try to discern what's on the screen or handout. For more information about choosing color, see the FYI feature. And always test your color choices on an audience before you give the real presentation.

Cost. Although cost continues to drop for color printing and copying, a color overhead or handout still costs more than a black-and-white one. If you are working for an organization where color presentations are expected and where the company will pay for color printing, that is one thing, but if you are a student giving a presentation for class, you may not be able to afford color.

In Summary: Visual versus Verbal Information

Visual communication is an important component of oral presentations in technical communication. Diagrams, drawings, photographs, charts, and selective color use can make scientific and technical topics more understandable and interesting for an audience, and they can clarify ideas that words alone cannot. In addition, international communication often requires visuals to help span the language gap. Graphics and presentation software make visual communication easy to incorporate into presentations.

QUESTIONS / EXERCISES / ASSIGNMENTS

1. Locate a newsletter or other printed document that contains text and information useful for a presentation you might give. Identify how you would change the print material into an effective presentation slide. Would you use different fonts? Would you use fewer colors or more colors? Would you add any other visual elements to your overhead versions of this printed document?

2. Locate a body of statistics that you might use for a presentation. For example, if you were giving a presentation about gun safety, you might locate statistics on the number of gun-related homicides in the United States for a given period. With another student, discuss the appropriate visuals you could use to convey these statistics to your audience. When would you use a bar chart? A line graph? A table?

Presentations and Cyberspace. Many excellent Web sources illustrate how complex information can be relayed in understandable visual formats. For example, the U. S. Census site (www.census.gov/hhes/income/income97/ incxrace.html) shows a line chart of U.S. median household income for 1967–1997. Locate other sources of charts and graphs on the Web for your topic of interest, and notice how these charts might be useful for your oral presentations.

Presentations and Teamwork. With two or three other students, locate a body of statistical information related to your field. If you have trouble finding this information, go to the U.S. Census site at www.census.gov and select some population data. Now, as a team, decide on a way to turn a portion of this data into a chart or graph. (You'll need to make up an audience and purpose for a sample presentation.) Using markers and a blank transparency sheet, or a computer program if you have time, create your chart or graph. Present it to your class, and explain what choices you made in creating your final design. Note the dynamics of how you worked together as a group.

Presentations and International Communication. Like language-based communication, visual communication is often culturally specific. Signs, symbols, diagrams, and charts that mean one thing to U.S. citizens might mean another thing to someone from a different culture. One author suggests, for example, that communicators should not use "any body parts or animals in icons and graphics," and that figures representing people should be androgynous (Coe, 1996, p. 304). A group called the International Standards Organization (ISO) has attempted to create cross-cultural icons; you've seen some of these in airports when you see no smoking or restroom signs. Learn more about ISO and cross-cultural visual communication by checking out the ISO Website at www.iso.ch/.

Presentations and Your Profession. Many professions have established standards for the visuals used in oral presentations: from rules about fonts and layout to standard ways of producing charts and graphs. Locate two or three people in your profession but at different organizations, and ask them about these topics. Present your findings to your class.

REFERENCES

Coe, M. (1996). *Human factors for technical communicators.* New York: Wiley.

Hay-Roe, H. (1999). How to sabotage a presentation. *Intercom, 46*(2), pp. 22–23.

Hoft, N. L. (1995). *International technical communication: How to export information about high technology.* New York: Wiley.

Horton, W. (1991). *Illustrating computer documentation: The art of presenting information graphically on paper and online.* New York: Wiley.

Houp, K., Pearsall, T. E., & Tebeaux, E. (1998). *Reporting technical information* (9th ed.). Boston: Allyn & Bacon.

Julesz, B. (1981). Textons, the elements of texture perception, and their interactions. *Nature, 290,* 91–97.

Kostelnick, C., & Roberts, D. D. (1998). *Designing visible language: Strategies for professional communicators.* Boston: Allyn & Bacon.

Legge, G. E., Gu, Y., & Luebeker, A. (1981). Efficiency of graphical perception. *Perception & Psychophysics, 46*(4), 365–374.

Tufte, E. R. (1990). *Envisioning information.* Cheshire, CT: Graphics Press.

Tufte, E. R. (1992). *The visual display of quantitative information.* Cheshire, CT: Graphics Press.

PRESENTING . . .

Peggy Durbin

Peggy Durbin has led a team of 25 technical communicators at Los Alamos National Laboratory. Before her stint in management, she was a technical writer-editor at the Laboratory for eleven years. Here are her thoughts about Part Four, Science, Technology, and Non-Expert Audiences.

Although Los Alamos National Laboratory communicates most information about its work on paper and on the Web, in my experience it also communicates much of what it does in presentations. I've helped many scientists and engineers with their presentations—particularly in managing hazardous and radioactive wastes. I've also given many presentations on safety issues.

The key to the success of the presentations is to tell a story, to put a human face on science or technology, to show how the science affects the audience's quality of life. Otherwise, such fascinating subjects as the reaction kinetics of lithium hydride can cause the audience's eyes to glaze over. It's one thing to say that responsible management of waste is important. It's quite another to tell the story of a child whose leg was blown off as she played with an unexploded munitions shell brought home from one of the canyons—before the area was cleaned up and such dangers were eliminated.

Much of the work done in the national laboratories is controversial and, of course, under taxpayer scrutiny, and a presenter must ensure that the presentation doesn't make the subject even more controversial.

For example, a comparison may make a technical concept easier for the audience to understand. However, I remind presenters to use comparisons—particularly those associated with risk—with great care. Often a presenter will compare an involuntary risk with a voluntary one—say, comparing the risk of hazardous or radioactive emissions from a waste incinerator with the risk of smoking or a high-fat diet. Such a comparison tends not to influence people's perceptions and in fact may make the audience more hostile. The audience members will say, "Smoking is my choice; having the wind blow emissions over my house is not." A better approach, I suggest to presenters, is to compare two involuntary risks: Tell how the level of a substance in a suspected contaminated area compares with natural background levels. How, for example, does the level of lead in someone's backyard compare with the average natural lead levels in soils in the United States?

When I review a presentation for a client, I look for the following elements, particularly if the technical presentation is on a potentially controversial subject:

- honesty;
- options, not answers, for the audience;
- language that the audience is comfortable with (simplify the language, not the content);
- the name of a contact person;

(continued)

PRESENTING. . . Continued

- actions that the audience can take;
- documents about the subject; the presenters can tell the audience why we wrote the documents, what the documents do, and what the audience can expect from the documents; and
- a list of related documents or other resources so that they can find more and different information.

I also do presentations myself on safety and health issues, which can be stupefyingly boring and dry. I use humor to get people's attention and make myself the butt of the joke. (As Herb Gardner, the American playwright, said, "Once you get people laughing, they're listening, and you can tell them almost anything.") I use rubber-stamped cartoons I've made myself to illustrate safety concepts. In one cartoon, I showed a bathtub dropping from the sky onto an oblivious woman. The caption was "Honoria knew that as long as she didn't use the hair dryer, the bathtub was safe."

I've used other visual aids as well. I cut the point off a push pin, affixed the head to a yellow stickie on which I had written "Safety first!" and stuck the stickie to my forehead. During my presentation on integrated safety management, my colleagues were alarmed—but attentive. The combination of humor and a hammy style seems to work: We haven't had a job-related accident or incident in almost two years.

Creating a vivid picture in the listener's mind and using humor appropriately help make controversial or dry subjects accessible to the audience.

PART FIVE

Presentations and Technologies

For many people, especially in the business world, presentation software such as PowerPoint or Lotus Freelance is their first introduction to giving an oral presentation. After all, the software, they assume, will do all the work. And with the fancy graphics and charts it can add, what else does a person need? Yet this is exactly the wrong attitude to take. Using presentation software without having basic speaking skills is like attempting to drive a fancy car before you know the rules of the road. All the technology in the world won't help if you don't know about stop signs or who has the right of way; similarly, fancy computer software won't make you a better speaker if you aren't organized, haven't done your research, or don't convey a professional ethos.

Think of presentation software as a tool to be used after you have mastered the basic principles of public speaking and after you have learned how to construct a presentation dealing with complex technical information. Once you understand and can work with these basics, presentation software will be the icing on the cake—it can enhance an already high-quality presentation.

CHAPTER

17 Using Presentation Software

CHAPTER OVERVIEW

In today's world of laptop computers and digitized images and sound, most presenters are expected at one time or another to use presentation software. This software can make a good presentation even better, but it isn't a substitute for the basic skills of an effective presenter. Chapter 17 reviews the pluses and minuses of using presentation software and offers you suggestions for making the software work to enhance your role as a powerful presenter. This chapter covers the following topics:

- What Is Presentation Software?
- The Two Faces of Presentation Software
- How to Make Presentation Software Work for You (and Not the Other Way Around!)
- Examples of Presentation Software

What Is Presentation Software?

Presentation software allows you to enter text, images, sound, and more, and turn this information into visually attractive presentation slides. These slides can be projected from your computer through a special computer projector onto a large screen. By simply clicking the mouse or pressing a keyboard key, you change the slides from one to another. You can make text and images move across the screen in various ways by using what are called transitions; you can use color, background images, numerous typefaces, and more, quite easily—and you can change these with little difficulty. There are several brands of presentation software on the market; Microsoft PowerPoint is probably the most widely used. Others include Lotus Freelance and Adobe Persuasion.

In general, presentation software works as follows. First, you design your presentation, according to the techniques you've learned so far—performing an audience and purpose analysis, researching the topic, and using appropriate rhetorical techniques. Next, you use the presentation software to create slides outlining your introduction, main points, and conclusion. You can scan images or import electronic clip art or other graphics files. Using the software's various features, you add color, a nice background image, graphics, and transitions. Sometimes, you rely on the software's easy-to-use templates and let the software choose fonts and layout. Then, you practice the presentation, much as you always would, but you practice with your electronic slide show.

Presentation software generally allows you to output your material in various forms. You can project images from the computer onto a screen, or you can print images and make overhead projection transparencies. Some software also lets you output images to standard 35mm slides for use with a traditional slide projector. You can also print images with speaker notes to help guide you through your talk, and you can make copies for use as audience handouts.

A note about the use of the word "slide" in this context: When you think of a slide, you probably think of the 35mm kind that fits into slide carousels. With presentation software, the word "slide" means the one-page image you create with the software and project on a screen or turn into a transparency (or even into a 35 mm slide). The word "slide" will be used in this way throughout this chapter.

The Two Faces of Presentation Software

Presentation software has, some might say, revolutionized the world of oral presentations. A presentation that might have taken days to prepare can now be put together in hours: color, formatting, visuals, and more are far easier to use with presentation software than with old-fashioned methods. In addition, the templates and wizards that come with some presentation software provide pre-arranged slides for the introduction, body, and conclusion. These templates basically walk the user through the designing of slides, inserting bullets, putting things in columns, and more.

Yet when presenters rely solely on presentation software to do their job, they usually come up short. As we've discussed throughout this book, excellent presentations come about because the presenter has a clear sense of his or her audience and purpose. The presenter has worked through basic nervousness and knows about creating credibility. The presenter understands the important and difficult task of making complex science and technology accessible to different audiences, and he or she has carefully used certain rhetorical techniques to make sure that audiences will be interested in the topic and will understand the material. In other words, good presentations are not made by presentation software. They are made by skilled communicators who use the presentation software as a tool to enhance their already well-designed presentation.

In this way, presentation software has two faces: a positive side, ready to work for you and help you give an even better presentation, and a negative side, ready to make your life more difficult and bring down even the finest presentations. The next sections review each side and discuss techniques you can use to avoid the negative side.

The Positive Side of Presentation Software

Relatively Easy to Use. Most presentation software has the look and feel of word processing software, so you don't need to learn many new features just to do basic slides. Notice in Figure 17.1 how the screen sample and menu features from Microsoft PowerPoint closely resemble Microsoft Word. The same is true for other presentation software: The buttons and icons will be familiar to most computer users.

Helps You Stay Organized and Aids Memory. Any kind of visual aid, especially slides and overhead transparencies, can keep you organized and help you remember. When you put your main points into a bulleted list, you give yourself memory joggers. By putting your presentation into a series of slides, you also force yourself to follow the format and stay organized.

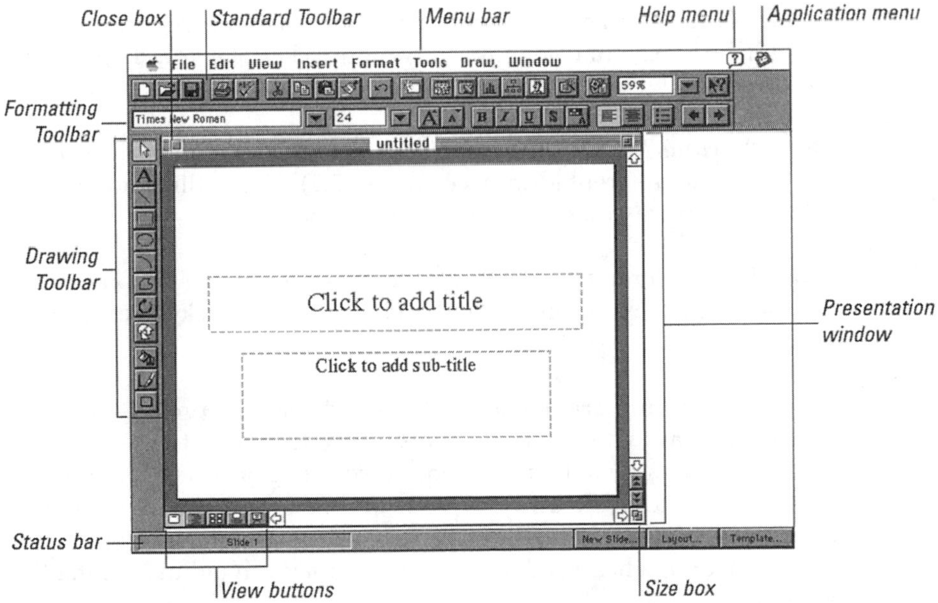

FIGURE 17.1 Presentation software screens resemble those of word processing software.

Source: Microsoft PowerPoint4 for the Macintosh Step by Step. (1994). Redmond, WA: Microsoft Press. Screenshots reprinted with permission from Microsoft Corporation.

Offers Speaker Notes. Presentation software lets you add something called speaker notes—notes to yourself that don't show up when you display your slides to your audience but can be seen when you are working on the presentation and will print out on whatever handouts you make for yourself. This feature is especially useful if you are preparing a presentation for someone else to give: You can include notes that might be things you'd remember to say but might not come naturally to another presenter.

Allows File Sharing. What if you are preparing a presentation for someone who works in a different physical location? Presentation software files can usually be sent as email attachments or on a disk. Also, what if some potential audience members couldn't attend the presentation? Although they'd miss the full experience of you presenting, you can still share your files with them so they at least get an idea of what you presented.

Provides Templates. The templates that are provided with presentation software essentially make many of the design decisions for you. These templates supply the layout, typeface, font, font sizes, and background. All you need to do is plug in your text.

Makes Color Cheap and Easy. Once you own a computer and projector, you never have to pay for color. Just a few mouse clicks let you change the color of text, backgrounds, bullets, and more.

Offers Various Modes to View Slides. Most presentation software lets you view your slides in different forms (see Figure 17.2). The outline mode is especially useful when you are first preparing a presentation.

Provides Numerous Backgrounds and Fonts. Even if you create your slides with a template, you can still add and change the backgrounds, fonts, and other visual features.

Offers Interesting Transitions. In the language of presentation software, transitions are ways you can make slides move from one to the other or make individual items on a slide appear on the screen. For example, you can make new slides appear to fizzle away, or you can make bulleted items move in, one at a time, from left to right on the screen. Transitions add life and motion to your presentation, and, when used in moderation, they can aid in keeping the audience's attention.

Imports Files from Other Applications. Most presentation software lets you import information you've created in other applications, such as charts and graphs from spreadsheets or drawings from paint programs.

Allows You to Scan Images. You can also scan diagrams, photos, or other illustrative material and include these items in your presentation.

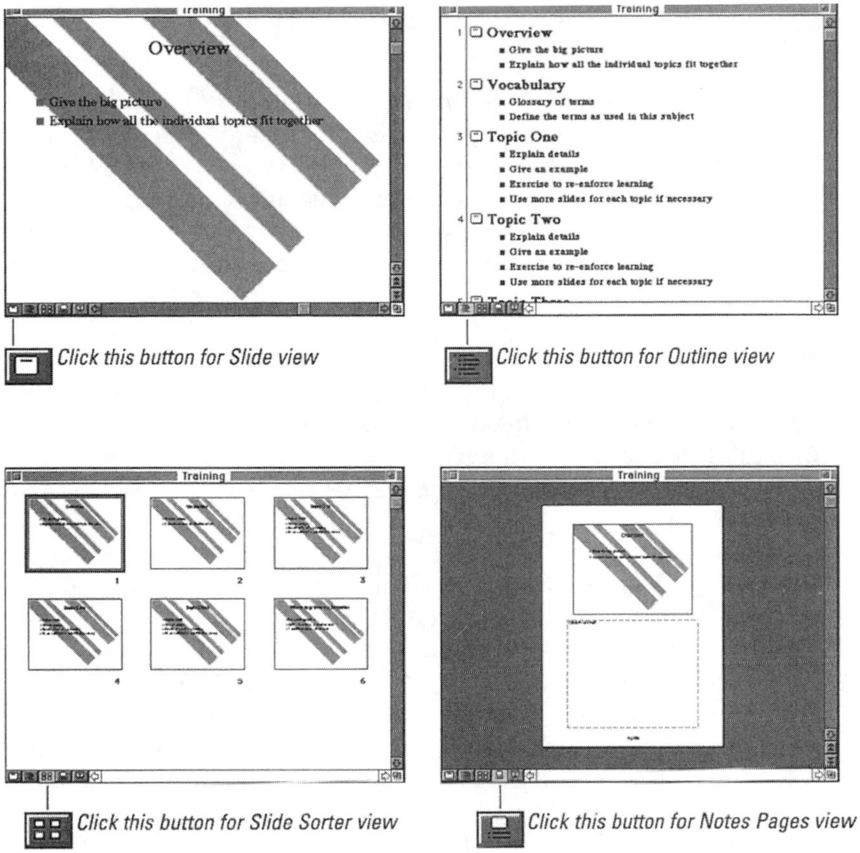

FIGURE 17.2 Presentation software permits you to view slides in different forms.
Source: Microsoft PowerPoint4 for the Macintosh Step by Step. (1994). Redmond, WA: Microsoft Press. Screenshots reprinted with permission from Microsoft Corporation.

Makes Handouts Easy to Prepare. It's easy to create handouts when you use presentation software. Once you've created the presentation slides, you simply print these slides in what's often called handout mode. Smaller-sized versions of your slide, from two to four on a page, will print onto a standard sheet of 8 ½ × 11 paper, so you can photocopy these for your audience.

Creates 35mm Slides. Most presentation software will allow you to output your slides to a special machine that can convert the data into traditional 35mm slides, for use in a standard carousel slide projector.

Converts to Web Pages. It's becoming common for presenters to put their presentations out on the Web. Presentations created in PowerPoint or other similar software can be converted to HTML with little difficulty.

The Negative Side of Presentation Software

Tempts Presenters to Be Unprepared. Too frequently, presenters now think that just because they have fancy presentation software, a great computer, and a nice computer projection device, they don't need to work very hard at being prepared. If you have done your research and are prepared, you might feel that way, but if you rely solely on the technology, you will not give a good presentation. Complex technical information of the sort presented by technical communicators needs to be planned, researched, and well designed *before* you count on the computer.

Tempts Presenters to Spend Too Much Time on Software. Sometimes, even when presenters know that they should be concentrating on the basics, they find the software too much fun and can't help playing around with the various features. It's fun to add color, transitions, and graphics, but remember that your main goal is to create a responsible, effective, well-organized presentation for a specific audience.

Downplays Other Features. In Chapter 3, you learned about delivery, which is the *bodily* part of your presentation; in other words, how you physically project yourself and your message. Recall that delivery includes gestures, vocal inflections, facial expressions, eye contact, and other nonverbal communication. Delivery is a key element in a good presentation. Yet when it appears as if the computer can do it all, people tend to skimp on delivery techniques. Often, people expect to be less nervous when they are shielded from the audience by a laptop computer. But good delivery is independent of the technology you use. In fact, when you use presentation software, you risk putting your audience into TV-watching mode. You may need to concentrate even more on delivery so that audiences focus on you and not just on the computer screen.

Causes Presenters to Talk to the Screen. One problem with delivery that presenters often face when using computers is the tendency to talk to the screen and not to the audience. Remember, don't turn your back on the audience and do maintain eye contact. Even with all the fancy computer displays, in the end, audiences are there to hear you, not to see the machine. Also, the more information you put on a slide, the more you will be tempted to focus on the screen, not your audience. One expert suggests that you have no more than six bulleted items (lines of text) per slide (Ringle, 1998, p. 125). By limiting your slides only to the main points, you will be more interactive with your audience and less dependent on the slide.

May Cause Technical Problems. Any professional you speak with will tell you the same thing: No matter how much experience you have with presentation software, something can easily go wrong. For example, you bring your laptop to a presentation site and discover that the laptop cables don't connect with the display unit at the site. Or, even though you've tested and retested your presentation, somehow, when you get to the site, your computer will not boot up. Or, when you press enter to switch to a new slide, nothing happens. The more technology you use, the greater the potential for such experiences.

May Cause File Sharing Problems. Even though the documentation for different programs may say that their files are compatible, you may discover otherwise. A certain spreadsheet may not import into your presentation, or your presentation software may not work with another brand.

May Cause Compatibility Problems. Even within the same product, such as PowerPoint, you may find that different versions are not completely compatible. What looked good using version 3 may not look so great using version 4. Or, what you create on a Macintosh may not appear the same on a PC.

What You See May Not Be What You Get. The fantastic colors and images you created at home, in the school computer lab, or at work may look one way on your computer screen but may look different when viewed on a big screen via a computer projection device.

Heavy to Cart Around. Although technology is getting smaller and lighter, it's still sometimes a heavy load to bring a computer and projector with you on a business trip, particularly if you are flying.

Templates May Not Be Suited to Your Audience. Templates are great, because they save you time and effort. But because templates are so easy, presenters may simply choose one instead of examining what sort of background, colors, and so on are appropriate for this particular audience.

How to Make Presentation Software Work for You (and Not the Other Way Around!)

Now that you've seen the two faces of presentation software, you may be wondering how to take advantage of the positive aspects while avoiding the negative ones. Here are a few tips for making the presentation software work for you and your audience.

Concentrate on the Basics. If you are still new to giving presentations, skip the technology at first. Because good presentations begin with the basics, not with technology, you should concentrate on rehearsing thoroughly and becoming an organized, sincere presenter before you begin working with presentation software. If you are new to giving presentations, and especially if you are new or unfamiliar with computers or presentation software, skip the technology the first few times and concentrate on the basics.

Utilize Professionals. Work with a professional designer if you are not confident. Many trained professionals specialize in using presentation software, and under certain circumstances, it may be more efficient for you to have one of them prepare the technology side of your presentation. Many companies have in-house graphics or support staff who can assist you; there are also many consultants and freelance communication professionals who can help. If you must use presentation software (if your company requires it, for example) but don't have time or feel comfortable learning it, hire someone else to do it for you.

Take a Training Course. If in the long run you would like to learn to use presentation software like the pros, you can take a training course through your college or university, through a neighborhood continuing education series, or at a private training company. Although you can easily learn the basics of using presentation software, training courses can teach you more advanced features and techniques.

Learn What's Expected. Find out what's generally done in your company or for this occasion. Before you decide to use presentation software, find out what is customary for this particular presentation. For example, at some companies it's expected that presenters will use a computer. For some conferences, presentation software is standard, especially conferences dealing with computers or technology. But for other conferences, a computer and presentation software would be considered overkill.

Consider Your Audience and Purpose. Even if you have the greatest idea for an electronic version of a presentation, there may be times when it's simply not appropriate for a given audience and purpose. As previously mentioned, certain conferences, companies, or other organizations may not require you to bring a computer. You may also find that for smaller audiences, too much technology gets in your way of being able to relate to each audience member. Some presentations require a more personal touch, and the computer may not fit in these settings.

Don't Overdo the Technical Features. Aim for presentation slides that are simple, clear, and easy to understand. Don't use too many colors, too many fonts, or too many icons or graphics scattered on each slide. You'll create visual noise and distract your audience; also, you may find that the nice little touches you added here and there don't show up when you try displaying your presentation. Simple layouts with well-planned color and graphics work best.

Think about Contrast. Unless you are sure about set up, aim for high contrast. High contrast means that you have a sharp distinction between the text, for example, and the backgrounds. That nice light blue background with white type may look okay on your computer screen at your desk, but it probably won't be distinctive enough when you project your slide.

Use Software Tools. Use spell check, outline mode, speaker notes, and other features. If you are going to create electronic presentations, you should avail yourself of the tools that come with the software. *Always* spell check your document; you can easily lose credibility with the audience by displaying slides that are full of spelling errors. Use the outline feature to help you organize the presentation, and use the speaker notes to help you remember other details you want to present.

Be Absolutely Sure about Technical Hookups. Find out everything you can about the technical hookups at the site where you'll be presenting. If you can, go to the site in advance and test your equipment. If you can't do this, at least test it on similar hookups if possible. Bring extra cables with different sorts of connections just in case. Talk to others at your company who regularly use presentation software and ask for advice.

Arrive Early and Test Everything. Even if you've tested everything in advance, arrive early and be sure the technology is working.

Always Have a Backup Plan. Always be prepared for the worst. In case the computer connections don't work, bring overhead projection transparencies. And in case the overhead projector fails, bring handouts. You should be prepared to give your presentation on your own, without any technology or visual aids, just in case. If you are prepared for the worst, you'll feel more confident than if you were relying on the technology to get you through.

Do the Background Work. Don't skimp on researching, organizing, preparing, and practicing. Even though you may have a wonderful electronic presentation, remember to do the background work: Good research, solid audience and purpose analysis, solid organization, and good delivery pay off. The technology won't help you if you skip these fundamental steps.

Don't Forget Your Primary Role. Remember that your main job is to connect with your audience and help them understand the many issues involved in science, technology, and the world. Stay enthusiastic, and maintain your personal connection to the audience. Don't let the technology get in the way.

Talk to Your Audience, Not the Screen. Your main focus should be your audience members, not the screen. There is no faster way to lose your audience and reduce your credibility than if you talk to the computer projection and ignore the live audience members who have come to hear and see you. Of course, it's important to look at the screen from time to time, to be sure that your slides are being properly displayed and to remind yourself about your next point. But make sure the bulk of your time is focused on your audience. Practicing with the computer setup will help you. Remember that there is no substitute for good delivery. Your gestures, vocal inflections, facial expressions, eye contact, and other nonverbal communication are always important aspects of a presentation, computer or no computer.

Move around the Room. When you use any system to project images onto a screen, you will be in the way of at least one audience member. Unfortunately, presentation software often requires that you be near the computer so you can change slides. There are two options here: one is to use a feature in the presentation software that will change the slide for you at a given interval. This option can be tricky, because if you have the slide set to change in two minutes but find that you are still speaking, you will need to quickly change the settings. The other option is a wireless mouse, like a regular computer mouse but without any cables. It works by sending a radio signal, much like your garage door opener, from the mouse to the computer.

Switch Slides when Ready. Be selective about when you put up each new slide. The moment you put up a new slide, your audience's attention will shift from you to the screen. So don't switch slides until you are ready to have them look at it.

Examples of Presentation Software

The best way to experience presentation software is to use it. You can take a training class, learn it hands-on, and practice at home. Only by experimenting with the various features will you see the full potential of how presentation software can enhance your presentations.

The screen samples in Figure 17.3 give you an idea of what an electronic presentation looks like. Each screen would be displayed one at a time as the presenter presses the mouse button or keyboard key. Individual bulleted items and graphics could appear all at once or could transition in from left to right, one at a time. Slides could also transition as they change from one to the next.

In Summary: Using Presentation Software

Presentation software allows you to enter text, images, sound, and more, and turn this information into presentation slides. These slides can be projected from the computer through a special camera and onto a projection screen. They can also be printed as handouts, originals for making transparency slides, or 35mm slides. Presentation software is a powerful tool, but like most technologies, it has two faces. On the positive side, this software offers you an almost endless choice of colors, clip art, borders, fonts, and transitions. On the negative side, however, these features can be overused and can confuse the audience. In addition, speakers may rely on the presentation software at the expense of their basic skills as a presenter.

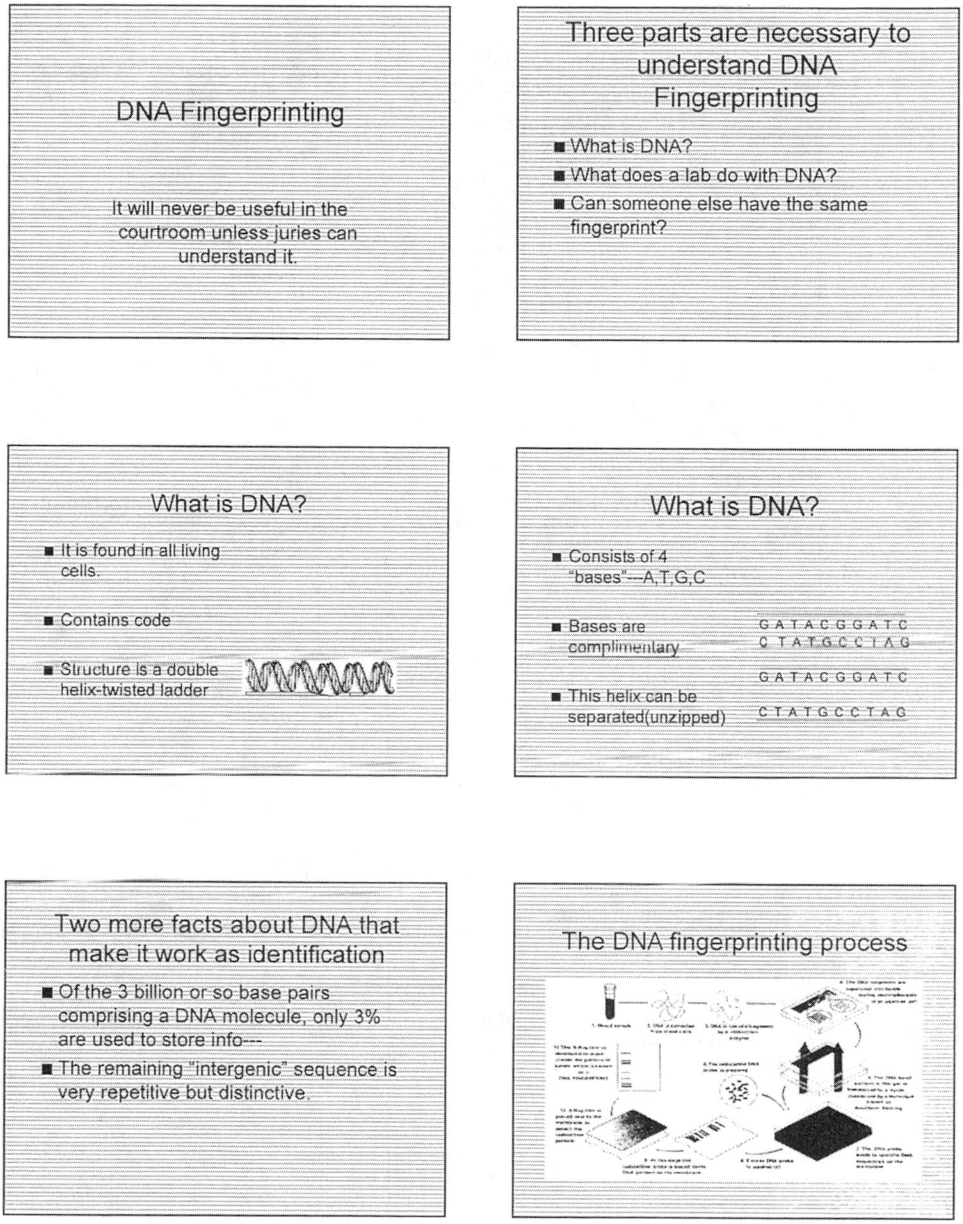
DNA Fingerprinting
It will never be useful in the courtroom unless juries can understand it.
Three parts are necessary to understand DNA Fingerprinting
What is DNA?
What does a lab do with DNA?
Can someone else have the same fingerprint?
What is DNA?
It is found in all living cells.
Contains code
Structure is a double helix-twisted ladder
What is DNA?
Consists of 4 "bases"---A,T,G,C
Bases are complimentary
G A T A C G G A T C
C T A T G C C T A G
This helix can be separated(unzipped)
G A T A C G G A T C
C T A T G C C T A G
Two more facts about DNA that make it work as identification
Of the 3 billion or so base pairs comprising a DNA molecule, only 3% are used to store info---
The remaining "intergenic" sequence is very repetitive but distinctive.
The DNA fingerprinting process

FIGURE 17.3 Snapshot of an Electronic Presentation.

Source: ©1998 Timothy J. Peters. Reprinted with permission.

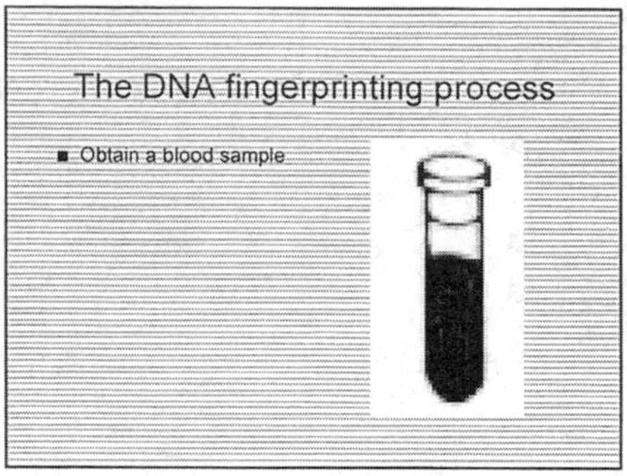

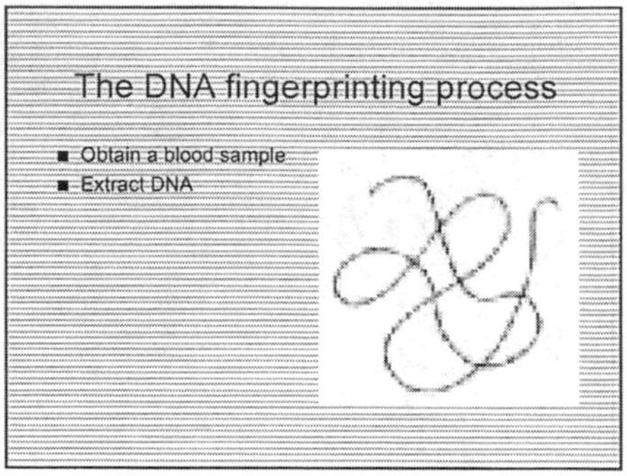

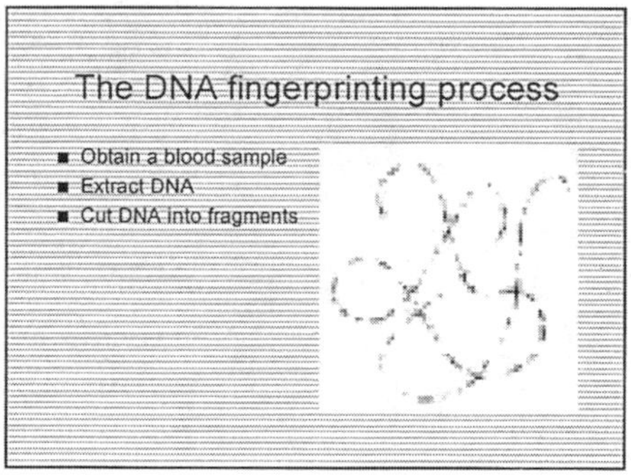

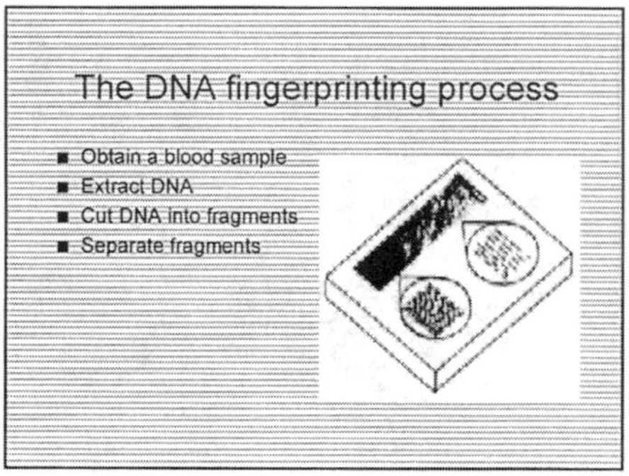

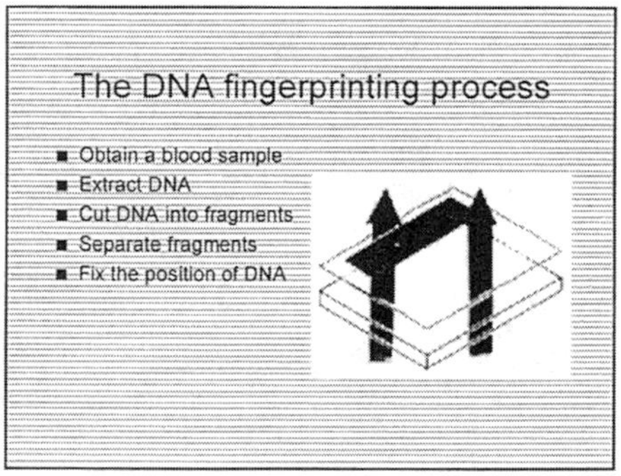

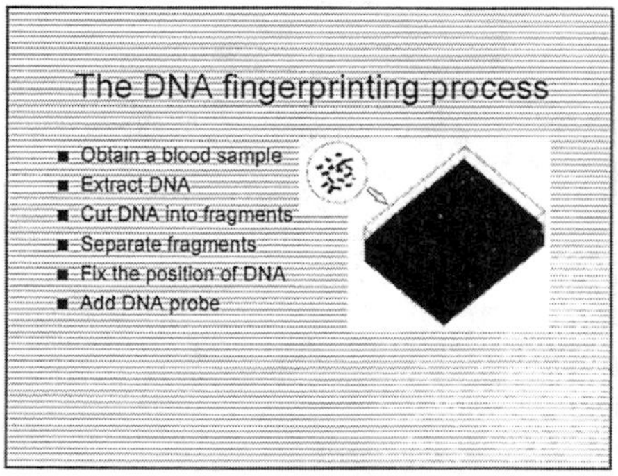

FIGURE 17.3 *(continued)*

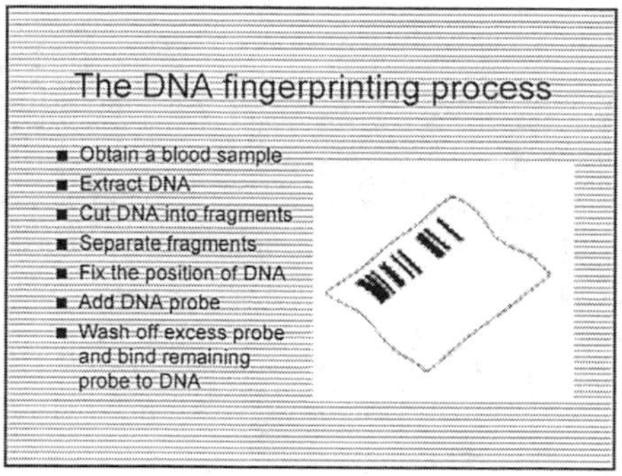

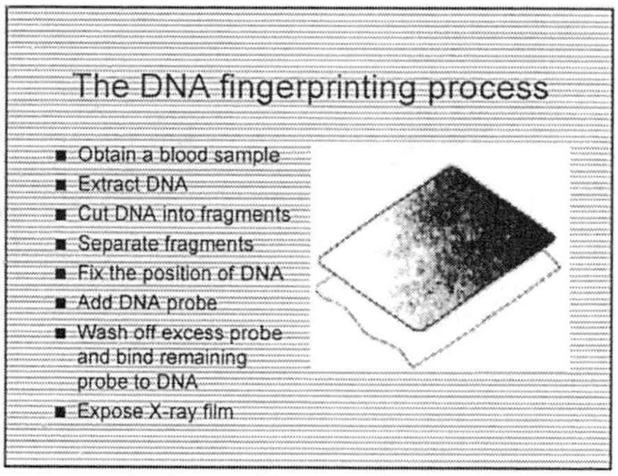

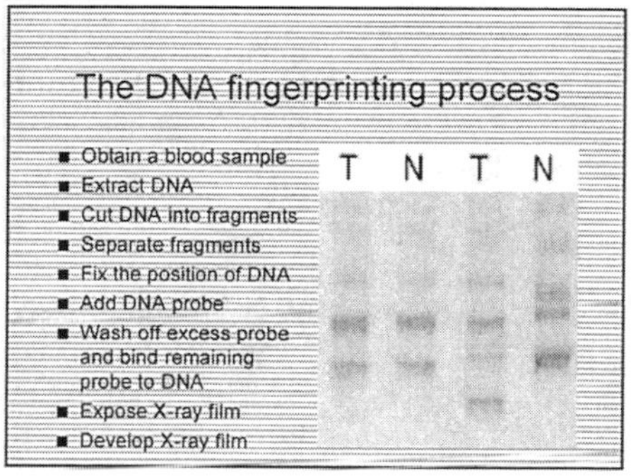

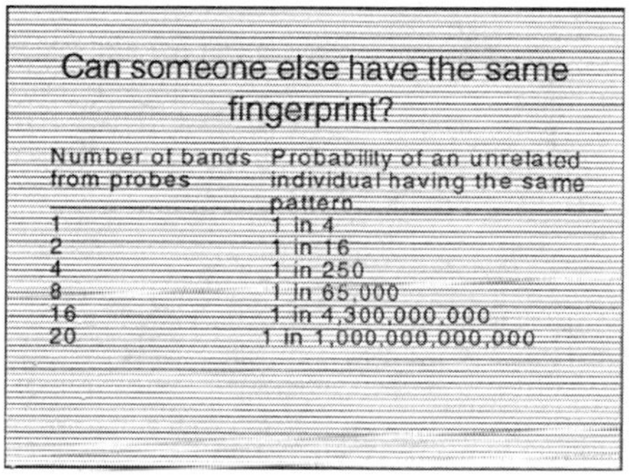

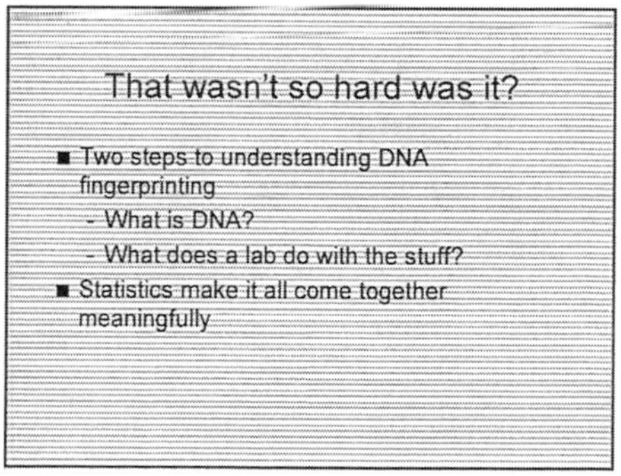

FIGURE 17.3 *(continued)*

QUESTIONS / EXERCISES / ASSIGNMENTS

1. Redesign an informative presentation that you have already given to include the use of presentation software.
2. Look through the various background images that are available in PowerPoint or other presentation software. Select two or three images and discuss the appropriateness of each for a given presentation situation.

Presentations and Cyberspace. Learn more about Microsoft PowerPoint at www.microsoft.com/powerpoint. Also, search the Web for PowerPoint information: You'll find sample presentations to download and comments by others. Find out what other presentation products, such as Lotus Freelance or Adobe Persuasion, are available and in use.

Presentations and Teamwork. You classmates may have a broad range of computer knowledge and experience with presentation software. There's no better way to learn than from each other, so divide up into teams of three to five people. Make sure that each team is balanced with people of different experience levels. Have each team select one aspect of PowerPoint (getting started; using clip art; importing graphs; using transitions), and, as a team, give a how-to presentation to your classmates.

Presentations and International Communication. Different countries possess different levels of general computer and Internet technologies. These technical limitations could greatly affect the tools that presenters can use in these countries. Devise a strategy for giving an electronic presentation to an overseas audience, and then formulate a backup plan of how you would give the same presentation if the technical limitations of the host country prevented you from using your electronic materials.

Presentations and Your Profession. Find out if people use presentation software in your profession, and ask about specifics. What type of software do they use? Is it used for all presentations? Do presenters prepare their own slides, or does the in-house graphics department handle this? Also, find out if presenters always present their own material, or if they tend to present the work of others.

REFERENCES

Microsoft PowerPoint4 for the Macintosh Step by Step. (1994). Redmond, WA: Microsoft Press.

Ringle, W. J. (1998). *Techedge: Using computers to present and persuade.* Boston: Allyn & Bacon.

CHAPTER

18 Other Technologies for Oral Presentations

CHAPTER OVERVIEW

Presentation software, described in the previous chapter, is becoming the most popular technology to use in conjunction with oral presentations for technical communication. But there are several other technologies with which you should become familiar. Like presentation software, each has its advantages and disadvantages. This chapter covers the following topics:

- Overhead Projectors
- 35mm Slides
- Flip Charts
- Multimedia and Computer-Based Training
- Teleconferencing
- Videotapes
- Web Technology

One rule applies to all of these technologies: *Always have a backup plan.* As you learned in the previous chapter, technologies can and do fail. No matter what technology you plan to use, you should be prepared to give your presentation on your own, without any technology or visual aids. The mark of a professional presenter is someone who, when faced with a series of technical difficulties, is able to keep on going.

Overhead Projectors

Overhead projectors are a tried-and-true technology for technical presentations (see Figure 18.1). In almost any presentation setting, you are sure to find one. To use an overhead projector, you need to make overhead transparency sheets, sometimes called overheads. These sheets are easy to make. You print originals on paper from your laser printer, then you use one of several methods to make the transparency sheets: a special machine that transfers the type and images from a laser-printed

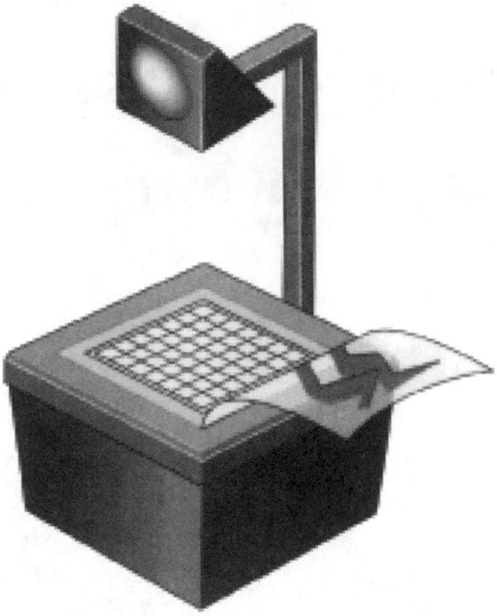

FIGURE 18.1 A Basic Overhead Projector.

page onto a clear plastic sheet, a photocopier that uses transparency plastic instead of paper, or special transparency sheets that you can print on directly from your laser printer. Transparencies can be black and white or color, depending on the ability of the copier or machine. Black-and-white overheads tend to cost a lot less than color ones.

Overhead projectors are easy to use and have fewer technical connections and potential problems than presentation software. At some conferences, presenters can use overhead projectors without charge but must pay a fee for computer hookups.

Tips for Using an Overhead Projector

Always Proofread First. Before you spend time and money making transparencies, be sure to spell check the text and proofread the entire page. Technical communicators pride themselves on accurate content; be sure your material is spelled correctly and does not contain any errors.

Use Graphics That Reproduce Well. Be sure that complex graphics or diagrams will reproduce well on your transparency. Sometimes, a visual that looks great in print just won't reproduce on an overhead transparency. Rather than subject your audience to transparencies that are hard to read and unappealing to look at, either find a new visual or simply do not use one.

Make Use of Typefaces, Clip Art. Use word processing or presentation software to create your originals. Good overheads require attention to all visual elements, and your word processing or presentation software can assist you by letting you use typefaces, clip art, and more. Presentation software is especially designed for output onto 8½ × 11 paper for reproduction on a transparency.

Don't Talk to the Overhead Projector. Especially for nervous presenters, it's easy to let the overhead projector act as a shield between you and the audience. We've all seen presenters who huddle over the projector, hands clenched tightly on the sides of the machine! Don't let the machine come between you and your audience.

Move around the Room. When you use any system to project images onto a screen, you will be in the way of at least one audience member. It's okay to ask if you are blocking anyone, and you should definitely not stand in the same location for the entire talk.

Know Where the Spare Bulb Is. One common technical problem with overhead projectors is that the bulb can suddenly burn out. Find out in advance where a spare bulb is located (often in a small compartment on the projector).

Know Where the On/Off Switch Is. There is nothing more unprofessional than a presenter who is fumbling around looking for the on/off switch. Locate this switch in advance and give it a few good practice clicks.

Use a Wipe-Off Marker to Write While Talking. It's often effective to write or draw on a transparency while you are speaking. If you want to emphasize a certain part of a map, for example, or dramatize some statistics on a chart, you can use a colored marker to underline or circle these areas. Using a marker in this fashion gives life to your presentation and draws your audience closely into the point you are making.

Practice the Reveal Method. Many presenters who use overhead projectors use the reveal method: They put up the entire transparency, then cover it with a sheet of paper and slide the paper down, line by line, to reveal each new point. This method is effective insofar as it allows you to keep the audience focused on the point at hand and not reading ahead. But it also can be complicated. The paper often slides off the slippery surface of the transparency; also, the transparency usually has a slight static charge (similar to the static that gives you a shock when you touch something), and this static can cause the paper to become crooked as you move it down the transparency. Finally, when presenters spend too much time working the paper and the overhead, they may distract the audience. So, if you choose to use the reveal method, be sure to practice in advance.

Be Selective about Switching Transparencies. The moment you put up a new transparency, your audience's attention will shift from you to the screen. So don't switch transparencies until you are ready to have your audience look at the new one.

Number Your Transparencies. If you accidentally dropped your transparencies in the middle of your talk, would you be able to put them back in order? Number each transparency in the corner so you can easily reorder them. Some transparencies are mounted in stiff cardboard frames that you can write on. Also, some presenters three-ring punch their transparencies and keep them in order in a standard three-ring binder.

35mm Slides

Another technology widely used in oral presentations is 35mm slides. As you probably know, these slides fit into a carousel tray and are projected through a slide projector onto a screen. The presenter controls when a slide is changed by clicking on a small handheld device. You make slides in a variety of ways: by taking photographs and having them developed into slides, by using presentation software and sending the output to a slide machine, or by working with sophisticated slide production equipment, usually done by a professional. Slides can be fun to look at, and the movie-like atmosphere often inspires audiences to stay very focused on the visual material.

Tips for Using 35mm Slides

Always Proofread First. 35mm slides are often more expensive than overhead transparencies, so be sure to spell check the text and proofread your original material.

Use Graphics That Reproduce Well. As is true with other presentation technologies, visuals that look great in print often won't reproduce well in 35mm slide format. Rather than subject your audience to transparencies that are hard to read and unappealing to look at, find a new visual or simply do not use one.

Use Presentation Software to Create Originals. The production of 35mm slides is a bit more complicated and expensive than that of overhead transparencies; instead of creating your own originals, you may have the production service do it. But, if you are going to produce original copy, presentation software such as PowerPoint is a good tool for creating professional 35mm slides.

Use Lighting to Focus the Audience on You. Slide presentations often require dimming the lights. If the room is too dark, your audience won't be able to see you very well, and likewise, you won't be able to see them or their reactions to your talk. They may also get drowsy sitting in the darkness. A 35mm slide presentation should be given in a room with lighting that can be modified so that the room lights can be dimmed but you can still have some light on you.

Move around the Room. Don't just stand there, tethered to the slide advance changer. If you can, move around a bit so you can be sure you are speaking to your entire audience and so you are not inadvertently blocking a portion of the screen.

Have a Second Carousel or Projector. Many a presenter who uses slides has struggled when the slide projector suddenly stopped working for some unknown reason. If possible, have a second carousel or projector nearby.

Be Selective about Switching Slides. Audiences will immediately focus on the slide, not you, when you switch slides. So don't switch until you are ready to make your next point.

Don't Present One Long Slide Show. Even though people enjoy the rich visuals that 35mm slides provide, the television-like atmosphere that is created in a slide show can easily put people into a passive listening mode. Try using slides selectively, with breaks in between where you turn away from the projector and connect with your audience.

Flip Charts

Flip charts are large pads of paper that are attached to an easel-like stand. Presenters may have the sheets of paper on a flip chart drawn out in advance, but these are normally used to take notes, draw, outline, or brainstorm during a presentation.

Tips for Using Flip Charts

Although flip charts and markers may seem rather low tech, they still require you to consider certain features.

Write Lengthy Material in Advance. Your audience will become bored and distracted if you spend too much time writing long sentences and ideas on the flip chart. Instead, prepare these pages in advance.

Use Different Marker Colors for Interest. As noted in Chapter 16, people like color. Color makes ideas come alive. So use different colored markers to make your flip charts. But don't overuse color; two to three colors per page is probably enough.

Carry Extra Markers. Markers have a strange habit of running out of ink just when you need them, so be sure to bring extra markers in a variety of colors with you.

Write on Flip Charts Selectively. Don't spend too much time in any one section of the presentation writing on the flip chart. Instead, intersperse your comments with items you wish to write.

Multimedia and Computer-Based Training

Some presentations are done without the presenter ever being in the room. Multimedia modules and computer-based training (CBT) are freestanding computer programs that present information, usually including sound, video, illustrations and other visuals, and sometimes including comprehension tests that users can take at the end of the module. You may be thinking that these are not really oral presentations as we've discussed them, and you are partly correct. Multimedia and CBT are not live presentations, and they certainly lack the real-life interactions between a presenter and an audience. But for many companies, putting a presentation into a reusable computer format is an efficient way to get a presenter's message out to the entire organization, without ever having to fly the presenter to those other sites. There are several software programs available for creating multimedia presentations; one popular program is called Macromedia Director. It allows you to incorporate video, sound, text, and more into what is essentially a movie that runs on the computer. Because there are so many types of multimedia presentations, and because these do not represent face-to-face presentations of the type being described in this book, this chapter does not discuss any specific tips for multimedia. However, you can learn more about multimedia by taking a class, learning from someone in your company's training or graphics groups, or searching on the Web.

Teleconferencing

Teleconferencing is another technology that connects presenters and audiences without any participants needing to leave their own locations. Unlike multimedia and CBT, teleconferencing is live in that it's happening in real time. The presenter may be at the New York office, for example, in front of an audience, while others in the audience are connected via a television system. These other audiences, in the Los Angeles, Atlanta, and Minneapolis locations are watching the presenter in real time but from their separate physical locations. Teleconferencing is based on television technology, but it can also allow multi-way discussions between all sites. Also known as interactive television, or ITV, teleconferencing is a way for companies to save travel costs while allowing employees to participate in a presentation at the moment it's being given. ITV is also popular in distance education, where students from different physical locations take courses together via the technology.

Tips for Teleconferencing

Teleconference technology and ITV require you to consider many factors when preparing your presentation, and you should rely on those with experience to give you the best advice. But in general, you can consider the following ideas.

Work with Trained Professionals. A good teleconference is not simply a camera aimed at a presenter. It requires the skills of teleconference professionals who know how to set up, run the camera, and so on. Usually, a team performs these tasks. If your presentation will be interactive, too, you'll need even more people on the team, because the interactive approach requires cameras at all sites, not just the outgoing one. If your company has a teleconference or ITV room, all the better. If not, consider going to a specialist and renting their services for the day. Professionals can teach you about the differences between face-to-face communication and communication via TV. Wearing a microphone, for example, requires adjustment in terms of your delivery. How and where you move around the room might need to be modified from your normal style so the cameraperson can follow you.

Find Out about Visuals and Overheads. The visual materials you prepare for a traditional face-to-face presentation may not be effective in a teleconference. Certain type sizes, colors, and graphical representations that appear fine in person may not show up well or at all when broadcast over the teleconference cameras. Investigate well in advance about the proper way to prepare visual material for a teleconference.

Learn about Your Different Audiences. The concept of audience takes on new meaning when your audience members are dispersed across the continent or the world. You may find it difficult to learn what you need to know about the audiences who are at various offsite locations, but do your best to complete a thorough audience analysis of all who will be attending your presentation.

Learn about Being in Front of a Camera. Television professionals know that there are certain elements that make a person look good when broadcast. Clothing is one example. Solid colors are preferable to clothing that has patterns, because these patterns—on jackets, shirts, and even ties—can come across as wavy lines or distortions on the television screen. Experts generally suggest that you avoid red (which can bleed outside the edges of the item when broadcast), pure white, or black, in favor of strong solid colors such as royal blue, green, gray, or plum. Also, the bright lights of broadcasting can make you look pale or make your facial features disappear; some powder or light makeup might be in order.

The background of the room is also important. An interesting background that is not too cluttered can add a certain feel to the situation, but it must be lit properly. Finally, make sure you have a wireless microphone, so you don't have to worry about tripping over the cord.

Videotapes

Presenters are commonly asked the following question nowadays: "Do you mind if we videotape your presentation so others can see it in the future?" Chapter 20 discusses the legal issues involved in this and similar questions. In terms of the technology, being videotaped requires you to consider items that are similar to those involved in teleconferencing: a professional or team of professionals will be in charge of taping your talk, and they can help you adjust to wearing a microphone, looking at the camera, moving around the room, and so on. They can also give you tips about preparing overheads and other visuals so that these visuals can be photographed by the videocamera. In terms of audience, it will probably be impossible to predict who will see your video in the long run. But if you ask questions about why someone wants to videotape your presentation, you may learn enough about who the immediate video audiences will be. Keep these audiences in mind as you give the presentation. Also, many of the suggestions given for television or video conference presentations (see Learn about Being in Front of a Camera) apply to being videotaped. And unlike live interactive television broadcasts, videotapes can be edited later, so it's possible to insert credits, music, other sound, and other graphics. A professional video producer will be your best resource should you want your taped presentation to be packaged and with more polish.

Web Technology

More and more, presentations are being given in conjunction with the Web. Although entire, live presentations can be transmitted on the Web, sending video in this fashion is still rather slow and uses too much storage and memory on the user's computer. More common is the use of the Web to augment and enhance a presentation. For example, you may present at a national conference for which organizers have set up an accompanying Website. This site might include small videoclips (but not the speaker's entire presentation), email discussion groups, real-time Internet chats, links to related information, speaker biographical information, and more. Later, when the conference has ended, such sites might post a summary of the presentations as well. Both those who attended and those who couldn't may visit such a site.

For any presentation, find out if there will be an accompanying Website, and ask if you can preview material related to your talk. Although your presentation itself is where you'll convey your true self, credibility is also established on Web pages (Hunt, 1996). Make sure your name is spelled correctly and that any summaries of your talk are accurate.

In Summary: Other Presentation Technologies

Although presentation software receives much attention these days, you have many choices when considering what types of presentation technologies to use for an oral presentation. These types include overhead projectors, 35mm slides, flip charts, multimedia, teleconferencing, videotape, and the Web. For any technology, remember to always have a backup plan. And for each specific technology, make sure you are set up and well prepared in advance.

QUESTIONS / EXERCISES / ASSIGNMENTS

1. If you can, attend an interactive video broadcast of a live presentation. If this is not possible, watch a television broadcast of a political or other type of presentation (CSPAN is a good channel for this, as are local public access cable channels). How is delivery (physical features, body language) enhanced or weakened when a presentation is broadcast via television?

2. Compare the costs of the same presentation using 35mm color slides, overhead transparency slides (color and black and white), and flip charts. Present your findings to your class.

Presentations and Cyberspace. Look at various Websites that accompany or augment live presentations. The Website for National Public Radio (www.npr.org) is a good place to start. Several of NPR's shows, such as Talk of the Nation or the National Press Club, often provide Websites for listeners to learn more, email questions and comments, and listen after the fact.

Presentations and Teamwork. As a class, discuss the difficulties that different presentation technologies might add to a group presentation. Determine what strategies you might use to avoid these problems. Form teams of three to four people, and select one of the technologies discussed in this chapter. Use this technology to give a short informative presentation. Afterward, write a short critique of the presentation, commenting on the technology and how it affected the presentation.

Presentations and International Communication. Contact someone from a government office, an educational institution, or a corporate office, that is located outside the United States. Ask what kinds of technologies and facilities they have available for giving a presentation and what kinds of visual and technological aids they expect to be a part of a presentation. Use these responses to design a list of technological expectations that presenters can use for planning and giving speeches in different cultures and to different institutions.

Presentations and Your Profession. Make a list of the presentation technologies listed in this chapter plus any others you can think of, and ask a professional in your field to rank this list from 1 to 10, with 1 being the least commonly used technology and 10 being the most. Have one or two students collect these surveys and report the findings to your class.

REFERENCES

Hunt, K. (1996). "Establishing a presence on the World Wide Web: A rhetorical approach." *Technical Communication, 43*(4), 376–387.

Ringle, W. J. (1998). *Techedge: Using computers to present and persuade.* Boston: Allyn & Bacon.

CHAPTER

19 Can I Use This Clip Art? Legal and Ethical Issues When Creating Presentations

CHAPTER OVERVIEW

As the previous two chapters have made evident, there are many ways in which communication technologies can enhance your presentations. Of all these technologies, the Web provides a rich and exciting source of information. However, although the Web encourages a sense of shared information, most Web text, sound, and artwork is probably copyrighted. In fact, much of the material, Web and otherwise, that you might use for a presentation probably belongs to someone else. Yet just because this material is copyrighted does not necessarily mean you cannot use it—four conditions, known as fair use, allow you to use material under certain conditions without requesting permission. This chapter will explore the legal and ethical issues you need to consider before using someone else's material in your own presentation.* This chapter covers the following topics:

- Copying and Scanning Images: A Scenario
- Copyright: An Overview
- When and How You Can Use Copyrighted Material
- Using Material from the Web
- Using Visuals from Printed Material
- Even If It's Legal, Give Credit

Copying and Scanning Images: A Scenario

Why should you care about copyright? Imagine the following situation. After much work and planning, you locate the perfect image for your classroom presentation: a full-color map in a magazine. You decide that this map will be helpful in two

*This chapter is not a substitute for the advice of an attorney. If you have specific questions about a project or topic, you should seek professional advice. Also, legal issues change as new cases develop and laws are passed; this chapter is current as of this publication date.

ways: as an image in your PowerPoint presentation and as handouts for your audience. So, you ask the local copy shop to scan the image and save it as a file (so you can use it in PowerPoint) and to make twenty-five color copies. "No," they tell you, "we can't do this. It's a violation of copyright, and unless you have the author's permission, we won't scan the image or make the copies for you." Without any knowledge of copyright or your rights in this situation, you simply might walk away and never know that because your use was for educational purposes, you actually had a right to scan and copy the image. To empower yourself in these and similar situations, it helps to have a basic understanding of copyright.

Copyright: An Overview

> The Congress shall have Power . . . To promote the Progress of Science and useful Arts, by securing for limited Times to Authors and Inventors the exclusive Right to their respective Writings and Discoveries. (Article 1, Section 8 of the United States Constitution)

This section of the U.S. Constitution establishes the basis for current U.S. copyright laws. Although you may be familiar with the © symbol, you may not be familiar with certain details about copyright, details that are important to you as you prepare oral presentations. Most presenters want to use someone else's material—a photograph, some clip art, a diagram—but few know whether they can legally use the material. Should you request permission to use it? What if it is only for classroom use? Or what if you scan the image and change it first? To answer these and other questions you will encounter about copyright and preparing oral presentations, the next section provides a brief introduction to copyright and the concept of fair use.

Copyright: What Is It?

In general, copyright is the right of the author or creator of a work. It gives that person complete legal control over who can reproduce, display, sell, or distribute her or his material. No one else can do this without the author's permission. As you'll learn, everything you produce that is "fixed in a tangible medium" is copyrighted. Sometimes, you own the copyright, and other times, your employer owns the copyright (this is established by the works for hire doctrine, something you can research further if you are interested).

One key concept to understand right away—you can only copyright the expression of an idea, not the idea itself. What does this mean? As one author puts it, ideas or facts cannot be owned, "but the unique description of the idea or fact in original terms can be" (Cavazos & Gavino, 1994, p. 50). In other words, you cannot copyright the idea of whales, but if you had written *Moby Dick,* you could copyright your expression of that idea (e.g., the actual book you wrote).

Some Background on Copyright

Congress established copyright to create a balance between those who create things and those who want to use things. The idea behind U.S. copyright law (originally based on British law) is that people who produce art, music, books, and other creative material should be given the right to control how their work is used, reproduced, or displayed. However, if authors and other creators were given this right indefinitely, the public would not have access to any information or would pay enormous amounts to use this information. In the same spirit that Congress recognized the right to free speech, Congress also recognized that in a democracy, people need open access to information; furthermore, they recognized that this information often helps spur the creative energies of whole new groups of authors and artists (Herrington, 1998). So Congress stated that authors would be given rights to their works, but only "for limited Times." After that time, material would go into public domain, where it can be freely accessed without permission from the author.

Copyright law has been modified many times since the Constitution was written; currently, an author or creator holds the rights to his or her work for the life of the creator plus 75 years. This means that during your entire lifetime, you own the work you create, and after you die, your estate owns the work for another 75 years. After 75 years, your work would enter public domain, thus balancing the rights of the original creators with the rights of the general public.

How Copyright Is Established

Prior to 1976, an author or creator needed to register his or her material with the Library of Congress in order to establish copyright. Since legislation in 1976, however, anything you create is automatically copyrighted to you the moment the item becomes "fixed in a tangible medium." In other words, the moment you type, write on paper, paint, or record something, you automatically own the copyright. It helps you if you add the line

© 1998 Matthew P. Wheeler

because this line reminds people that the work is yours. And if you feel there is a chance that your material might be infringed, you can go the extra step and register your material with the Library of Congress. Should you need to sue for infringement, this registration gives you extra weight.

But even if an author does not add the © symbol, the work is automatically copyrighted. This means that everything you see on the Web, in print, and in email, is copyrighted. And only the copyright holder has the right to reproduce this material. For this reason, you see copyright statements posted near most photocopy machines, and you may even see these notices near scanners, too. Copying, scanning, making transparencies—all of these technologically common tasks are potential violations of someone else's rights to their works.

When and How You Can Use Copyrighted Material

Any time you reproduce something that isn't yours, you may be violating copyright. Yet there are times when reproducing something is not a violation at all. As noted earlier, Congress wanted copyright to be a balance between authors/creators and the public. In order to give people incentives for producing material, Congress established rights to that material for a limited time. This thinking makes sense—why would people write books, make movies, record songs, or design artwork if they knew that others could come along and use their material, making money on their hard work? Because copyright holders have rights to their material for a limited time, they have the financial motivation to produce interesting, creative, important works. After the original holders have died and their heirs have exercised their rights for 75 years, the material enters public domain. At that time, anyone can reproduce, record, perform, or otherwise use the material without the permission of the heirs or estate. (The same general concepts apply if the copyright is held by a corporation, but the terms of ownership are generally longer.)

Items in the public domain are only one category of materials you can freely use for your presentations. The next section examines the instances when you can use materials.

Items You Have Permission to Use

Just because someone holds the copyright to a work does not mean you cannot use it. Copyright holders are free to give their permission for others to use their work. For example, many of the drawings and cartoons you see in this textbook were not created by the author. They were created by others, who are, therefore, the copyright holders. The author and publisher asked these others for what are called one time rights—the right to use the material one time, for this book. Copyright holders can say yes or no, and they can ask for money or other conditions if they grant the right to use their material.

Public Domain

As discussed moments ago, you can freely use works that are in the public domain, and you do not need to ask permission to use these works. How do you know if a work is public? Many public domain items, such as collections of clip art or certain software programs, announce on their front page that they are in the public domain. You can also ask someone affiliated with these items.

Fair Use

Probably your most powerful tool for using copyrighted materials in your presentations is your right to what's called the fair use doctrine. Congress recognized that there should be times when people didn't need to ask permission to use copyrighted materials; that in a democracy, where citizens value free access to information and where use of that information helps to educate and enhance people's lives, there should be room for flexibility. So the doctrine of fair use was established. This doctrine states that, under certain conditions, the use of copyrighted material without permission is considered fair. How is this fairness established? Over the years, courts have defined certain conditions to help them determine fair use:

- Purpose of the use. Is your use commercial or educational? If educational, courts will view it more favorably than if the use is for profit.
- Publication status. If the material has been published (as a book, an article, or electronically), it will be viewed more favorably than if it has not been published (like a personal letter or diary, for example).
- Amount used. If you are using only part of a text or work, this use will be viewed more favorably than if you are reproducing the entire work.
- Competition. If your use of the work will not damage the potential market of the original, this use will be viewed more favorably than if it would cause damage.
  (based on Patry, 1985, p. vii)

In general, courts tend to look favorably upon cases where you are using material in an educational setting, where the material has already been published, where you are not using the entire item, and where your use will not affect the market of the original. For this reason, classroom use has almost always been considered fair. Your instructors rarely ask author permissions in order to put something up on an overhead projector or copy it for handouts. For classroom projects, you can usually assume that your use of the material is fair, and that you don't need to ask permission. But each case is unique, so it's worth returning to the copy shop scenario for a closer look.

Recall that the copy shop would not allow you to scan an image or make a color copy for your classroom presentation, because they felt that such scanning would violate copyright. Who is right? The copy shop is correct in one sense: scanning and copying could be considered copyright infringements, because both are acts of reproducing the image, and only the copyright holder has the right to reproduce the material. But because your use is for the classroom, it would be considered fair. So you return to the clerk and explain that your use is fair use, a right given to all U.S. citizens. The clerk doesn't agree and again tells you no, but invites you to use the scanner and copier yourself instead.

What is happening here? In this typical scenario, one that many of you may already have experienced, the copy shop is being overly cautious. During the 1990s, many copy shops were sued by publishers for violating copyright. Although the copy shops were copying material for classroom use, they were also binding and packing the material and selling it in coursepacks for a profit, a clear violation. So today, copy shops are wary of lawsuits and often implement strict policies.

Your best answer in this situation would be to scan the image and make the copies yourself. Because you are not making a profit on the use of the image, and because you are using it for the classroom, there is no violation. If this scenario were changed, and you were now a professional communicator or engineer working for a company, you could not use the educational fair use condition to argue for your right to make the copy. Instead, you would need to consider the other three factors. If the material has already been published, and if you are only using a small part of the work and will not damage the market for the original, you may still have a fair use claim. Usage in educational settings is the most straightforward; for a corporate setting, you may need to check with your legal department.

Using Material from the Web

If you've used the Web at all, you've noticed that people tend to borrow and use information from other Web pages. If someone sees a graphic on one Web page and would like to use the graphic, she or he simply links to that image or obtains it from the source file. Most Web browsers have a show source command that lets you look at the HTML source code, the structure behind a Web page: Once you've seen the source code, it's easy to copy something from that page to your own. In addition, the very structure of the Web, where pages contain links to many other pages, encourages the idea of shared information. However, even though the Web promotes the use of information from a variety of sources, most Web text, sound, and artwork is in fact copyrighted—remember, even if there is no copyright mark, anything fixed in a tangible medium (print or digital) becomes copyrighted to the author or creator. So you can assume that, in most cases, the work is copyrighted.

How, then, can you use a graphic or illustration from another's Web page in your own presentations without violating copyright? There are several ways.

Exercise Your Fair Use Rights

First and foremost, if you are creating a presentation for a class project, your use of a copyrighted work will almost always be covered by the fair use doctrine. Because your use is educational, not commercial, you can use almost any copyrighted work in your classroom presentation. Always compare your use to the four conditions previously listed; if you feel your use complies, then exercise your legal rights to fair use.

Ask Permission

Second, if you are not covered by fair use, that is, if you are creating a presentation for commercial purposes, you can write to the author/creator of the original image and ask permission to use it. Often, people are flattered to know that someone would like to use their material and gladly give you permission. However, in other cases, especially where the copyright holder is a large corporation with concern for control over the use of its images, you will not have as much luck. A lone Web page designer is probably more apt to give you permission to use his or her drawing of a mouse, for example, than is Disney Corporation to use Mickey Mouse.

Use Material in the Public Domain

Although most material on the Web is copyrighted, some is not. When looking for clip art or other sources of material on the Web, you can look for pages that are clearly marked free or public domain. The owners of these pages are indicating that material on their pages is in the public domain; thus, anyone can use the images or sound without permission. Because of the Web's interconnectedness to other images and pages, beware of images on a Web page that are actually links to other pages. Although the main page may consist of items in the public domain, the linked pages may not.

Using Visuals from Printed Material

Often, books, magazines, newspapers, and other printed material contain excellent visuals (illustrations, diagrams, maps) in support of your presentation topic. As with Web pages, much of what you find in printed material is also copyrighted. Sometimes, the copyright is owned by the author of the work; other times, the publisher owns the rights. To use printed material in an oral presentation, consider the same points as for using material from the Web.

If you need permission you will need to determine the copyright holder, and that can sometimes be difficult. An advertisement in a magazine, for example, may be owned by the magazine or by the company it's advertising. Or, the copyright may belong to the advertising agency that created the ad. You can write to the general editor of the magazine to find out. Allow plenty of time to receive a reply—although some publishers respond quickly, many forward such requests to the legal department, and you will need to follow up.

Many print images are in the public domain. Dover Publishing Company, for example, publishes a large series of clip art books, each containing hundreds of copyright-free images. Government documents are almost always copyright free as are many government issued maps and charts. You can ask a reference librarian to assist you in finding printed material that is in the public domain.

Even If It's Legal, Give Credit

Even if your use is legal, because

- your use is covered by fair use doctrine, or
- you have obtained permission, or
- you are using material from the public domain,

there is still an ethical side to the matter. Remember plagiarism, which was discussed in Chapter 8? Even if your use of someone else's material is not an infringement of their copyright, it's always appropriate and ethical to give the original creator credit for her or his work. Returning to the example of the map, before you copy it and make handouts, be sure to add a citation indicating the author of the map and the copyright holder. If you obtained written permission, you would add

© 1998 Matthew P. Wheeler. Used with permission.

If the map was taken from the public domain, you might add:

United States topographical map. From the public domain Website www.freemaps.org/.

If you did not obtain permission because your use of the material is in the public domain, a traditional citation such as the following would do:

Illustration from Field, A. R., et al. (1987, 9 Feb.). "Big brother inc." may be closer than you thought. *Business Week,* pp. 84–86.

In any case, the point is this: Even though you are able to use a work legally (that is, without violating copyright), you should still give the original author credit for the work.

In Summary: Copyright and Fair Use

Visual information—clip art, maps, diagrams, charts, and more—is a necessary feature of oral presentations in technical communication. Visuals can enhance your presentation, make important points even clearer, and help hold an audience's attention. You will find a wide range of sources for visuals, from Websites to books to magazines. It's important to understand the basic legal principles about copyright so that you can be informed about how to choose and use visuals. As some have noted, the laws involving copyright and computerized communication can be a "labyrinth" of complexity (Helyar & Doudnikoff, 1994), but by understanding the basics, you'll be able to ask the right questions and exercise your right to fair use of copyrighted materials.

QUESTIONS / EXERCISES / ASSIGNMENTS

1. Your manager asks you to scan an image, then modify this image and use it in a company presentation. If you were to perform this action, would you be infringing copyright? Why or why not?

2. Even if you were not infringing copyright in question 1, would you be comfortable with performing what your boss has requested? Why or why not?

Presentations and Cyberspace. Using any search engine you like, do a search on the phrase "clip art." You will probably locate at least twenty-five pages. Carefully look at each page and see if you can determine which pages offer copyright-free images and which do not. Notice how many of the pages are actually advertisements for clip art services. Make a list of copyright-free pages and share this list with your class.

Presentations and Teamwork. Go to the Library of Congress copyright Website (lcweb.loc.gov/copyright/). Have some team members read "Copyright Basics" (lcweb.loc.gov/copyright/circs/circ1.html) and other copyright circulars. Have other team members read information about recent copyright legislation. Prepare an informative presentation for your class.

Presentations and International Communication. This chapter discussed U.S. copyright law. Yet every country has its own views on ownership of intellectual property and its own copyright laws. Given how technologies like the Web allow access to information that crosses national boundaries, a group called the World Intellectual Property Organization (WIPO) has been formed to consider ways that intellectual property (copyright, patent, trademark) law can be dealt with at a global level. With one or two other students, go to the WIPO Website (www.wipo.org/) and to an online list of embassy contact information (www.embassy.org/ embassies/index.html) and learn what you can about the different concepts and laws of copyright in other countries.

Presentations and Your Profession. A legal doctrine called works for hire states that in most cases, work you do for an employer is automatically owned by that employer, whereas work you do as a consultant is usually owned by you (unless your contract with a client states otherwise). Interview two professionals in your field—one employed full time by an organization and one who works as a consultant—and ask each professional about how he or she deals with copyright issues.

REFERENCES

Cavazos, E. A., & Gavino, M. (1994). *Cyberspace and the law: Your rights and duties in the on-line world.* Cambridge: MIT Press.

Gurak, L. J. (1997). Technical communication, copyright, and the shrinking public domain. *Computers & Composition, 14,* 329–342.

Helyar, P. S., & Doudnikoff, G. M. (1994). Walking the labyrinth of multimedia law. *Technical Communication, 41*(4), 662–671.

Herrington, T. K. (1998). The interdependency of fair use and the first amendment. *Computers & Composition, 15*(2), 125–144.

Patry, W. F. (1985). *The fair use privilege in copyright law.* Washington, DC: Bureau of National Affairs.

CHAPTER

20 Privacy, Censorship, and Oral Presentations

CHAPTER OVERVIEW

The use of computer technologies in oral presentations forces people to ask questions not only about copyright but also about issues of privacy and censorship. As more and more information becomes available on the Web, personal privacy becomes compromised. And as more and more information of every sort finds its home on a Website, it will be important to think about whether this information should or shouldn't be censored. These issues are crucial for all technical communicators. This chapter discusses the following topics:

- Privacy and Oral Presentations
- Censorship and Oral Presentations

Privacy and Oral Presentations

At first, you may be wondering how the topic of privacy has anything to do with giving oral presentations. Actually, many aspects of a presentation directly involve privacy. For instance, if you are researching a presentation and wish to find out more about your topic, you may conduct an informal survey on the Web or through email. What obligations do you have to the people who respond to this survey? Should you keep their names private, or do you even need to protect their privacy? Or, maybe your company decides that your presentation is so good that it wants to package the presentation into a Web-based multimedia site, available to users who are willing to type their credit card information into the computer. Is this credit card information safe? Will users perceive it to be safe and thus be willing to type in their credit card numbers? These and other scenarios are quite likely as computer technologies play increasingly important social and economic roles. Oral presentations and privacy therefore have much to do with each other.

What Is Privacy?

It helps to begin by defining privacy. Although the United States Bill of Rights does not actually use the word "privacy," a famous Supreme Court decision in 1965 known as Griswold v. Connecticut established privacy as a constitutional guarantee (Trubow, 1991, pp. 19-3). The right to privacy was first defined as "the right to be let alone," by Justices Louis Brandeis and Samuel Warren in a famous 1890 Supreme Court decision. If you speak to most Americans, they probably would readily admit that they feel they have a right to privacy and want their private lives protected. Yet in practice, what actually constitutes privacy is a complicated matter. Concepts of privacy change with the times and with the available technologies; as two experts note, "[i]deas about privacy have often been challenged by new technologies" (Agre & Rotenberg, 1997, p. 7). Technologies such as caller ID, supermarket scanning systems, and the Internet raise new and important questions about privacy. For your work as a technical communicator giving presentations, you must consider the specific situation. Two such situations are discussed in the following sections.

Privacy and Interviews/Surveys

One situation where you may need to ask yourself about privacy is the use of surveys. In Chapter 8, you learned about various ways to perform research for your presentation. One way is to conduct a survey or informal interview with experts in your field. Yet in conducting surveys or interviews, you need to take personal privacy into consideration. Have you completely informed these experts about why you are conducting the survey, and have they consented to give you this information? Have you explained how you will use the information? These and other such questions are important, and in most research settings, a group usually called the Human Subjects Review Board is available to assist you. For a simple classroom presentation, you may not need the advice of this group, which is designed to review experiments involving humans, such as psychology experiments, to be sure the subjects are adequately protected. But you may wish to consult an experienced researcher or professor for advice about how to set up your informal survey and how to take the privacy rights of your experts into consideration. For something simple, you may be able to send them a note explaining your classroom project and asking permission to interview them. For a more complicated survey or series of interviews, work with a skilled researcher to be sure you are not violating any privacy guidelines.

Is Information on the Web Private?

As more and more Web pages transform from simple text pages to more complex pages requesting credit card and personal information, the question of privacy becomes high on the list of considerations when using the Internet. There are many instances when, as a communicator preparing or giving an oral presentation, you might wish to stop and consider the privacy implications of your interactions with this technology. For example, consider an issue raised in Chapter 18. Your presentation is going to be videotaped, and parts of the video will be turned into a Web page, complete with additional information, links to other sites, and more. You or your organization decide to collect the names, addresses, and other information from each user who signs on and also to collect a fee for those who want to see the entire video. Is it a violation of personal privacy to request this personal information from each person who accesses the page? On the one hand, they don't need to give it to you—they can simply click off the page. But on the other hand, perhaps your presentation topic is important enough that you want to share it widely. Should you make people provide you personal information in order to access your presentation site?

For many companies, using the Web to collect personal information is a great marketing technique. They take the personal information and use it to create mailing lists; they also sell this information to other marketers. By U.S. law, they are not doing anything illegal. But it may be unethical if your Website does not indicate where or how the information will be used. You will need to decide if you want to collect this information at all, and if so, if you wish to inform users about how this information will or won't be used. Also, if you are collecting credit card numbers, you will need to be sure that your site is *encrypted;* that is, protected against unauthorized entry to the site, so that people with mischievous or even criminal motives cannot access your site and illegally obtain credit card and other information.

As a presenter, you may not be involved in these decisions. But you should find out what you can and ask to have input. If a Website is to be a companion site to your presentation, it reflects on you and your credibility.

Censorship and Oral Presentations

Along with privacy, another issue to consider is censorship. As a technical communicator preparing a presentation, you need access to as much information as possible. The Web is an excellent tool for this task. As discussed in Chapter 8, if you become adept at learning how to filter the inaccurate information from the credible, you can use the Web effectively for finding information. And, you can also use the Web to promote your presentation topic and make your presentation available to a vast audience around the globe. Yet should certain information be censored, so it is not available to children, for example? This topic is receiving a great deal of attention at the time of publication of this book, and it will continue to be important as information technologies expand and grow.

What Is Censorship?

In general, information is considered censored when parts of it are left out or otherwise made unavailable to everyone. If you have ever looked at declassified government documents, you will notice that portions of these documents have black marks drawn through them. By blocking out parts of the document, government censors have blocked information that is still considered too sensitive to be released.

On the Internet, censorship is being proposed in the form of what are called filters—software that can be configured to stop certain Web pages from loading into your Web browser. The most widely discussed form of censorship of recent has been something called a v-chip, which would allow parents to block certain types of television shows from their children.

What Should and Should Not Be Censored?

In a democracy that values freedom of information, there is an ongoing debate about the balance between censoring information and making everything free and open. U.S. citizens value a free approach to information but may also be concerned about violence, pornography, or other topics that may be a problem for children or for society at large. In the United States, freedom of information usually wins out over censorship, but it is often a struggle. An excellent example of this struggle is how the report of independent counsel Kenneth Starr, released in September 1998, was made public via the Internet. Although the House of Representatives had been concerned with children seeing pornography on the Internet, they voted in favor of releasing the Starr Report online, despite its graphic descriptions of sexual activity. In this case, the idea of freedom of information seemed to win out over the idea of censorship (though parts of the Report were, in fact, kept out of the online version). Though there are some laws about what can be said or talked about, especially on broadcast television and radio, there are still very few laws regulating Internet content.

Censorship and Technical Presentations

When determining what information you will present as part of your talk, you'll need to consider what, if anything, you wish to censor. If you are speaking to a group of children, for example, you may not want to include certain information. And, if you are placing your presentation on the Web, you'll need to decide if any part of this needs to be left off the Website. You may wish to censor your information for a variety of reasons—information may be sensitive to corporate or political issues of the time; you may not want children to hear or see certain aspects of your topics; your information may come from classified sources. On the other hand, you may believe that free access to all information is important, and that other factors, such as parental control, should be responsible for screening this information. Whatever you decide, you should know that the decision about how much information to make available is important, and you should treat it seriously.

In Summary: Privacy and Censorship

Although it may not seem immediately apparent, privacy and censorship are topics that pertain to you as a technical communicator giving oral presentations. Should you choose to conduct interviews or surveys as part of the research for your presentations, you'll need to consider the privacy of those you interview or survey. Also, if your conference or presentation has a Website, it should be made secure to protect the privacy of those who connect to it. Along with privacy issues, you'll also need to consider whether to censor the information you are presenting.

QUESTIONS / EXERCISES / ASSIGNMENTS

1. Consider a topic discussed in Chapter 18—videotaping of presentations. If you are approached before a presentation and asked permission to have your presentation taped, what privacy issues should you consider?
2. Review the presentations you have given for class so far, and ask yourself if you needed to censor information in any of these presentations. Why or why not?

Presentations and Cyberspace. You can learn a lot more about privacy and censorship by connecting to the Web page for the Electronic Privacy Information Center at www.epic.org and the site for Computer Professionals for Social Responsibility at www.cpsr.org. Go to these two sites and connect to other links on these sites. Create a short, informative presentation explaining some of the concepts you learn and how these concepts may affect your work as a communicator giving oral presentations.

Presentations and Teamwork. In your study group, identify types of information in your field of interest that you might be expected to censor in an oral presentation. Discuss the possible reasons for such censorship and whether you agree or disagree with it. To facilitate the discussion, you may wish to divide into two teams, with one team agreeing and the other disagreeing.

Presentations and International Communication. The concepts of privacy and censorship change with cultures and countries. U.S. citizens have a very high expectation of privacy; citizens of other countries do not. U.S. citizens also have a very open standard for free information, whereas in other countries, information is regularly censored. Go to the privacy Websites listed under Presentations and Cyberspace and find out about differences in privacy and censorship expectations in different countries. How do you think these rights (or lack of rights) affect each country's national policies or views on privacy? How do these policies and views differ from the privacy rights guaranteed under U.S. law? What do such differences mean for what the presenter can do or say when giving a presentation in these countries? Imagine how you might work with these differences if you were preparing a Website for your presentation that would be available to audiences from at least one other country.

Presentations and Your Profession. Identify a company in your planned profession that maintains a Website and collects information from those who visit the site; arrange to talk with the person responsible for deciding what information the company will collect. Determine what their policy is and what information they collect, why they collect data, who has access to the data, how long the company stores the information, and whether they share the data with other companies. In an oral presentation, report your findings to your class; share your opinions about this data collection and whether you believe it invades people's privacy.

REFERENCES

Agre, P. E., & Rotenberg, M. (Eds.). (1997). *Technology and privacy: The new landscape.* Cambridge: MIT Press.

Trubow, G. B. (Ed.). (1991). *Privacy law and practice.* New York: Matthew Bender.

PRESENTING . . .

Lisa Kattan

Lisa Kattan is a lawyer with interests in intellectual property and technology. She studied scientific and technical communication before going to law school. Here are her thoughts about Part Five, Presentations and Technologies.

Nobody likes how lawyers communicate. Not even lawyers. "Pursuant to the aforementioned motion on behalf of the party of the first part": nobody communicates like this naturally, but that's how many lawyers have been trained to speak and write. Lawyers have to give many types of oral presentations, whether it is the opening statement in a trial, a pitch to a new client, or explaining a position in a negotiation. In more formal settings, and especially with technical topics, using presentation software can be an invaluable way to clarify difficult concepts, speak persuasively, and keep your audience from falling asleep. So why don't more lawyers use presentation software? Old habits die hard, and that's especially true in the legal community. Even most lawyers who have devoted their careers to new issues about privacy, intellectual property, and the Internet are slow to incorporate their subject matter of choice into their daily practice. I have met with top-notch technology lawyers who do not use email, have never surfed the Net, and a few who don't even have computers in their offices!

Perhaps their keen knowledge of the legal issues surrounding these technologies is the very reason why these lawyers are slow to adapt to new technologies in their practices. Email may not be the most secure method for transmitting confidential client information. A lawyer's Website may lead to charges of the unauthorized practice of the law, or of an unwanted attorney/client relationship. A copy of a court's opinion found on the Internet may not be the official version. Just thinking about using copyrighted materials in a presentation without permission can lead to big headaches for lawyers.

I have noticed two extreme reactions in my technical communicator friends to the thought of figuring out copyright, privacy, and other legal issues that touch them. The first reaction is denial. Some people plaster their Websites with copyrighted images, use "borrowed" software, and carelessly (i.e., without encryption) send personal or sensitive information over email. Others react with paralysis; afraid to exercise their right to fair use or reluctant to contact authors for permission to use their works. Neither reaction is appropriate. As a student, you may feel fairly secure that your classroom projects are fair use; in fact conforming to your university's policies on plagiarism is probably a bigger concern than getting copyright permission for those golden arches you used in your presentation on the history of hamburgers. As a professional technical communicator, following your company's policies on the use of copyrighted material and the protection of your

(continued)

PRESENTING. . . Continued

copyrighted material should help you to sleep easier at night.

In the end, lawyers are just technical communicators and the law is just another technical subject. The law changes, just as technology changes, and you have to be aware of new legal issues that may affect your work just as you would be aware of developments in your chosen area of expertise. As I begin my legal career, I have not abandoned my training as a technical communicator; rather I think of it as, first and foremost, a way, means, method, or mechanism, by which I, the party of the first part, may cease and desist from using convoluted, enigmatic, obscure, or obtuse language. Oops, there I go again.

Index